American Hegemony: Preventive War, Iraq and Imposing Democracy

Edited by

DEMETRIOS JAMES CARALEY

THE ACADEMY OF POLITICAL SCIENCE
NEW YORK

Published by
The Academy of Political Science
475 Riverside Drive, Suite 1274
New York, NY 10115

Cover design: Loren Morales Kando

Cover credits: U.S. Marine Photo

Library of Congress Cataloging-in-Publication Data

American hegemony : preventive war, Iraq, and imposing democracy/edited by Demetrios James Caraley.
    p. cm.
    ISBN 1-884853-04-8
    1. United States—Foreign relations—2001- 2. Iraq War, 2003. 3. Terrorism—Government policy—United States. 4. United States—Military policy. 5. Unilateral acts (International law) 6. Intervention (International law) I. Caraley, Demetrios.
E902.A56 2004
327.73'009'0511—dc22

                                                                    2004006796

Printed in the United States of America
p 5 4 3 2 1

For Lisa, Wyatt, and Lucy

Contents

Editor's Foreword: Some Early Lessons

DEMETRIOS JAMES CARALEY

The purpose of *American Hegemony* is to bring within one volume essays that examine the post-September 11 "Bush doctrine," which declares that as the world's sole remaining superpower—or hegemon—the United States has the right to launch preventive wars against any nation in order to end a military or terrorist threat that might materialize in the future. Under this doctrine, the U.S. also assumes responsibility for converting as many nondemocratic nations as possible to democracies. Implementing this last responsibility, the doctrine's defenders argue, will bring many benefits: the people of those currently non-democratic nations will gain a better life; tyrannical, rogue states once converted to democracies will have no incentive to develop weapons of mass destruction that might be a threat to the United States; and democratic states will have no tolerance for terrorist groups that might organize and launch attacks from their soil.

This volume is a sequel to *September 11, Terrorist Attacks, and U.S. Foreign Policy*, published by the Academy of Political Science in the summer of 2002. In the Overview to that work, Alexander Cooley and I showed concern, first, that President Bush's 2002 State of the Union message, which defined as an "axis of evil" Iraq, Iran, and North Korea, defocused the real war on the September 11 terrorists and second, that the preventive war doctrine that President Bush first made public in the 2002 graduation exercises at West Point would antagonize many allies if it were to be implemented.[1] Now that preventive war is a reality, it remains to be seen whether the impact of the 2003–2004 Iraq war will cause anti-American terrorist attacks to increase or decrease and whether

---

[1] Demetrios James Caraley, ed., *September 11, Terrorist Attacks, and U.S. Foreign Policy* (New York: The Academy of Political Science, 2002), 14.

DEMETRIOS JAMES CARALEY is the Janet Robb Professor of the Social Sciences at Barnard College, professor of international and public affairs at Columbia University, and the editor of *Political Science Quarterly*. He has published numerous books on national security policy including, as author, *The Politics of Military Unification*, and as editor and contributor, *The President's War Powers*, *The New American Interventionism*, and *September 11, Terrorist Attacks, and U.S. Foreign Policy*.

other Arab and Muslim states as well as traditional European allies will cooperate more or less with our intelligence agencies to frustrate new attacks on the United States. What has already been seen in the two and one-half years since September 11, 2001 is that the almost worldwide view of the United States as a victim of terrorism that deserved the world's sympathy and support has given way to a widespread vision of America as an imperial power that has defied world opinion through the unjustified and unilateral use of military force. In this foreword, I paint in very broad strokes some troubling implications of the doctrine of world hegemony and some very early lessons that might be drawn from the preventive war launched in the spring of 2003 against Iraq, reporting also on some events that took place after the essays in the book went to press. As of this writing, eleven months after the declaration of military victory, internal security is still weak, as suicide bombers and remnants of the Hussein regime carry out, seemingly at will, attacks against coalition forces. They also attack and kill, again seemingly at will, Iraqis seen to be cooperating with American forces, such as the newly organized Iraqi police and even neutrals like UN and Red Cross staff, causing those organizations to withdraw their helpful personnel from Iraq. There have been three major suicide attacks on Shiite mosques during major high holy days; the last attack, on March 2nd, caused the deaths of some 200 Iraqis in a single day.[2] The attacks continue even though the United States, to show that it does not intend to stay as a permanent occupier, has agreed to transfer sovereignty to an Iraqi authority by 30 June 2004. The following are, in my judgment, some early lessons to be drawn and should be read as being prefaced by the words "in my opinion" or "so far."

THE UNITED STATES AS THE SOLE REMAINING SUPERPOWER IS NOT INVINCIBLE OR IRRESISTIBLE

The view of the United States as the world's sole remaining superpower seemed to be confirmed by its quick and easy victory over Iraq's organized military forces. Once again, it was also confirmed that American superpower is primarily the power to destroy and, at the extreme, to create chaos but not necessarily to assure compliance with its will, even after it proclaimed military victory. When victory was announced in May of 2003, there was virtually no security for the Iraqi people except in the northern, Kurdish areas. Basic services, such as water and electricity, had been cut, and hospitals, schools, factories, museums, and offices had been looted. Coalition forces that relied so heavily and successfully on air attacks with smart bombs, Special Forces, tanks, and other heavy weapons were unable to restore security. In part, this was because the Pentagon never had in their military plan the possibility that the Iraqi military

---

[2] John F. Burns, "At Least 143 Die in Attacks At Two Sacred Sites in Iraq," *New York Times*, 3 March 2004. After the publication of this article, it was reported that around 200 people had been killed.

would simply dissolve and some of it re-emerge as guerrilla fighters, and there were not enough coalition ground troops to saturate the Sunni triangle and stop the attacks. Before the war was launched, the chief of staff of the Army, General Eric Shinseki, warned that "several hundred thousand" U.S. troops would be required to secure Iraq against internal opposition. Shinseki was sharply criticized by Secretary of Defense Donald Rumsfeld and others at the Pentagon, who incorrectly decided that peaceful occupation could be established with less than half of that force. General Shinseki was then forced out of his post.[3]

With respect to exhibiting military invincibility, again, as in the 1991 Gulf war, the war against Serbia, and the war against the Taliban in Afghanistan, this quick U.S. military victory was scored over a fourth-rate power without an air force, navy, or sophisticated antiaircraft or antimissile defenses. If there were to be a war against real military powers, like China, Russia, France, Germany, India, Japan, or even North Korea, U.S. military victory would be uncertain and there might be military retaliation against the American homeland. In short, the Iraqi war proved only that U.S. military superiority can be guaranteed against small states that lack nuclear weapons, and even that does not guarantee that after victory over a state's military forces, there will be compliance by the defeated state and opposition attacks will stop. Small states can also draw a different lesson from this scenario—that developing or buying a few nuclear bombs would act as a deterrent to the possibility of a U.S. preventive attack and therefore spur, instead of curb, proliferation. It is important to understand these caveats because there is a danger that continuous proclamations about the U.S. being the world's sole remaining superpower might lead to delusions among American officials and the American people that the United States can go to war against any power on earth and score a quick victory with few casualties.

THE UNITED STATES CANNOT SUCCEED MILITARILY WHEN "GOING IT ALONE"

The fact that the Iraq war was opposed by all of the U.S.'s traditional allies, except Britain, Italy, Spain, and some smaller, new American partners, does not prove the dictum that the United States can win even if it has to go it virtually alone. In reality, even against a weak state like Iraq, the U.S. did not go it alone. It used military bases and received overflight permissions from many of its traditional allies in NATO and on the Arab peninsula who were strongly against the war. The major military hospital where all seriously wounded American soldiers were sent for more sophisticated treatment than could be offered in field hospitals was in Landstuhl, Germany, despite that nation's vociferous opposition to the Iraq war.

---

[3] David Rieff, "Blueprint for a Mess," *New York Times*, 2 November 2003.

The United States maintains some 725 military and naval installations abroad[4] that are integral to the U.S. being able to deploy, supply, and resupply American ground, air, and naval forces over 6,000 miles from its shores.

How responsibly the United States chooses to exercise its superpower affects the deference and respect that it will be accorded by other nations and international organizations. The more alienated other nations feel by an exercise of American unilateralism over their objections, the more likely it is that they may start denying the U.S. even tacit cooperation. Turkey, for example, refused to allow American military forces to cross its territory to invade northern Iraq or even to use the major American air base at Incirlik.

U.S. MILITARY INTERVENTIONS AGAINST ROGUE STATES AND TYRANNIES WILL NOT GUARANTEE THE RISE OF DEMOCRACIES

At the outset of Operation Iraqi Freedom, the United States claimed its intelligence showed that there would be only a short war and that quickly following the war, a democracy would be successfully imposed. This was to be a pro-Western democracy supportive of U.S. policies, and this new Iraqi democracy would become a pillar—an oil-rich pillar—of security for the U.S. in the Middle East.

This vision proved to be a mirage. Especially because of the complete collapse of security and basic services to the civilian population, the United States failed to generate good will even among those Iraqis who hated Saddam. Even when services and security were partially restored, an Iraqi governing council established, and movement for transferring sovereignty was underway, the differences among Kurdish, Sunni, and Shia Iraqis prevented any quick agreement as to how a new, permanent government should be organized.[5] Those Iraqi factions who thought that they would be electoral minorities were opposed to having a transitional government elected and functioning only by simple majority rule, much as the less-populous American states did while creating a new constitution in 1787. At the Constitutional Convention in Philadelphia, those less-populous states insisted as "the price of union"[6] on adding to the original proposal of a single-chamber legislature with representation based on population, a second chamber with equal representation for each state. Also, to further prevent sheer democratic "tyranny of the majority" from arising, the new constitution provided for an independent judiciary and a written constitution that established certain liberties and rights as supreme law of the land, which were not changeable by ordinary legislative majorities.

Democracies require very special social, historical, and economic prerequisites, including the cultural values of being willing to compromise and to accept unpopular decisions when they come from a legitimate process. It is as yet un-

---

[4] Joshua Micah Marshall, "Power Rangers," *The New Yorker*, 2 February 2004, 84.

[5] Chibli Mallat, "East Meets West, at Least on Paper," *New York Times*, 11 March 2004.

[6] See Herbert Agar, *The Price of Union* (Boston: Houghton Mifflin, 1966).

known how tightly the Iraqi civilian population will embrace the plan for democratization and the rule of law, especially considering the deep divisions among Sunnis, Shiites, and Kurds. Furthermore, insurgents are systematically assassinating Kurdish, Shiite, and even Sunni political leaders, professors, and other intellectual elites in order to undercut the leadership needed to operate a democracy.[7] Their objective is, precisely, to prevent the organization of a stable, new, democratic Iraqi government.

Even when elections are held and a de jure democracy is organized, it seems clear that the United States will have to de facto occupy Iraq for an indeterminate period of time and absorb continued deaths and other casualties among its forces in order to provide backup to an indigenous Iraqi police and army. There is as yet no evidence that even if a new democratic Iraq can be established, it will serve as a "beacon" of democracy and freedom in the Middle East, resulting in the people of other nondemocracies in the region demanding democracies of their own. Nor is there evidence that such a movement would always be desirable for the United States—as it might not be in Jordan, if its monarchy were to be replaced by a majority-rule, fundamentalist Islamic republic.

IN PURSUING WHAT WILL BE A PERPETUAL "WAR ON TERRORISM" INCLUDING LAUNCHING PREVENTIVE WARS, WE MAY BE WEAKENING THE AMERICAN CONSTITUTIONAL DEMOCRACY AT HOME

The case made to Congress for a resolution authorizing the use of force in Iraq has been shown to have been based on false and misleading readings of intelligence reports.[8] On the basis of those reports, the administration claimed that Iraq had weapons of mass destruction that could be given to terrorists to be used against the U.S., that Saddam Hussein was connected with the attacks of September 11, and that the Iraqis so hated their government that they would immediately welcome American forces as liberators and not see them as an army of occupation with plans to "steal" Iraq's oil.

Through a joint resolution that authorized the president in the broadest terms "to use the Armed Forces of the United States as he determines to be necessary and appropriate in order to defend the national security of the United States against the continuing threat posed by Iraq,"[9] majorities in Congress transferred to the president the power to decide whether and when the United States would go to war. Not only did Congress in effect abdicate its constitutional rights in the Iraq resolution, but it did so in haste, without sufficient debate and deliberation and over strong arguments that the case against Iraq had not been proven. The haste was the result of the president arguing that the

---

[7] Jeffrey Gettleman, "The Struggle for Iraq: Killings; Assassinations Tear Into Iraq's Educated Class," *New York Times*, 7 February 2004.

[8] Douglas Jehl, "Weapons: U.S., Certain That Iraq Had Illicit Arms, Reportedly Ignored Contrary Reports," *New York Times*, 6 March 2004.

[9] House Joint Resolution 114, Use of Force, 11 October 2002.

danger was increasing daily and of the congressional leadership wanting, for a variety of reasons, to get the vote "out of the way" before the 2002 midterm elections.

It would have been inconceivable to our Framers that congressional leaders would have abdicated their constitutional powers essentially for reasons of convenience. The Founders were all ambitious politicians, jealously guarding their prerogatives, and they expected their successors to be the same. Madison wrote in *The Federalist, No. 51* that they counted on this ambition to control overreaching branches:

> Ambition must be made to counteract ambition. The interest of the man must be connected with the constitutional rights of the place. It may be a reflection on human nature, that such devices should be necessary to control the abuses of government. But what is government itself, but the greatest of all reflections on human nature? . . . In framing a government which is to be administered by men over men, the great difficulty lies in this: you must first enable the government to control the governed; and in the next place oblige it to control itself.[10]

Not all members of Congress were willing to roll over. Senator Robert C. Byrd of West Virginia, the Senate's senior constitutional expert, challenged at length both the wisdom and constitutionality of the war resolution.[11] Nevertheless, majorities in Congress, including a Democratic majority in the Senate, did not heed the warnings. Among the Senate majority was the leading Democratic aspirant to the presidency in 2004, who voted for the resolution but later turned against the war, claiming that he had not been given accurate information and intelligence. Other notable senators, however, including Democrats Edward Kennedy, Patrick Leahy, Paul Wellstone, Carl Levin, Barbara Boxer, and Bob Graham; Republican Lincoln Chaffee; and sole Independent James Jeffords, felt they had enough information to justify voting "no."

By launching a war without having convinced majorities in Congress of the case's merits—as opposed to claiming support on the basis of party loyalty and "not being soft on terrorism"—the president not only violated the spirit of the Constitution but also lost the intellectual advantage of a give-and-take with officials who were independently elected and not beholden to him. From informed members of Congress, especially those serving on the Joint Intelligence, Foreign Affairs, and Foreign Relations committees, the president could have gained fresh perspectives to balance those generated and debated by his subordinates in the secret recesses of the Office of the Secretary of Defense, the National Security Council, the CIA, and the State Department. It was such a failure of past presidents to consult more broadly and to rely instead on executive branch "groupthink" that played a large part in the 1961 Bay of Pigs fiasco

---

[10] James Madison, *The Federalist Papers, No. 51*.

[11] Senator Robert C. Byrd, "Threats and Responses: Excerpts of Speeches Made on Senate Floor Regarding Resolution on Iraq," *New York Times*, 4 October 2002.

and in the disastrous decisions starting in 1964 to expand the war in Vietnam.[12] It appears that it was this kind of "groupthink" that prevented intelligence officers who had a different take on the danger of Iraq from getting their views to the top decision makers in the executive branch and in Congress.[13]

In exit polls during the early 2004 primary elections for choosing a Democratic presidential nominee, the issue of the war was deemed by the voters to be less important than jobs, health care, and education.[14] If how the U.S. went to war in 2003 against Iraq becomes accepted as a legitimate precedent, we run this risk: any president could find misleading and allegedly very confidential intelligence with which to frighten Congress into giving him some authority for using the military against "terrorism"(or even worse, claim that he could do so on his own, as part of his inherent power as Commander in Chief).[15] Furthermore, having an all-volunteer military force means that no great part of the public will be concerned about the danger to themselves or their children of being drafted to serve in the war and object, as they did during the Vietnam War. Finally, funding the war entirely by issuance of debt instead of by raising taxes keeps the broad general public from complaining because of a financial pinch.

Another element that may be weakening our traditional constitutional democracy is the wide range of powers given to the attorney general right after the attacks of September 11 by the USA PATRIOT Act.[16] Among other things, this legislation gave the Justice Department the authority to monitor communications by phone and by email of anyone at any time and to incarcerate even American citizens arrested on American soil by designating them as "enemy combatants." Clearly, some of this authority is necessary for detecting and incapacitating terrorists in the U.S. and foiling their plans to launch attacks. But to apprehend an American citizen within the U.S. and hold him indefinitely, without filing charges against him, without giving him access to a lawyer, and without allowing him to apply for

---

[12] See Irving Janis, *Groupthink: Pyschological Studies of Policy Decisions and Fiascoes* (Boston: Houghton Mifflin, 1983) and David Halberstram, *The Best and The Brightest* (New York: Random House, 1972).

[13] Jehl, "Weapons," and Seymour Hersh, "The Stovepipe," *The New Yorker*, 27 October 2003, 77–87.

[14] Robin Toner, "Whoever is Chosen, Democrats Spoil for a Fight," *New York Times*, 30 January 2004.

[15] Alexander Hamilton explained in *The Federalist Papers, No. 69* that there is a clear distinction intended between the president's powers as commander-in-chief and the power of Congress to declare war. "The President is to be commander-in-chief of the army and navy of the United States. In this respect his authority would be nominally the same with that of the king of Great Britain, but in substance much inferior to it. It would amount to nothing more than the supreme command and direction of the military and naval forces, as first General and admiral of the Confederacy; while that of the British king extends to the DECLARING of war and to the RAISING and REGULATING of fleets and armies, all which, by the Constitution under consideration, would appertain to the legislature." As shown by Hamilton, the Founders designed our government so that the president as commander-in-chief would not be endowed with the power to declare war and raise and regulate military forces.

[16] The Uniting and Strengthening America by Providing Appropriate Tools to Intercept and Obstruct Terrorism Act of 2001 (USA PATRIOT Act), P.L. 107-05, 115 Stat. 2721.

a writ of habeas corpus, is a major departure from the protections of the Bill of Rights. Fortunately, as of this writing, very few Americans have been so detained, and the Supreme Court has agreed to take the matter up for consideration in its Spring 2004 session.

WHAT IS AHEAD?

Realistically, the United States cannot leave Iraq before it has a stable government that can provide good internal security and some capacity to protect itself against foreign foes. It was the United States that claimed it could deliver major benefits to the Iraqi people. It is as yet unknown and unknowable how long an American security presence will be necessary in Iraq. As explained earlier, even with the U.S.'s presence there, there has been a failure to squelch violence not only against coalition armed forces but also against foreign contractors, ethnic and religious factions, major Shiite mosques, hotels, and Iraqi police stations and police training facilities. Indeed, more Iraqis have been killed by these attacks than coalition forces. Richard Betts, a preeminent scholar on terrorism,[17] has written:

> Guerrilla attacks and assassinations in this postconventional phase of the war can profit tactically from the advantage of choosing the time and place to engage isolated elements of the U.S. military. The attackers may evade capture with the assistance of the civilian population if the latter simply refuse to inform on them to the Americans. Such civilian cooperation may flow from identification with the resistance, or from fear of being killed by the resistance if they cooperate with the occupation. Terror thus plays a role in limiting the intelligence available to the American counterinsurgency forces. . . .
>
> Many of the challenges and dilemmas of counterterrorism in Iraq are represented in the ongoing postconventional phases of the war in Afghanistan as well. To defeat the resistance movements, the counterinsurgents must convince the populations to dry up the sea in which the insurgent fish swim, to provide timely information that allows rapid action to find and eliminate the resistance organization. In Iraq, that means convincing the population that the occupation forces will leave them with their own government, one better than the Baathists trying to make a comeback. It also means convincing the populations—especially the indigenous police, militia, and other organizations—that if they collaborate with the occupation and the new governments that follow it, they will be protected against reprisals by the resistance. The record of counterterrorism and counterinsurgency in other cases is sufficiently mixed that neither success nor failure in the current cases can be guaranteed.[18]

In his memoirs, former President George H. W. Bush argued that he did not send ground forces to occupy Iraq and topple Saddam Hussein after having driven

---

[17] See Richard Betts, "Surprise Despite Warning: Why Sudden Attacks Succeed," *Political Science Quarterly* 95 (Winter 1980–81): 551–572, and "The Soft Underbelly of American Primacy: Tactical Advantages of Terror" in Demetrios James Caraley, ed., *September 11, Terrorist Attacks, and U.S. Foreign Policy* (New York: The Academy of Political Science, 2002), 33–50.

[18] Private communication to the writer, 30 December 2003.

Iraqi military forces out of Kuwait in the 1991 Gulf war because he believed the U.S. would have wound up being "an occupying power in a bitterly hostile land."[19] Having the U.S. leave the Iraqis in the lurch now in order to prevent further casualties could precipitate a civil war along ethnic and religious lines, and many sects already have heavily armed private militias. A civil war in Iraq would be disastrous to the entire region and might draw in other nations, such as Iran, Turkey, and Syria, as well as more al-Qaeda-type terrorists.

To create a stable Iraq, the United States will need to enlist the support of the United Nations, our historical allies, and the Muslim nations in the Middle East. It is difficult now to gain assistance from those governments and organizations whose advice the U.S. did not abide by prior to the invasion, and indeed showed contempt for. But there is an underlying, even if unspoken, common interest to appeal to. If the UN and other nations do not help with the security and economic problems in Iraq, and it remains perilous for U.S. forces to stay there, the U.S. may be tempted to remove them. Were that to happen, there would probably be devastating levels of chaos and violence in the Middle East that would, in turn, disrupt most of the world, because it is in the Middle East that much of the world's oil supply originates. If the Middle East erupts into chaos, only the true terrorists—al Qaeda, Osama bin Laden, and their religious and tactical allies—will benefit. They have already profited by the war in Iraq having drawn energy, attention, and Special Forces away from northwest Afghanistan where the true September 11 terrorists were based. Because of force used in Iraq, the U.S. has also increased the number of angry Muslims who may attack Americans both in the Middle East and in the United States. But having to use the threat of withdrawing from Iraq, even if only implicitly, as leverage to garner the support of allies and international organizations is far from ideal for enhancing the U.S.'s reputation as a responsible and fair hegemon. The United States was seen as a responsible, fair, and trustworthy hegemon by its Western allies and much of the rest of the world from the end of World War II to the collapse of the Soviet empire. And the United States as a hegemon that is seen as responsible, fair, and trustworthy is more necessary than ever in the post-September 11 world.

One possible silver lining is that the United States will heed as an expensive lesson its experience in Iraq in 2003–2004 and will not repeat it. Specifically, it might learn not to embark on war so rapidly when the threat to the U.S. is remote in time and place, the intelligence reports are murky and inconclusive, the cost of the war is substantial, and the international community fails to see the threat and thus refuses to provide support. Another good lesson to be learned is that the human and monetary costs of a war may turn out to be many times greater than originally projected, especially if, as is inevitable, the war

---

[19] George H. W. Bush and Brent Scowcroft, *A World Transformed* (New York: Knopf, 1998), 489–490.

takes costly turns that were not originally foreseen. The final lesson is to also have a plausible exit strategy, particularly if the war doesn't go according to optimistic predictions.[20]

Acknowledgments

I thank the authors of the essays in this collection, some of which are also being published in *Political Science Quarterly.* As is normal, the views expressed in the essays are those of the authors and not of the institutions with which they are affiliated. I am especially grateful to Robert Jervis and Robert Shapiro, two colleagues and members of *PSQ's* editorial advisory board, not only for helping me organize this book, but also for having, over the years, provided assistance and advice. A special thanks also goes to editorial board member Walter LaFeber for writing the introduction and for helping me over the years above and beyond the call of duty. I thank my wife, Vilma Caraley, who reads, edits, and therefore improves everything I write and did so again here. Others who warrant my warm thanks are Kathleen Doherty, my research assistant and organizer; Kristin Zellmer, *PSQ's* managing editor; and Loren Morales Kando, who, as business manager, production manager, and vice president for operations at the Academy of Political Science, does everything she can to make my professional life easier. Mrs. Kando also designed the book's cover. Finally, I dedicate this book to Lisa Paterson, my daughter, and to Wyatt and Lucy Paterson, my grandchildren, with love and with the earnest hope and fervent prayer that neither they nor anyone like them will ever again be dealt a savage blow like the one they received on September 11, 2001.

April 6, 2004

[20] President George H. W. Bush is reported to have asked during the run-up to the war, "But do they have an exit strategy?" Michiko Kakutani, "Father, Son, Freud and Oedipus," *New York Times*, 29 March 2004.

Introduction

WALTER LAFEBER

In the seemingly ever-present debates over the "American empire," the wished-for payoffs from "imperialism," and the lessons to be learned from supposedly "small wars," the focus has usually been on foreign lands Americans and their governments are targeting rather than the effects of the "empire" on Americans and their political societies at home. Alexis de Tocqueville was uncomfortably correct in many of his warnings about the future of American democracy. It is possible, however, to be less fearful than he but to worry nevertheless over his famous formulation that the democracy stood less chance of being undone by "victorious generals . . . after the manner of Sulla and Caesar" than by the people's own search for security: "all those who seek to destroy the liberties of a democratic nation ought to know that war is the surest and the shortest means to accomplish it. This is the first axiom of the science."[1]

The essays in this volume, written by some of our most respected and articulate scholars, deserve to be at the center of the debate over "American empire" precisely for the reasons Tocqueville set out nearly 170 years ago. They explore the

---

[1] Alexis de Tocqueville, *Democracy in America*, 2 vols (New York: Oxford University Press, 1948), I: 268–269. For contemporary versions of Tocqueville's concern, note Elaine Tyler May, "Echoes of the Cold War: The Aftermath of September 11 at Home," in Mary L. Dudziak, ed., *September 11 in History: A Watershed Moment?* (Durham, NC: Duke University Press, 2003), 35–54; and Amy Kaplan, "Homeland Insecurities: Transformation of Language and Space," Ibid., 55–69. Various points of the debate over "American empire" are helpfully brought together in Andrew J. Bacevich, ed., *The Imperial Tense: Prospects and Problems of American Empire* (Chicago, IL: Ivan R. Dee, Inc., 2003), and typified by the front-page story on historian Bernard Lewis, Peter Waldman, "A Historian's Take on Islam Steers U.S. in Terrorism Fight," *The Wall Street Journal*, 3 February 2004, as well as by Niall Ferguson's many attempts to convince readers that Americans should embrace their "empire" as the rightful heir to the British Empire and its long-set sun's cold glow; note, for example, his "The Empire Slinks Back," *New York Times Magazine*, 27 April 2003.

WALTER LAFEBER is the Marie Underhill Noll Professor of American History at Cornell University. He is the author of thirty books and articles, the most recent of which, *The Clash: U.S. Relations with Japan from the 1850's to the Present*, received the Bancroft Prize and the Ellis Hawley Prize. He is the president-elect of the Society of Historians of American Foreign Relations.

center of the ongoing discussion over how the world's only superpower should define and act out its role in the world. This debate has deep roots. As Tocqueville's writings indicated, the attacks of September 11 only accelerated arguments that go back more than two centuries. The horror of the events in New York, Washington, DC, and Pennsylvania, however, did make Americans finally aware that they had long been involved in foreign policies that could cost them their lives as well as their dollars. Those events radically changed the environment in which American foreign policy was defined, discussed, and formulated, while providing the consensus, not apparent before that point, for the use of massive military force, if necessary, to create an "American empire."

In the 1990s, during the rush of triumphalism that affected both American political debate and scholarship, fewer than 10 percent of those polled (and sometimes fewer than 5 percent) could name a national security issue of importance to them. By October 2001, however, 90 percent supported President George W. Bush's policies—policies he defined as not only aiming to destroy terrorist networks but also moving globally to attack, if necessary, sovereign states harboring terrorists.[2] The public's support gave him one of the broadest informal mandates in recent American history for an active, militaristic foreign policy, and probably the broadest since Congress and the American people seemed to rally around President Harry Truman's 1947 doctrine of containing totalitarianism (read: communism) wherever it tried to push out.

If this volume's essays are important because of their relevance and special contributions to the ongoing debate, they are also notable because most are marked by a pessimism—or, to use a more neutral term, a realism. The main thrust of post–September 11 coverage, especially in the mainstream U.S. media, has been on the why and how of the American military efforts in Afghanistan and the Middle East, with some attention given to military commitments in areas such as the Philippines and central Asia. Considerable attention has also been paid to the response by other powers, above all, France, Germany, and members of the United Nations Security Council. These stories are usually those of American success, quick military triumphs over Afghanistan and Iraqi resistance, effective deployments in other areas, and successful defiance of nations that attempted to slow up the pace of the march. These mainstream debates are obviously important. By focusing on U.S. military power and on the effects of the Bush administration's policies overseas, however, the debates are also too narrow and too safe. The overwhelming superiority that the nation's military enjoys over any combination of other national forces is indisputable and can be clearly measured by noting how the U.S. military budget more than matches the next dozen highest such budgets in the world. American forces effortlessly cut through Iraqi defenses (even given the accuracy of one observer's comment that "we were at war with the

[2] See Ivo H. Daalder and James M. Lindsay, *America Unbound: The Bush Revolution in Foreign Policy* (Washington, DC: The Brookings Institution, 2003), 48 for quotes from the so-called Bush doctrine and the context. Also note Robert Jervis, "Understanding the Bush Doctrine," in this volume.

Flintstones").[3] In Afghanistan, it was also true that the U.S. military won a quick victory because of its close working relationship with the Northern Alliance, a collection of warlords' forces that were effective, but, as it turned out, not interested in either American-style democracy or working with a Washington-imposed regime. Certainly the one-time allies of the Northern Alliance failed to see the attractions of a long-term American empire in their home areas.[4] But the U.S. effort in Afghanistan was, nevertheless, as the Bush administration defined it and most Americans believed, a significant victory.

So why should this volume's essays be pessimistic? Because they go well beyond the military victories to ask the necessary next and more complex questions about Washington's plans (or lack thereof) for the reconstruction, stabilization, and even democratization of the invaded countries. The invasions of Afghanistan to some degree, and of Iraq to a greater degree, have been justified on the grounds of destroying rogue regimes who harbored terrorists and/or had designs to use weapons of mass destruction (WMD) and replacing them with democracies that (again according to the conventional wisdom) are less interested in waging wars.

These essays, then, are important because they go beyond Americans' beliefs in their military security to deal with the inevitable questions of what has to follow economically and politically. But they are especially important because many of them focus on the United States, where the decisions are made about the political and economic follow-through, and where (at least according to the Constitution) officials who make war and claim the power for making the peace are to be held responsible by the U.S. Congress and the people who elect it. As Tocqueville indicated, moreover, in a protracted conflict it would be the American homeland, not an overseas locale, where the most important question of all—the viability of this particular democracy—would be decided.

Robert Jervis defines the broad background for this struggle at home by exploring the implications of the Bush doctrine abroad. The U.S. response to September 11, he argues, emanated, in part, from how great powers usually act, how they define the world (their "neighborhoods"), and how effectively they use their political and military might. "All this means that under the Bush doctrine, the United States is not a status quo power," he concludes. Instead, "the combination of power, fear, and perceived opportunity leads it to reshape world politics and the societies of many of its members." The last seven words of that formulation also force the reader to consider the effect such an effort has on the politics and society of the nation doing the reshaping. The remainder of the essays, indeed, deal with different aspects of that seven-word phrase.

Louis Fisher is the most incisive, comprehensive, concerned, and published analyst of that phrase as it relates to how waging war and creating an "empire"

---

[3] Daalder and Lindsay, *America Unbound*, 147.

[4] An important and, again, deeply pessimistic discussion of Afghanistan two years after the overthrow of the Taliban is found in Ahmed Rashid, "The Mess in Afghanistan," *New York Review of Books*, 12 February 2004, 24–27.

changes, sometimes for the worse, the U.S. constitutional system.[5] Among other contributions, he notes here how in the twenty-first-century wars against terrorism, intelligence information is crucial and how corrupted intelligence can lead not only to corrupted policy but also to corrupt constitutional processes. Fisher's conclusion is unequivocal: "U.S. political institutions failed in their constitutional duties when they authorized war against Iraq." As is too often the case in the making of modern American foreign relations, the failure of constitutional restraints on the exercise of war powers was due in important respects to the failure of the media to present accurate or sufficiently full analyses of events.

Steven Kull, Clay Ramsay, and Evan Lewis provide a highly important dissection, and in parts condemnation, of how the media misinformed the American public after September 11. Some parts of the media, especially the Fox Network, appear more guilty than others. The authors further contend that "the public had so many of these misperceptions" of what was occurring, and who was responsible, because "the Bush administration made numerous statements that could easily be construed as asserting these falsehoods"—not least in its interpretation of intelligence estimates about Iraqi ties to al-Qaeda terrorists. Thus, a misinformation loop was formed: the administration's misleading statements were picked up by media, which uncritically repeated them and thus misinformed the public and its elected officials who, in Fisher's formulation, not surprisingly failed to exercise proper restraints on the administration's war powers. One of the stunning conclusions in the essay is that Americans pay considerably more attention to the news than pundits have believed. The problem is less in the viewers than in what they viewed. Or to underline the famous dictum, the point was not that the medium was the message, but that the medium corrupted the message. And in a modern democracy, the implications of such corruption are especially far-reaching and ominous.

Andrew Flibbert notes that the phrase at the center of the heated and politically inflammable debate over the major reason the Bush administration offered for invading Iraq, the weapons of mass destruction, has become less a scientific or technical phrase than "a distinctly political term." While U.S. officials "never refer to the U.S. military's development, possession, and potential use of WMD," the phrase is used "with the clear purpose of describing the kinds of weapons that American adversaries may seek." Flibbert's questioning that the WMD genie can never again be put "back in its early twentieth-century bottle" and—more importantly—his argument that democracies known for supposedly not wanting to fight are willing in reality to sacrifice a great deal in order to obtain such weapons are highly significant. His probing adds an important dimension to Jervis's international arena, while providing a crucial set of examples to support the theses of the previous two essays.

---

[5] In regard to his arguments in this volume, note especially Louis Fisher, *Constitutional Conflicts Between Congress and the President* (Lawrence, KA: University Press of Kansas, 1997); Louis Fisher and Nada Mourtada-Sabbah, *Is War a Political Question?* (Huntington, NY: Nova Science Publishers, 2001); and Louis Fisher, *Presidential War Power* (Lawrence, KA: University Press of Kansas, 1995).

The success of U.S. foreign policy will depend not only on the effectiveness with which the nation's power is used, but, when necessary, with the restraint that Americans place on that power. Joseph S. Nye, Jr. spells out components of that power, the "hard" military as well as, in his well-known formulation, the "soft" cultural and economic power the United States exercises globally (too often with its citizens not understanding the sometimes unwelcome consequences of that exercise of soft power in various parts of the world). Sections of this essay, and most of the next by Charles A. Kupchan, argue that the restraint on U.S. power will be imposed by other nations if it is not imposed by Americans. While some experts see China as the potential leader of opposition to Washington's leadership, Kupchan argues that a cohesive Europe will be better positioned to take such a lead. He worries that American behavior might lead "other nations to rally against rather than with U.S. power." More precisely, he fears that such an alignment, along with other developments his essay outlines, will inevitably result in "a diminishing appetite for liberal internationalism" in the United States. This liberal internationalism has been the dynamic ideological center of the nation's power since World War II, but the appetite for it can also be diminished by the overreach of the Bush doctrine (as Jervis indicates), disillusionment with Congress and the media (as Fisher and Kull-Ramsay-Lewis emphasize), and the misunderstanding of the nature and limits of U.S. power (as Flibbert and Nye observe.)

The world in which American power operates is not only incredibly complex, but, as Samuel Huntington concludes, it is complex because it is also local. That is, the problems with which U.S. power is involved can be far removed and deeply isolated from the cultural and political assumptions that guide most Americans. Democracy, Huntington argues, is not imposed by outsiders but only—if they are lucky (for example, by having bad leaders die at an appropriate moment)—by the indigenous population. Nor, he emphasizes, has democracy in the recent past evolved when even a superpower might desire, but as part of a long cycle, a "wave," over which Americans have little control. Along with the external restraints on U.S. empire building that Jervis, Kupchan, and Nye underline, Huntington adds the complicated transformation taking place in other societies which Washington officials often do not understand, let alone guide.

One of the most instructive examples of how even a superpower cannot control such internal processes is the Iranian Revolution of 1979. Fareed Zakaria believes that many of the problems U.S. officials have had to deal with since September 11, especially those posed by Islamic fundamentalism, began after the upheaval in Iran. Resembling Huntington, Zakaria asks how the transition to democracy can work, especially in the Middle East, and what role Americans can play. Also resembling Huntington, his answer is that any transformation will be determined primarily within the local societies. He emphasizes that "economic reforms must come first, for they are fundamental." Zakaria's formulation is highly important, not least because he undermines the popular assumptions of Americans and some of their leaders that democracy involves mainly the development of a political process. Such processes have resulted in some of the century's worst rulers. As Zaka-

xxii | WALTER LAFEBER

ria has argued elsewhere in detail, such political processes are much less important than the power of a legitimate legal system and the institutionalization of the law along with democratic checks and balances, not least in the economic realm.[6]

Americans like to think that democracy is not difficult to practice (even if many of them often do not participate in that practice) and thus is a universal good that others can also easily enjoy. The ghost of Woodrow Wilson's happy if ahistorical faith that if the world can only be made safe for democracy, democracy will easily follow, refuses, unfortunately, to die. Americans want to share such faith (defined in one important source as being based on the evidence of things not seen), and they make such easy assumptions in part because their economic base has allowed their peculiar kind of democracy to evolve since at least the 1830s. This collection of essays raises the central questions of whether Americans can continue to maintain such a system in the face of the terror, distortions, corrupted intelligence, an unquestioning mainstream media, and international complexities that they have had to confront since the September 11th attacks. Once again, Tocqueville's prediction is tested.

[6] Fareed Zakaria, *The Future of Freedom: Illiberal Democracy at Home and Abroad* (New York: W.W. Norton and Company, 2003).

Part I:
THE RATIONALE FOR PREVENTIVE WAR

Understanding the Bush Doctrine

ROBERT JERVIS

The invasion of Iraq, although important in itself, is even more noteworthy as a manifestation of the Bush doctrine. In a sharp break from the President's pre-September 11 views that saw American leadership, and especially its use of force, restricted to defending narrow and traditional vital interests, he has enunciated a far-reaching program that calls for something very much like an empire.[1]

The doctrine has four elements: a strong belief in the importance of a state's domestic regime in determining its foreign policy and the related judgment that this is an opportune time to transform international politics; the perception of great threats that can be defeated only by new and vigorous policies, most notably preventive war; a willingness to act unilaterally when necessary; and, as both a cause and a summary of these beliefs, an overriding sense that peace and stability require the United States to assert its primacy in world politics. It is, of course, possible that I am exaggerating and that what we are seeing is mostly an elaborate rationale for the overthrow of Saddam Hussein that will have little relevance beyond that. I think the doctrine is real, however. It is quite articulate, and American policy since the end of the military campaign has been consistent with it. Furthermore, there is a tendency for people to act in accord with the explanations they have given for their own behavior, which means that the doctrine could guide behavior even if it were originally a rationalization.[2]

---

[1] For somewhat similar analyses, but with quite different evaluations, see James Chace, "Imperial America and the Common Interest," *World Policy* 19 (Spring 2002): 1–9; Charles Krauthammer, "The Unipolar Moment Revisited," *National Interest* 70 (Winter 2002/03): 5–17; Stephen Peter Rosen, "An Empire, If You Can Keep It," ibid 71 (Spring 2003): 51–62; Robert Art, *A Grand Strategy for America* (Ithaca, NY: Cornell University Press, 2003), 87–92.

[2] See Deborah Larson, *Origins of Containment: A Psychological Explanation* (Princeton: Princeton University Press, 1985), which draws on Bem's theory of self-perception. See Daryl Bem, "Self-Perception Theory" in Leonard Berkowitz, ed., *Advances in Experimental Social Psychology*, vol. 6 (New York: Academic Press, 1972), 1–62.

ROBERT JERVIS, Adlai E. Stevenson Professor of International Politics at Columbia University, served as president of the American Political Science Association in 2000–01. He is the author of numerous books and articles on international politics. His most recent book is *System Effects: Complexity in Political and Social Life.*

I will describe, explain, and evaluate the doctrine. These three tasks are hard to separate. Evaluation and explanation are particularly and perhaps disturbingly close. To see the doctrine as a response to an unusual external environment may verge on endorsing it, especially for Realists who both oppose the doctrine and see states as rational. In the end, I believe it to be the product of idiosyncratic and structural factors, both a normal reaction to an abnormal situation and a policy that is likely to bring grief to the world and the United States. The United States may be only the latest in a long line of countries that is unable to place sensible limits on its fears and aspirations.[3]

DEMOCRACY AND LIBERALISM

This is not to say that the doctrine is entirely consistent, and one component may not fit well with the rest despite receiving pride of place in the "The National Security Strategy of the U.S.," which starts thusly: "The great struggles of the twentieth century between liberty and totalitarianism ended with a decisive victory for the forces of freedom—and a single sustainable model for national success: freedom, democracy, and free enterprise." The spread of these values opens the path to "make the world not just safer but better," a "path [that] is not America's alone. It is open to all."[4] This taps deep American beliefs and traditions enunciated by Woodrow Wilson and echoed by Bill Clinton, and it is linked to the belief, common among powerful states, that its values are universal and their spread will benefit the entire world. Just as Wilson sought to "teach [the countries of Latin America] "to elect good men," so Bush will bring free markets and free elections to countries without them. This agenda horrifies Realists (and perhaps realists).[5] Some mid-level officials think this is window dressing; by contrast, John Gaddis sees it as the heart of the doctrine,[6] a view that is endorsed by other officials.

---

[3] Paul Kennedy, *The Rise and Fall of the Great Powers: Economic Change and Military Conflict from 1500 to 2000* (New York: Random House, 1987); Robert Gilpin, *War and Change in World Politics* (New York: Cambridge University Press, 1981); Geoffrey Parker, *The Grand Strategy of Philip II* (New Haven: Yale University Press, 1998).

[4] White House, "The National Security Strategy of the United States" (Washington, DC: September 2002), i, 1. Bush's West Point speech similarly declared: "Moral truth is the same in every culture, in every time, and in every place. . . . We are in a conflict between good and evil. . . . When it comes to the common rights and needs of men and women, there is no clash of civilizations." "Remarks by the President at 2002 Graduation Exercise of the Unites States Military Academy," White House Press Release, 1 June 2002, 3; Paul Allen, *Philip III and Pax Hispanica, 1598–1621: The Failure of Grand Strategy* (New Haven: Yale University Press, 2000).

[5] Thus, Samuel Huntington, who agrees that a state's foreign policy is strongly influenced by its domestic regime, argues that conflict can be reduced only by not pushing Western values on other societies. See his *The Clash of Civilizations and the Remaking of the World Order* (New York: Simon and Schuster, 1996).

[6] John Lewis Gaddis, "Bush's Security Strategy," *Foreign Policy* 133 (November/December 2002): 50–57.

The administration's argument is that strong measures to spread democracy are needed and will be efficacious. Liberating Iraq will not only produce democracy there, but it will also encourage democracy in the rest of the Middle East. There is no incompatibility between Islam or any other culture and democracy; the example of political pluralism in one country will be emulated. The implicit belief is that democracy can take hold when the artificial obstacles to it are removed. Far from being the product of unusually propitious circumstances, a free and pluralist system is the "natural order" that will prevail unless something special intervenes.[7] Furthermore, more democracies will mean greater stability, peaceful relations with neighbors, and less terrorism, comforting claims that evidence indicates is questionable at best.[8] Would a democratic Iraq be stable? Would an Iraq that reflected the will of its people recognize Israel or renounce all claims to Kuwait? Would a democratic Palestinian state be more willing to live at peace with Israel than an authoritarian one, especially if it did not gain all of the territory lost in 1967? Previous experience also calls into question the links between democracy and free markets, each of which can readily undermine the other. But such doubts do not cloud official pronouncements or even the off-the-record comments of top officials. The United States now appears to have a faith-based foreign policy.

This or any other administration may not act on it. No American government has been willing to sacrifice stability and support of U.S. policy to honor democracy in countries like Algeria, Egypt, Saudi Arabia, and Pakistan.[9] But the current view does parallel Ronald Reagan's policy of not accepting a detente with the Union of Soviet Socialist Republics (USSR) that was limited to arms control and insisting on a larger agenda that included human rights within the Soviet Union and, thus, implicitly called for a new domestic regime. The Bush administration is heir to this tradition when it declares that any agreement with North Korea would have to address a range a problems in addition to nuclear weapons, including "the abominable way [the North] treats its people."[10] The argument is that, as in Iraq, regime change is necessary because tyrannical governments will always be prone to disregard agreements and coerce their neighbors just as they mistreat their own citizens. Notwithstanding their being Realists in their views about how states influence one another, Bush and his colleagues are Liberals in their beliefs about the sources of foreign policy.

---

[7] For the concept of natural order, see Stephen Toulmin, *Foresight and Understanding: An Enquiry into the Aims of Science* (Bloomington: Indiana University Press, 1961).

[8] Edward Mansfield and Jack Snyder, *Democratization and War* (Cambridge, MA: MIT Press, forthcoming).

[9] It can be argued that Carter's policy toward the shah's regime in Iran is an exception. There is something to this, but the conflict between his policy and stability is more apparent in retrospect than it was at the time.

[10] Quoted in David Sanger, "U.S. to Withdraw From Arms Accord With North Korea," *New York Times*, 20 October 2002.

Consistent with liberalism, this perspective is highly optimistic in seeing the possibility of progress. A week after September 11, Bush is reported to have told one of his closest advisers: "We have an opportunity to restructure the world toward freedom, and we have to get it right." He expounded this theme in a formal speech marking the six-month anniversary of the attack: "When the terrorists are disrupted and scattered and discredited, . . . we will see then that the old and serious disputes can be settled within the bounds of reason, and goodwill, and mutual security. I see a peaceful world beyond the war on terror, and with courage and unity, we are building that world together."[11] In February 2002, the President responded to a reporter's question about the predictable French criticism of his policy by saying that "history has given us a unique opportunity to defend freedom. And we're going to seize the moment, and do it."[12] One month later, he declared, "We understand history has called us into action, and we are not going to miss that opportunity to make the world more peaceful and more free."[13]

The absence of any competing model for organizing societies noted at the start of the National Security document is part of the explanation for the optimism. Another is the expectation of a benign form of domino dynamics, as the replacement of the Iraqi regime is expected to embolden the forces of freedom and deter other potential disturbers of the peace. Before the war, Bush declared that when Saddam is overthrown "other regimes will be given a clear warning that support for terror will not be tolerated. Without this outside support for terrorism, Palestinians who are working for reform and long for democracy will be in a better position to choose new leaders—true leaders who strive for peace."[14] After the war, Bush reaffirmed his belief that "a free Iraq can be an example of reform and progress to all the Middle East."[15] Even some analysts like Thomas Friedman, who are skeptical of much of the administration's policy, believe that the demonstration effect of regime change in Iraq can be large and salutary.

The mechanisms by which these effects are expected to occur are not entirely clear. One involves establishing an American reputation for opposing tyranny. But the power of reputation is questioned by the Bush administration's skepticism toward deterrence, which works partly by this means. Another

[11] Quoted in Frank Bruni, "For President, a Mission and a Role in History," ibid. 22 September 2001; "President Thanks World Coalition for Anti-Terrorism Efforts," White House Press Release, 11 March 2002, 3–4; also see "Remarks by the President at 2002 Graduation Exercise," 4–5.

[12] "President Bush, Prime Minister Koizumi Hold Press Conference," White House Press Release, 18 February 2002, 6.

[13] "President, Vice President Discuss the Middle East," White House Press Release, 21 March 2002, 2.

[14] Speech to the American Enterprise Institute, 26 February 2003. For a general discussion of the administration's optimism about the effects of overthrowing Saddam on the Middle East, see Philip Gordon, "Bush's Middle East Vision," *Survival* 45 (Spring 2003): 155–165.

[15] Quoted in David Sanger and Thom Shanker, "Bush Says Regime in Iraq is No More; Syria is Penalized," *New York Times*, 16 April 2003.

mechanism is the power of example: people will see that tyrants are not invulnerable and that democracy can provide a better life. But seeing one dictator overthrown (not an unusual occurrence) may not have much influence on others. The dynamics within the Soviet bloc in 1989–1991 were a product of special conditions, and while contagion, tipping, and positive feedback do occur, so does negative feedback. We may hope for the former, but it is unreasonable to expect it.

THREAT AND PREVENTIVE WAR

The second pillar of the Bush doctrine is that we live in a time not only of opportunity, but also of great threat posed primarily by terrorists and rogue states. Optimism and pessimism are linked in the belief that if the United States does not make the world better, it will grow more dangerous. As Bush said in his West Point address of 1 June 2002: "Today our enemies see weapons of mass destruction as weapons of choice. For rogue states these weapons are tools of intimidation and military aggression against their neighbors. These weapons may also allow these states to attempt to blackmail the U.S. and our allies to prevent us from deterring or repelling the aggressive behavior of rogue states. Such states also see these weapons as their best means of overcoming the conventional superiority of the U.S."[16]

These threats cannot be contained by deterrence. Terrorists are fanatics, and there is nothing that they value that we can hold at risk; rogues like Iraq are risk-acceptant and accident prone. The heightened sense of vulnerability increases the dissatisfaction with deterrence, but it is noteworthy that this stance taps into the longstanding Republican critique of many American Cold War policies. One wing of the party always sought defense rather than deterrence (or, to be more precise, deterrence by denial instead of deterrence by punishment), and this was reflected in the search for escalation dominance, multiple nuclear options, and defense against ballistic missiles.[17]

Because even defense may not be possible against terrorists or rogues, the United States must be ready to wage preventive wars and to act "against . . . emerging threats before they are fully formed," as Bush puts it.[18] Prevention is not a new element in world politics, although Dale Copeland's important

[16] Also see White House, *National Strategy to Combat Weapons of Mass Destruction* (Washington, DC: December 2002), 1.

[17] It is no accident that the leading theorist of this school of thought, Albert Wohlstetter, trained and sponsored many of the driving figures of the Bush administration, such as Paul Wolfowitz and Richard Perle.

[18] Letter accompanying "National Security Strategy of the United States," ii. Calling this aspect of the doctrine as our policy against Iraq "preemptive," as the Bush administration does, is to do violence to the English language. No one thought that Iraq was about to attack anyone; rather, the argument was that Iraq and perhaps others are terrible menaces that eventually will do the United States great harm and must be dealt with as soon as possible, before the harm has been inflicted and while prophylactic actions can be taken at reasonable cost. For a study of cases, see Robert Litwak, "The New Calculus of Pre-emption," *Survival* 44 (Winter 2002–03): 53–79.

treatment exaggerates its previous centrality.[19] Israel launched a preventive strike against the Iraqi nuclear program in 1981; during the Cold War, U.S. officials contemplated attacking the USSR and the Peoples' Republic of China (PRC) before they could develop robust nuclear capabilities.[20] The Monroe doctrine and westward expansion in the nineteenth century stemmed in part from the American desire to prevent any European power from establishing a presence that could menace the United States.

The United States was a weak country at that time; now the preventive war doctrine is based on strength and on the associated desire to ensure the maintenance of American dominance. Critics argue that preventive wars are rarely necessary because deterrence can be effective and many threats are exaggerated or can be met with strong but less militarized policies. Libya, for example, once the leading rogue, now seems to be outside of the axis of evil. Otto von Bismarck called preventive wars "suicide for fear of death," and, although the disparity of power between the United States and its adversaries means this is no longer the case, the argument for such wars implies a high degree of confidence that the future will be bleak unless they are undertaken or at least a belief that this world will be worse than the likely one produced by the war.

This policy faces three large obstacles. First, by definition, the relevant information is hard to obtain because it involves predictions about threats that reside sometime in the future. Thus, while in retrospect it is easy to say that the Western allies should have stopped Hitler long before 1939, at the time it was far from clear that he would turn out to be such a menace. No one who reads Neville Chamberlain's speeches can believe that he was a fool. In some cases, a well-placed spy might be able to provide solid evidence that the other had to

[19] Dale Copeland, *The Origins of Major War* (Ithaca, NY: Cornell University Press, 2000); also see John Mearsheimer, *Tragedy of Great Power Politics* (New York: Norton, 2001). For important conceptual distinctions and propositions, see Jack Levy, "Declining Power and the Preventive Motivation for War," *World Politics* 40 (October 1987): 82–107; for a study that is skeptical of the general prevalence of preventive wars but presents one example, Jack Levy and Joseph Gochal, "Democracy and Preventive War: Israel and the 1996 Sinai Campaign," *Security Studies* 11 (Winter 2001/2): 1–49. On the U.S. experience, see Art, *A Grand Strategy for America*, 181–197. Randall Schweller argues that democratic states fight preventively only under very restrictive circumstances: "Domestic Structure and Preventive War: Are Democracies More Pacific?" *World Politics* 44 (January 1992): 235–269; he notes the unusual nature of the Israeli cases. For the argument that states are generally well served resisting the temptation to fight preventively, see Richard Betts, "Striking First: A History of Thankfully Lost Opportunities," *Ethics and International Affairs* 17 (2003): 17–24. For a review of power transition theory, which in one interpretation is driven by preventive motivation, see Jacek Kugler and Douglas Lemke, *Parity and War: Evaluations and Extensions of The War Ledger* (Ann Arbor: University of Michigan Press, 1996).

[20] Marc Trachtenberg, *History and Strategy* (Princeton: Princeton University Press, 1991), chap. 3; William Burr and Jeffrey Richelson, "Whether to 'Strangle the Baby in the Cradle': The United States and the Chinese Nuclear Program, 1960–64," *International Security* 25 (Winter 2000/01): 54–99. Gregory Mitrovich shows how much of American early Cold War policy was driven by the fear that it could not sustain a prolonged confrontation: *Undermining the Kremlin: America's Strategy to Subvert the Soviet Bloc, 1947–1956* (Ithaca, NY: Cornell University Press, 2000).

be stopped, but in many other cases—perhaps including Nazi Germany—even this would not be sufficient, because leaders do not themselves know how they will act in the future. The Bush doctrine implies that the problem is not so difficult, because the state's foreign policy is shaped, if not determined, by its domestic political system. Thus, knowing that North Korea, Iran, and Syria are brutal dictatorships tells us that they will seek to dominate their neighbors, sponsor terrorism, and threaten the United States. But while the generalization that states that oppress their own people will disturb the international system fits many cases, it is far from universal, which means that such short-cuts to the assessment process are fallible. Second and relatedly, even information on capabilities and past behavior may be difficult to come by, as the case of Iraq shows. Saddam's links to terrorists were murky and remain subject to debate, and while much remains unclear, it seems that the United States and Britain not only publicly exaggerated, but also privately overestimated, the extent of his weapons of mass destruction (WMD) program.

Third, unless all challengers are deterred by the exercise of the doctrine in Iraq, preventive war will have to be repeated as other threats reach a similar threshold. Doing so will require sustained domestic, if not international, support, which is made less likely by the first two complications. The very nature of a preventive war means that the evidence is ambiguous and the supporting arguments are subject to rebuttal. If Britain and France had gone to war with Germany before 1939, large segments of the public would have believed that the war was not necessary. If it had gone badly, the public would have wanted to sue for peace; if it had gone well, public opinion would have questioned its wisdom. While it is too early to say how American opinion will view Saddam's overthrow (and opinion is likely to change over time), a degree of skepticism that will inhibit the repetition of this policy seems probable.

National leaders are aware of these difficulties and generally hesitate to take strong actions in the face of such uncertainty. While one common motive for war has been the belief that the situation will deteriorate unless the state acts strongly now, and indeed this kind of fear drives the security dilemma, leaders usually put off decisions if they can. They know that many potential threats will never eventuate or will be made worse by precipitous military action, and they are predisposed to postpone, to await further developments and information, to kick the can down the road. In rejecting this approach in Iraq, if not in North Korea, Bush and his colleagues are behaving unusually, although this does not mean they are wrong.

Part of the reason for their stance is the feeling of vulnerability and the consequent belief that the risks and costs of inaction are unacceptably high. Note one of the few lines that brought applause in Bush's Cincinnati speech of 7 October 2002 and that shows the powerful psychological link between September 11 and the drive to depose Saddam: "We will not live in fear." Taken literally, this makes no sense. Unfortunately, fear is often well founded. What it indicates is an understandable desire for a safer world, despite that fact that the United States did live in fear throughout the Cold War and survived quite well. But if the sentence has little logical meaning, the emotion it embodies is an understandable fear of fear, a drive to gain certainty, an impulse to assert control by acting.[21]

This reading of Bush's statement is consistent with my impression that many people who opposed invading Iraq before September 11, but altered their positions afterwards, had not taken terrorism terribly seriously before September 11, a category that includes George Bush.[22] Those who had studied the subject were, of course, surprised by the timing and method of the attacks, but not that they took place; they changed their beliefs only incrementally. But Bush frequently acknowledges, indeed stresses, that he was shocked by the assault, which greatly increased his feelings of danger and led him to feel that drastically different policies were necessary. As he put it in his Cincinnati speech: "On September 11th, 2001, America felt its vulnerability." It is no accident that this sentence comes between two paragraphs about the need to disarm Iraq. Three months later, in response to an accusation that he always wanted to invade Iraq, Bush replied: "prior to September 11, we were discussing smart sanctions. . . . After September 11, the doctrine of containment just doesn't hold any water. . . . My vision shifted dramatically after September 11, because I now realize the stakes, I realize the world has changed."[23] Secretary of Defense Donald Rumsfeld similarly explained that the United States "did not act in Iraq because dramatic new evidence of Iraq's pursuit of weapons of mass murder. We acted because we saw the existing evidence in a new light, through the prism of our experience on September 11."[24] The claim that some possibilities are unlikely enough to be put aside lost plausibility in face of the obvious retort: "What could be less likely than terrorists flying airplanes into the World Trade Center and the Pentagon?" During the Cold War, Bernard Brodie expressed his exasperation with wild suggestions about military actions the USSR might

[21] A minor illustration of the power of fear was the closing of a New York subway station when a first-year art student taped to the girders and walls thirty-seven black boxes with the word "fear" on them, an unlikely thing for a bomber to do. See Michael Kimmelman, "In New York, Art Is Crime, And Crime Becomes Art," *New York Times*, 18 December 2002. For a study of how people's willingness to sacrifice civil liberties are affected by their fear of a future attack, see Darren Davis and Brian Silver, "Civil Liberties vs. Security: Public Opinion in this Context of the Terrorist Attacks on America" (unpublished manuscript); Leonie Huddy, Stanley Feldman, Charles Taber, and Gallya Lahav, "The Politics of Threat: Cognitive and Affective Reactions to 9/11" (paper presented at the annual meeting of the American Political Science Association, Boston, 29 August–1 September 2002); Leonie Huddy, Stanley Feldman, Theresa Capelos, and Colin Provost, "The Consequences of Terrorism: Disentangling the Effects of Personal and National Threat," *Political Psychology* 23 (September 2002): 485–510. For a general theory of the impact of feelings of vulnerability on policy, see Charles Kupchan, *The Vulnerability of Empire* (Ithaca, NY: Cornell University Press, 1994).

[22] According to Robert Woodward, George Tenet believed that "Bush had been the least prepared of all of [the administration leaders] for the terrorist attacks." See *Bush at War* (New York: Simon and Schuster, 2002), 318. Before then, his administration had concentrated on Russia and the PRC.

[23] *New York Times*, 1 February 2003.

[24] Quoted in James Risen, David Sanger, and Thom Shanker, "In Sketchy Data, Trying to Gauge Iraq Threat," ibid., 20 July 2003.

undertake: "All sorts of notions and propositions are churned out, and often presented for consideration with the prefatory words: 'It is conceivable that. . . .' Such words establish their own truth, for the fact that someone has conceived of whatever proposition follows is enough to establish that it is conceivable. Whether it is worth a second thought, however, is another matter."[25] Worst-case analysis is now hard to dismiss.

The fact that no one can guarantee that an adversary with WMD will not use them means that fear cannot be banished. Although administration officials exaggerated the danger that Saddam posed, they also revealed their true fears when they talked about the possibility that he could use WMD against the United States or its allies. At least some of them may have been insensitive to the magnitude of this possibility; what mattered was its very existence. Psychology plays an important role here because people value certainty and are willing to pay a high price to decrease the probability of a danger from slight to none.[26] Bush's choice of words declaring a formal end to the organized combat in Iraq was telling: "this much is certain: No terrorist network will gain weapons of mass destruction from the Iraqi regime."[27] Concomitantly, people often feel that uncertainty can be best eliminated by taking the initiative. As Bush put it in his letter accompanying the submission of his National Security Strategy, "In the new world we have entered, the only path to peace and security is the path of action." The body of the document declared that "The greater the threat, the greater is the risk of inaction."[28] In the past, a state could let a potential threat grow because it might not turn into a major menace. Now, if one follows this cautious path and the worst case does arise, the price will be prohibitive. Thus, Senator Orrin Hatch dismissed the argument that since the threat from Iraq was not imminent the United States could afford to rely on diplomacy and deterrence by saying, "Imminence becomes murkier in the era of terrorism and weapons of mass destruction."[29] It then makes sense to strike much sooner and more often, even though in some cases doing so will not have been necessary.

UNILATERALISM

The perceived need for preventive wars is linked to the fundamental unilateralism of the Bush doctrine, since it is hard to get a consensus for such strong

[25] Bernard Brodie, "The Development of Nuclear Strategy," *International Security* 2 (Spring 1978): 83.

[26] Daniel Kahneman and Amos Tversky, eds., *Choices, Values, and Frames* (New York: Cambridge University Press, 2000).

[27] "Transcript of President Bush's Remarks on the End of Major Combat in Iraq," *New York Times*, 2 March 2003. (Emphasis added.) He used a similar formulation three months later: "President Meets with Small Business Owners in New Jersey," 16 June 2003, White House Press Release.

[28] "National Security Strategy of the United States," ii, 15; also see "In President's Words: Free People Will Keep the Peace of the World," *New York Times*, 27 February 2003; "Bush's Speech on Iraq: 'Saddam Hussein and His Sons Must Leave," ibid., 18 March 2003; Tony Blair's statement quoted in Emma Daly, "Both Britain and Spain Dismiss Offer On Iraq Missiles," ibid., 1 March 2003.

[29] Quoted in Carl Hulse, "Senate Republicans Back Bush's Iraq Policy, as Democrats Call it Rash and Bullying," ibid., 8 March 2003.

actions and other states have every reason to let the dominant power carry the full burden.[30] Unilateralism also has deep roots in the non-northeastern parts of the Republican party, was well represented in the Reagan administration, draws on long-standing American political traditions, and was part of Bush's outlook before September 11. Of course, assistance from others was needed in Afghanistan and Iraq. But these should not be mistaken for joint ventures, as the United States did not bend its policy to meet others' preferences. In stressing that the United States is building coalitions in the plural rather than an alliance (the mission determines the coalition, in Rumsfeld's phrase), American leaders have made it clear that they will forego the participation of any particular country rather than compromise.

The seeming exception of policy toward North Korea, in which the United States refuses to negotiate bilaterally and insists that the problem is one for the international community, is actually consistent with this approach. Others were not consulted on the policy and in fact resisted it. The obvious purpose of the American stance was to get others to apply pressure on the adversary. While this is a legitimate aim and, perhaps, the best policy, it is one the United States has selected on its own. Multilateralism here is purely instrumental, a way to avoid giving what the United States regards as a concession to North Korea and a means of further weakening and isolating it, despite others believing this is unwise.

Even before September 11, Bush displayed little willingness to cater to world public opinion or to heed the cries of outrage from European countries as the United States interpreted its interests and the interests of the world in its own way. Thus, the Bush administration walked away from the Kyoto treaty, the International Criminal Court, and the protocol implementing the ban on biological weapons rather than try to work within these frameworks and modify them. The United States also ignored European criticisms of its Middle Eastern policy. On a smaller scale, it forced out the heads of the Organization for the Prohibition of Chemical Weapons and the Intergovernmental Panel on Climate Change. In response to this kind of behavior, European diplomats can only say: "Big partners should consult with smaller partners."[31] The operative word is "should." When in the wake of the overthrow of Saddam, Chirac declares: "We are no longer in an era where one or two countries control the fate of another country," he describes the world as he would like it to be, not as it is.[32]

---

[30] One of those outside the government who helped formulate the Bush doctrine denies that it is unilateralist. See Philip Zelikow, "The Transformation of National Security," *National Interest* 71 (Spring 2003): 24–25.

[31] Quoted in Steven Erlanger, "Bush's Move On ABM Pact Gives Pause to Europeans," *New York Times*, 13 December 2001; also see Suzanne Daley, "Many in Europe Voice Worry that U.S. Will Not Consult Them," ibid., 31 January 2002; Erlanger, "Protests, and Friends Too, Await Bush in Europe," ibid., 22 May 2002; Elizabeth Becker, "U.S. Unilateralism Worries Trade Officials," ibid., 17 March 2003.

[32] Quoted in Karen DeYoung, "Chirac Moves To Repair United States Ties," *Washington Post*, 16 April 2003.

The administration has defended each of its actions, but not its general stance. The most principled, persuasive, and perhaps correct defense is built around the difficulty in procuring public goods. As long as leadership is shared, very little will happen because no one actor will be willing to shoulder the costs and the responsibilities. "At this moment in history, if there is a problem, we're expected to deal with it," is how Bush explains it. "We are trying to lead the world," is what one administration official said when the United States blocked language in a UN declaration on child health that might be read as condoning abortion.[33] This is not entirely hypocritical: many of the countries that endorsed the Kyoto protocol had grave reservations but were unwilling to stand up to strongly committed domestic groups.

Real consultation is likely to produce inaction, as was true in 1993, when Clinton called for "lift and strike" in Yugoslavia (that is, lifting the arms embargo against Bosnia and striking Serbian forces). But because he believed in sharing power and was unwilling to move on his own, he sent Secretary of State Warren Christopher to ascertain European views. This multilateral and democratic procedure did not work because the Europeans did not want to be put on the spot; in the face of apparent American indecision, they refused to endorse such a strong policy. If the United States had informed the Europeans rather than consulted them, they probably would have complained, but gone along; what critics call unilateralism often is effective leadership. Could Yasir Arafat have been moved from his central position if the United States had sought consensus rather than staking out its own position? Bush could also argue that just as Reagan's ignoring the sophisticated European counsels to moderate his rhetoric led to the delegitimation of the Soviet system, so his insistence on confronting tyrants has slowly brought others around to his general perspective, if not to his particular policies.

In this context, the strong opposition of allies to overthrowing Saddam was an advantage as well as a disadvantage to Bush. While it exacted domestic costs, complicated the effort to rebuild Iraq, and perhaps fed Saddam's illusion that he could avoid a war, it gave the United States the opportunity to demonstrate that it would override strenuous objections from allies if this was necessary to reach its goals. While this horrified multilateralists, it showed that Bush was serious about his doctrine. When Kofi Annan declared that an American attack without Security Council endorsement "would not be in conformity with the [UN] charter," he may not have realized that for some members of the Bush administration this would be part of the point of the action.[34]

---

[33] Quoted in Bob Woodward interview with Bush in ibid., 19 November 2002; also see Woodward, *Bush at War*, 281; quoted in Somini Sengupta, "U.N. Forum Stalls on Sex Education and Abortion Rights," *New York Times*, 10 May 2002.

[34] Patrick Tylor and Felicity Barringer, "Annan Says U.S. Will Violate Charter if It Acts Without Approval," ibid., 11 March 2003.

AMERICAN HEGEMONY

The final element of the doctrine, which draws together the others, is the establishment of American hegemony, primacy, or empire.[35] In the Bush doctrine,
there are no universal norms or rules governing all states.[36] On the contrary,
order can be maintained only if the dominant power behaves quite differently
from the others. Thus the administration is not worried that its preventive war
doctrine or attacking Iraq without Security Council endorsement will set a
precedent for others because the dictates do not bind the United States. Similarly, the United States sees no contradiction between expanding the ambit of
nuclear weapons to threaten their employment even if others have not used
WMD first on the one hand and a vigorous antiproliferation policy on the other.
American security, world stability, and the spread of liberalism require the
United States to act in ways others cannot and must not. This is not a double
standard, but is what world order requires.

Hegemony is implied when the Nuclear Posture Review talks of dissuading
future military competitors. At first glance, this seems to refer to Russia and
China. But the point applies to the countries of Western Europe as well, either
individually or as a unit. This was clear in the draft defense guidance written
by Paul Wolfowitz for Dick Cheney at the end of the first Bush administration
and also was implied by President George W. Bush when he declared to the
graduating cadets at West Point: "America has, and intends to keep, military
strengths beyond challenge—thereby making the destabilizing arms races of
other eras pointless, and limiting rivalries to trade and other pursuits of
peace."[37] This would mean not only sustaining such a high level of military

[35] Paul Schroeder sharply differentiates hegemony from empire, arguing that the former is much
more benign and rests on a high degree of consent and respect for diverse interests: "Empire or Hegemony?" address given to the American Historical Association meeting, Chicago, 3 January 2003. I
agree that distinctions are needed, but at this point both the terms and the developing American policy
are unclear. I have a soft spot in my heart for primacy because it has the fewest connotations. Ten
years ago I argued that the United States did not need to seek primacy (at least I was sensible enough
to avoid saying whether the United States would be sensible): Jervis, "The Future of World Politics:
Will it Resemble the Past?" *International Security* 16 (Winter 1991/92): 39–73; "International Primacy:
Is the Game Worth the Candle?" ibid., 17 (Spring 1993): 52–67. For discussions about what an empire
means today, whether it necessarily involves territorial control and how it can be maintained, see Rosen, "An Empire if You Can Keep It"; also see Kurth, "Migration and the Dynamics of Empire,"
National Interest 71 (Spring 2003): 5–16; and Anna Simons, "The Death of Conquest," ibid., 41–49.

[36] Only after World War I was lip-service paid to the concept that all states had equal rights. The
current United States stance would be familiar to any nineteenth-century diplomat.

[37] "Remarks by the President at 2002 Graduation Exercise," 4. The Wolfowitz draft is summarized
in stories in the *New York Times*, 8 March and 24 May 1992. Also see Zalmay Khalilzad, *From Containment to Global Leadership? America and the World After the Cold War* (Santa Monica, CA: RAND,
1995); and Robert Kagan and William Kristol, eds., *Present Dangers: Crisis and Opportunity in American Foreign and Defense Policy* (San Francisco: Encounter Books, 2000). This stance gives others incentives to develop asymmetric responses, of which terrorism is only the most obvious example. For
possible PRC options, see Thomas Christensen, "Posing Problems Without Catching Up: China's Rise
and Challenges for U.S. Security Policy," *International Security* 25 (Spring 2001): 5–40.

spending that no other country or group of countries would be tempted to challenge it, but also using force on behalf of others so they will not need to develop potent military establishments of their own. In an implicit endorsement of hegemonic stability theory, the driving belief is that the world cannot afford to return to traditional multipolar balance of power politics, which would inevitably turn dangerous and destructive.[38]

Although many observers, myself included, were taken by surprise by this turn in American policy, we probably should not have been. It is consistent with standard patterns of international politics and with much previous American behavior in the Cold War. As early as the start of World War II, American leaders understood that the United States would emerge as the prime architect of the new international politics.[39] In the years before the Soviet Union was perceived as a deadly menace, American leaders understood that theirs would be the major role in maintaining peace and prosperity.

Even had the Soviet Union been more benign, instability, power vacuums, and the anticipation of future rivalries would have led the United States to use and increase the enormous power it had developed.[40] The task could not be done by the United States alone, however. The world was not strictly bipolar, especially because the United States sought to limit its defense spending, and the prime target of the conflict was the allegiance of West Europe. The United States knew that allied, and especially European, support was necessary to resist Soviet encroachments. Allies, fearing a return to American isolationism, reciprocally made great efforts to draw the United States in.[41] Although American power was central and consent often was forthcoming only because of veiled (or

[38] It is noteworthy that hegemonic stability theory comes with both a malign and a benign version. See Duncan Snidal, "The Limits of Hegemonic Stability Theory," *International Organization* 25 (Autumn 1985): 579–614; for the applicability of these theories to the pre-Bush post-Cold War world, see Michael Mastanduno, "Preserving the Unipolar Moment: Realist Theories and United States Grand Strategy after the Cold War," *International Security* 21 (Spring 1997): 49–88; see the exchange between Mark Sheetz and Mastanduno in ibid., 22 (Winter 1997/98): 168–174; Ethan Kapstein and Michael Mastanduno, eds., *Unipolar Politics: Realism and State Strategies After the Cold War* (New York: Columbia University Press, 1999); G. John Ikenberry, ed., *America Unrivaled: The Future of the Balance of Power* (Ithaca, NY: Cornell University Press, 2002).

[39] See, for example, David Reynolds, *From Munich to Pearl Harbor: Roosevelt's America and the Origins of the Second World War* (Chicago: Dee, 2001); Warren Kimball, *The Juggler: Franklin Roosevelt as Wartime Statesman* (Princeton: Princeton University Press, 1991).

[40] Melvyn Leffler, *A Preponderance of Power: National Security, the Truman Administration, and the Cold War* (Stanford, CA: Stanford University Press, 1992); Thomas Christensen, *Useful Adversaries: Grand Strategy, Domestic Mobilization, and Sino-American Conflict, 1947–1958* (Princeton: Princeton University Press, 1996); for the domestically imposed limits on this process, see Aaron Friedberg, *In the Shadow of the Garrison State: America's Anti-Statism and Its Cold War Grand Strategy* (Princeton: Princeton University Press, 2000); Michael Hogan, *A Cross of Iron: Harry S. Truman and the Origins of the National Security State, 1945–1954* (New York: Cambridge University Press, 1998).

[41] Geir Lunstestad, "Empire by Invitation? The United States and Western Europe, 1945–1952," *Journal of Peace Research* 23 (September 1986): 263–277; James McAllister, *No Exit: America and the German Problem, 1943–1954* (Ithaca, NY: Cornell University Press, 2002).

not so veiled) rewards and threats, on fundamental issues the United States had to take allied interests and views to heart. Thus, Charles Maier exaggerates only slightly when he refers to "consensual American hegemony" within the West.[42]

As Europe stabilized and the American deterrent force became concentrated in intercontinental bombers and missiles, the need for allies, although still considerable, diminished. The United States could rebuff Britain and France at Suez in a way that it could not have done five years earlier. Twenty-five years later, Reagan could pay even less heed to allied wishes than Eisenhower had. Of course, the United States could not do everything it wanted. Not only was it restrained by Soviet power, but to go it alone would have alienated domestic opinion, risked policy setbacks, and endangered an international economic system already under great pressure. But the degree to which the United States sought consensus and respected allied desires varied from issue to issue and president to president. Above a significant but limited minimum level, cooperation with allies had become a matter of choice, not necessity.

The required minimum level of cooperation decreased with the end of the Cold War and the emergence of unipolarity. The United States now has a greater share of world power than any state since the beginning of the state system, and it is not likely to lose this position in the foreseeable future.[43] Before the first Bush's presidency, the United States used a mixture of carrots and sticks and pursued sometimes narrower but often broader conceptions of its interest. Clinton, and Bush before him, cultivated allies and worked hard to maintain large coalitions. Most scholars approve of this mode of behavior, seeing it as the best if not the only way for the United States to secure desired behavior from others, minimize the costs to itself, and most smoothly manage a complex and contentious world.[44] But the choice of this approach was indeed

---

[42] Charles Maier, *In Search of Stability: Explorations in Historical Political Economy* (New York: Cambridge University Press, 1987), 148. Also see John Lewis Gaddis, *We Now Know: Rethinking Cold War History* (New York: Oxford University Press, 1997); and Thomas Risse-Kappen, *Cooperation Among Democracies: The European Influence on U.S. Foreign Policy* (Princeton: Princeton University Press, 1995).

[43] William Wohlforth, "The Stability of a Unipolar World," *International Security* 24 (Summer 1999): 5–41; see also Kenneth Waltz, "Structural Realism After the Cold War," ibid. 25 (Summer 2000): 5–41. For a dissenting view, see Immanuel Wallerstein, "The Eagle Has Crash Landed," *Foreign Policy* 131 (July/August 2002): 60–68. The well-crafted argument by Robert Kudrle that the United States does not always gets its way even on some important issues is correct, but I think does not contradict the basic structural point: "Hegemony Strikes Out: The U.S. Global Role in Anti-Trust, Tax Evasion, and Illegal Immigration," *International Studies Perspectives* 4 (February 2003): 52–71.

[44] See, for example, G. John Ikenberry, "After September 11: America's Grand Strategy and International Order in the Age of Terror," *Survival* 43 (Winter 2001–2002): 19–34; Ikenberry, *After Victory: Institutions, Strategic Restraint, and the Rebuilding of Order After Major War* (Princeton: Princeton University Press, 2000); John Gerard Ruggie, *Winning the Peace: America and the New World Order* (New York: Columbia University Press, 1996); Joseph Nye, *The Paradox of American Power: Why the World's Only Superpower Can't Go It Alone* (New York: Oxford University Press, 2002); John Steinbrunner, *Principles of Global Security* (Washington, DC: Brookings Institution, 2000). More popular treatments are Clyde Prestowitz, *Rogue Nation: American Unilateralism and the Failure of Good Intentions* (New York: Basic Books, 2003); and Michael Hirsh, *At War With Ourselves: Why America Is Squandering Its Chance to Build a Better World* (New York: Oxford University Press, 2003).

a choice, revocable upon the appearance of changed circumstances and a differ-ent leader. The structure of world power meant that there was always a possibil-ity that the United States would act on its own.

Until recently, however, it did not seem clear that the United States would in fact behave in a highly unilateral fashion and assert its primacy. The new American stance was precipitated, if not caused by, the interaction between the terrorist attacks and the election of George W. Bush, who brought to the office a more unilateral outlook than his predecessor and his domestic opponents. Bush's response to September 11 may parallel his earlier religious conversion and owe something to his religious beliefs, especially in his propensity to see the struggle as one between good and evil. There is reason to believe that just as his coming to Christ gave meaning to his previously aimless and dissolute personal life, so the war on terrorism has become, not only the defining charac-teristic of his foreign policy, but also his sacred mission. An associate of the President reports: "I believe the president was sincere, after 9/11, thinking 'This is what I was put on this earth for.'"[45] We can only speculate on what President Al Gore would have done. My estimate is that he would have invaded Afghani-stan, but not proceeded against Iraq; nor would he have moved away from trea-ties and other arrangements over a wide range of issues. To some extent, the current assertion of strong American hegemony may be an accident.

But it was an accident waiting to happen. To start with, there are structural reasons to have expected a large terrorist attack. Bin Laden had attacked American interests abroad and from early on sought to strike the homeland. His enmity stemmed primarily from the establishment of U.S. bases in Saudi Arabia, which was a product of America's worldwide responsibilities. Ironi-cally, the overthrow of Saddam is likely to permit the United States to reduce its presence in Saudi Arabia, although I doubt if bin Laden expected this result to follow from his attack or that he will now be satisfied. Furthermore, al Qaeda was not the only group targeting the United States; as Richard Betts has argued, terrorism is the obvious weapon of weak actors against the leading state.[46]

Even without terrorism, both internal and structural factors predisposed the United States to assert its dominance. I think structural factors are more important, but it is almost a truism of the history of American foreign relations that the United States rarely if ever engages in deeply cooperative ventures with equals.[47] Unlike the European states who were surrounded by peers, once

---

[45] Quoted in James Harding, "Conflicting Views From Two Bush Camps," *Financial Times*, 20 March 2003; for a perceptive analysis, see Bruni, "For President, a Mission and a Role in History." Also see Woodward, *Bush at War*, 102, 205, 281.

[46] Richard Betts, "The Soft Underbelly of American Primacy: Tactical Advantages of Terror," *Political Science Quarterly* 117 (Spring 2002): 19–36.

[47] See, for example, Jesse Helms's defense of unilateralism as the only way consistent with Ameri-can interests and traditions: "American Sovereignty and the UN," *National Interest* 62 (Winter 2000/01): 31–34. For a discussion of historical, sociological, and geographical sources of the moralistic out-look in American foreign policy, see Arnold Wolfers, *Discord and Collaboration* (Baltimore: Johns Hopkins University Press, 1962), chap. 15; and Louis Hartz, *The Liberal Tradition in America* (New York: Harcourt, Brace, 1955), chap. 11. For a discussion of current U.S. policy in terms of its self-image as an exceptional state, see Stanley Hoffmann, "The High and the Mighty," *American Prospect* 13 (January 2003): 28–31.

the United States had established its dominance first over its neighbors and then over the rest of the New World, it had great choice about the terms on which it would work with others. Thus, when the United States intervened in World War I, it insisted that the coalition be called the "Allied and Associated Powers"—that is, it was an associate with freedom of action, not an ally. The structure of the American government, its weak party system, its domestic diversity, and its political traditions, all make sustained cooperation difficult. It would be an exaggeration to say that unilateralism is the American way of foreign policy, but there certainly is a strong pull in this direction.

More importantly, the United States may be acting like a normal state that has gained a position of dominance.[48] There are four facets to this argument. First and most general is the core of the Realist outlook that power is checked most effectively and often only by counterbalancing power. It follows that states that are not subject to external restraints tend to feel few restraints at all. As Edmund Burke put it, in a position endorsed by Hans Morgenthau: "I dread our *own* power and our *own* ambition; I dread our being too much dreaded. It is ridiculous to say that we are not men, and that, as men, we shall never wish to aggrandize ourselves."[49] With this as one of his driving ideas, Kenneth Waltz saw the likelihood of current behavior from the start of the post-Cold War era:

> The powerful state may, and the United States does, think of itself as acting for the sake of peace, justice, and well-being in the world. But these terms will be defined to the liking of the powerful, which may conflict with the preferences and the interests of others. In international politics, overwhelming power repels and leads others to try to balance against it. With benign intent, the United States has behaved, and until its power is brought into a semblance of balance, will continue to behave in ways that annoy and frighten others.[50]

Parts of the Bush doctrine are unique to the circumstances, but it is the exception rather than the rule for states to stay on the path of moderation when others do not force them to do so.[51]

---

[48] Thus, it is not entirely surprising that many of the beliefs mustered in support of United States policy toward Iraq parallel those held by European expansionists in earlier eras: Jack Snyder, "Imperial Temptations," *National Interest* 71 (Spring 2003): 29–40.

[49] Quoted in Hans Morgenthau, *Politics Among Nations*, 5th ed. (New York: Knopf, 1978), 169–170. (Emphasis in the original.)

[50] Kenneth Waltz, "America as a Model for the World? A Foreign Policy Perspective," *PS: Political Science and Politics* 24 (December 1991): 69; also see Waltz's discussion of the Gulf War: "A Necessary War?" in Harry Kriesler, ed., *Confrontation in the Gulf* (Berkeley, CA: Institute of International Studies, 1992), 59–65. Charles Krauthammer also expected this kind of behavior, but believed that it will serve the world as well as the American interests. Krauthammer, "The Unipolar Moment," *Foreign Affairs, America and the World, 1990–91* 70 (no. 1, 23–33); also see Krauthammer, "The Unipolar Moment Revisited." For a critical analysis, see Chace, "Imperial America and the Common Interest." As Waltz noted much earlier, even William Fulbright, while decrying the arrogance of American power, said that the United States could and should "lead the world in an effort to change the nature of its politics": quoted in *Theory of International Politics* (Reading, MA: Addison-Wesley, 1979), 201.

[51] Alexander Wendt and, more persuasively, Paul Schroeder, would disagree or at least modify this generalization, arguing that prevailing ideas can and have led to more moderate and consensual behav-

Second, states' definitions of their interests tend to expand as their power does.[52] It then becomes worth pursuing a whole host of objectives that were out of reach when the state's security was in doubt and all efforts had to be directed to primary objectives. Under the new circumstances, states seek what Arnold Wolfers called "milieu goals."[53] The hope of spreading democracy and liberalism throughout the world has always been an American goal, but the lack of a peer competitor now makes it more realistic—although perhaps not very realistic—to actively strive for it. Seen in this light, the administration's perception that this is a time of great opportunity in the Middle East is the product, not so much of the special circumstances in the region, but of the enormous resources at America's disposal.

More specifically, the quick American victory in Afghanistan probably contributed to the expansion of American goals. Likewise, the easy military victory in Iraq, providing the occupation can be brought to a successful conclusion, will encourage the pursuit of a wider agenda, if not threatening force against other tyrants ("moving down the list," in the current phrase). Bush's initial speech after September 11 declared war on terrorists "with a global reach." This was ambitious, but at least the restriction to these kinds of terrorists meant that many others were not of concern. The modifier was dropped in the wake of Afghanistan, however. Not only did rhetoric shift to seeing terrorism in general as a menace to civilization and "the new totalitarian threat,"[54] but the United States sent first military trainers and then a combat unit to the Philippines to attack guerrillas who posed only a minimal threat to Americans and who have no significant links to al Qaeda. Furthermore, at least up until a point, the exercise of power can increase power as well as interests. I do not think that the desire to control a large supply of oil was significant motivation for the Iraqi war, but it will give the United States an additional instrument of influence.

A third structural explanation for American behavior is that increased relative power brings with it new fears. The reasons are both objective and subjec-

---

ior: Wendt, *Social Theory of International Politics* (New York: Cambridge University Press, 1999); Schroeder, *The Transformation of European Politics, 1763–1848* (New York: Oxford University Press, 1994); and "Does the History of International Politics Go Anywhere?" in David Wetzel and Theodore Hamerow, eds., *International Politics and German History* (Westport, CT: Praeger, 1997), 15–36. This is a central question of international politics and history that I cannot fully discuss here, but believe that at least the mild statement that unbalanced power is dangerous can easily be sustained.

[52] See, for example, Fareed Zakaria, "Realism and Domestic Politics: A Review Essay," *International Security* 17 (Summer 1992): 177–198; Robert Tucker, "The Radical Critique Assessed" in Tucker, *The Radical Left and American Foreign Policy* (Baltimore: Johns Hopkins University Press, 1971), 69–77, 106–111. For a discussion of alternative possibilities suggested by American history, see Edward Rhodes, "The Imperial Logic of Bush's Liberal Agenda," *Survival* 45 (Spring 2003): 131–154.

[53] Wolfers, *Discord and Collaboration*, chap. 5.

[54] "President Thanks World Coalition for Anti-Terrorism Efforts"; David Sanger, "In Reichstag, Bush Condemns Terror as New Despotism," *New York Times*, 24 May 2002. Also see "Remarks by President at 2002 Graduation Exercise." The question of how broad the target should be was debated within the administration from the start, with Bush initially insisting on a focus on al Qaeda: Woodward, *Bush at War*.

tive. As Wolfers notes in his classic essay on "National Security as Ambiguous Symbol," the latter can diverge from the former.[55] In one manifestation of this, as major threats disappear, people psychologically elevate ones that were previously seen as quite manageable.[56] People now seem to be as worried as they were during the height of the Cold War despite the fact that a terrorist or rogue attack, even with WMD, could cause only a small fraction of a possible World War III's devastation. But there is more to it than psychology. A dominant state acquires an enormous stake in the world order, and interests spread throughout the globe. Most countries are primarily concerned with what happens in their immediate neighborhoods; the world is the hegemon's neighborhood, and it is not only hubris that leads it to be concerned with anything that happens anywhere. The result is a fusion of narrow and broad self-interest. At a point when most analysts were worried about the decline of American power, not its excesses, Waltz noted that for the United States, "like some earlier great powers. . . . the interest of the country in security came to be identified with the maintenance of a certain world order. For countries at the top, this is predictable behavior. . . . Once a state's interests reach a certain extent, they become self-reinforcing."[57]

The historian John S. Galbraith explored the related dynamic of the "turbulent frontier" that produced the unintended expansion of colonialism. As a European power gained an enclave in Africa or Asia, usually along the coast or river, it also gained an unpacified boundary that had to be policed. This led to further expansion of influence and often of settlement, and this in turn produced a new area that had to be protected and a new zone of threat.[58] There were few natural limits to this process. There are not likely to be many now. The wars in Afghanistan and Iraq have led to the establishment of U.S. bases and security commitments in central Asia, an area previously beyond reach. It is not hard to imagine how the United States could be drawn further into politics in the region and to find itself using force to oppose terrorist or guerrilla movements that arise there, perhaps in part in reaction to the American presence. The same dynamic could play out in Colombia.

The fourth facet can be seen as a broader conception of the previous point. As Realists stress, even states that find the status quo acceptable have to worry

[55] Wolfers, *Discord and Collaboration*, chap. 10.

[56] John Mueller, "The Catastrophe Quota: Trouble after the Cold War," *Journal of Conflict Resolution* 38 (September 1994): 355–375; also see Frederick Hartmann, *The Conservation of Enemies: A Study in Enmity* (Westport, CT: Greenwood Press, 1982).

[57] Waltz, *Theory of International Politics*, 200.

[58] John S. Galbraith, "The 'Turbulent Frontier' as a Factor in British Expansion," *Comparative Studies in Society and History* 2 (January 1960): 34–48; *Reluctant Empire: British Policy on the South African Frontier, 1834–1854* (Berkeley: University of California Press, 1963). Also see Ronald Robinson and John Gallager with Alice Denny, *Africa and the Victorians: The Official Mind of Imperialism* (London: Macmillan, 1961). A related imperial dynamic that is likely to recur is that turning a previously recalcitrant state into a client usually weakens it internally and requires further intervention.

about the future.[59] The more an actor sees the current situation as satisfactory, the more it will expect the future to be worse. Psychology plays a role here too: prospect theory argues that actors are prone to accept great risks when they believe they will suffer losses unless they act boldly. The adoption of a preventive war doctrine may be a mistake, especially if taken too far, but is not foreign to normal state behavior. It appeals to states that have a valued position to maintain. However secure states are, only rarely can they be secure enough, and if they are currently very powerful, they will have strong reasons to act now to prevent a deterioration that could allow others to harm them in the future.[60]

All this means that under the Bush doctrine the United States is not a status quo power. Its motives may not be selfish, but the combination of power, fear, and perceived opportunity leads it to seek to reshape world politics and the societies of many of its members. This tracks with and extends traditional ideas in American foreign relations held by both liberals and conservatives who saw the United States as a revolutionary country. As the first modern democracy, the United States was founded on principles of equality, progress, and a government subordinate to civil society that, while initially being uniquely American, had universal applicability. Because a state's foreign policy is inseparable from its domestic regime, a safe and peaceful world required the spread of these arrangements.[61] Under current conditions of terrorism and WMD, tyrannical governments pose too much of a potential if not actual danger to be tolerated. The world cannot stand still. Without strong American intervention, the international environment will become more menacing to America and its values, but strong action can increase its security and produce a better world. In a process akin to the deep security dilemma,[62] in order to protect itself, the United States is impelled to act in a way that will increase, or at least bring to the surface, conflicts with others. Even if the prevailing situation is satisfactory, it cannot be maintained by purely defensive measures. Making the world safe for American democracy is believed to require that dictatorial regimes be banished, or at least kept from weapons of mass destruction. Although not mentioned in the pronouncements, the Bush doctrine is made possible by the existence of a secu-

---

[59] See esp., Copeland, *Origins of Major War*; Mearsheimer, *Tragedy of Great Power Politics*.

[60] Waltz (*Theory of International Politics*) sees this behavior as often self-defeating; Mearsheimer (*Tragedy of Great Power Politics*) implies that it is not; Copeland's position is somewhere in between.

[61] George W. Bush would endorse Wilson's claim that America's goal must be "the destruction of every arbitrary power anywhere in the world that can separately, secretly, and of its single choice disturb the peace of the world" just as he would join Clinton in calling for "the spread of his revolt [i.e., the American revolution], this liberation, to the great stage of the world itself!" "An Address at Mount Vernon," 4 July 1918, in Arthur Link et al., eds., *The Papers of Woodrow Wilson*, vol. 48, *May 13–July 17, 1918* (Princeton: Princeton University Press, 1985), 516–517.

[62] Robert Jervis, "Was the Cold War a Security Dilemma?" *Journal of Cold War History* 3 (Winter 2001): 36–60; also see Paul Roe, "Former Yugoslavia: The Security Dilemma That Never Was?" *European Journal of International Relations* 6 (September 2000): 373–393. The current combination of fear and hope that produces offensive actions for defensive motives resembles the combination that produced the pursuit of preponderance in the aftermath of World War II.

rity community among the world's most powerful and developed states—the United States, Western Europe, and Japan.[63] The lack of fears of war among these countries allows the United States to focus on other dangers and to pursue other goals. Furthermore, the development of the security community gives the United States a position that it now wants to preserve.

HEGEMONY, IRAQ, AND EUROPE

This perspective on the Bush doctrine helps explain international disagreements about Iraq. Most accounts of the French opposition stress its preoccupation with glory and its traditional jealousy and disdain for the United States. Europe's resistance to the war is attributed to the peaceful world view produced by its success in overcoming historical rivalries and creating a law-governed society, summarized by the phrase "Americans are from Mars, the Europeans are from Venus."[64] Also frequently mentioned is the European aversion to the crude and bullying American style: "Bush is just a cowboy." There is something to these positions, but are Europeans really so averse to force and wedded to law? When faced with domestic terrorism, Germany and other European countries did not hesitate to employ unrestrained state power that John Ashcroft would envy, and their current treatment of minorities, especially Muslims, does not strike these populations as liberal. The French continue to intervene in Africa unilaterally, disregarded legal rulings to drop their ban on British beef, and join other European states in playing as fast and loose with trade regulations as does the United States. Most European states favored the war in Kosovo and supported the United States in Afghanistan; had they been attacked on September 11, they might not have maintained their aversion to the use of force.

Even more glaringly, the claims for a deep cultural divide overlook the fundamental difference between how Europe and the United States are placed in the international system. The fact that the latter is hegemonic has three implications. First, only the United States has the power to do anything about problems like Iraq; the others have incentives to ride free. Second, the large European states have every reason to be concerned about American hegemony and sufficient resources to seek to constrain it. This is not traditional power balancing, which is driven by security fears; the French are not afraid of an American attack, and the German worry is that the United States will withdraw too many of its troops. But they do fear that a world dominated by the United States would be one in which their values and interests would be served only at American sufferance. It is hardly surprising that an April 2002 poll showed that overwhelming majorities within many European countries felt that American policy toward Iraq and the Middle East in general was based "mainly on its own inter-

[63] Robert Jervis, "Theories of War in an Era of Leading Power Peace," *American Political Science Review* 96 (March 2003): 1–14.

[64] The best known statement of this position is Robert Kagan, *Of Paradise and Power: America and Europe in the New World Order* (New York: Knopf, 2003).

ests."[65] The National Security Advisor, Condoleezza Rice, has forgotten her knowledge of basic international politics when she expresses her shock at discovering that "there were times that it appeared that American power was seen [by France and Germany] to be more dangerous than, perhaps, Saddam Hussein."[66] The United States may be correct that American dominance serves Europe and the world, but we should not be startled when others beg to differ. The United States probably is as benign a hegemon as the world has ever seen. Its large domestic market, relatively tolerant values, domestic diversity, and geographic isolation all are helpful. But a hegemon it remains, and by that very fact it must make others uneasy.

Third, the Europeans' stress on the need to go through the Security Council shows less their abstract attachment to law and world governance than their appreciation of power. France especially, but also Russia and China (two countries that are not from Venus), will gain enormously if they can establish the principle that large-scale force can be used only with the approval of the Council, of which they are permanent members. Security Council membership is one of the major resources at these countries' disposal. The statement of a Russian leader that "if someone tries to wage war on their own account . . . without an international mandate, it means all the world is confusion and a wild jungle"[67] would carry more moral weight if Russia did not have a veto in the mandate-granting body. If the Council were not central, French influence would be much diminished.

The United Kingdom does not readily fit this picture, of course. Structure always leaves room for choice, and Tony Blair told Parliament on 24 September 2002 that "it is an article of faith with me that the American relationship and our ability to partner [with] America in these difficult issues is of fundamental importance, not just to this country but to the wider world." Blair's personal views may be part of the explanation, but this has been the British stance ever since World War II, which resisted becoming too much a part of Europe and sought to maintain a major role in the world through supporting rather than opposing the United States. But only one ally can seek to have a "special relationship" with the hegemon, and Britain's having taken this role makes it harder for others to emulate it.

Structure also explains why many of the smaller European countries chose to support the United States in Iraq despite hostile public opinion. The dominance they fear most is not American, but Franco-German. The United States is more powerful, but France and Germany are closer and more likely to menace them.[68] Seeking a distant protector is a standard practice in international politics. That France and Germany resented the resulting opposition is no more

---

[65] Adam Clymer, "European Poll Faults U.S. for its Policy in the Mid East," *New York Times*, 19 April 2002.

[66] Quoted in David Sanger, "Witness to Auschwitz Evil, Bush Draws a Lesson," ibid., 1 June 2003.

[67] Quoted in John Tagliabue, "France and Russia Ready to Use Veto Against Iraq War," ibid., 6 March 2003.

[68] This is a version of Stephen Walt's argument that states balance against threat, not power: *The Origins of Alliances* (Ithaca, NY: Cornell University Press, 1987).

surprising than the American dismissal of "old Europe," with the resulting parallel that while France and Germany bitterly decried the American effort to hustle them into line, they disparaged and bullied the East European states that sided with the United States—quite un-Venusian behavior.

CONCLUSION

Where we will go from here depends in part on unpredictable events such as economic shocks, the course of reconstruction in Iraq, the targets and success of future terrorist attacks, and the characteristics of the leaders that arise through diverse domestic processes. The war against Saddam, however, already marks out the path on which the United States is embarked and illuminates the links between preventive war and hegemony, which was much of the reason for the opposition at home and abroad. Bush's goals are extraordinarily ambitious, involving remaking not only international politics but recalcitrant societies as well, which is seen as an end in itself and a means to American security. For better or (and?) for worse, the United States has set itself tasks that prudent states would shun. As a result, it will be infringing on what adversaries, if not allies, see as their vital interests. Coercion and especially deterrence may be insufficient for these tasks because these instruments share with traditional diplomacy the desire to minimize conflict by limiting one's own claims to interests that others can afford to respect. States that seek more need to be highly assertive if not aggressive, which provides additional reasons to question the goals themselves. The beliefs of Bush and his colleagues that Saddam's regime would have been an unacceptable menace to American interests if it had been allowed to obtain nuclear weapons not only tell us about their fears for the limits of United States influence that might have been imposed, but also speak volumes about the expansive definition of United States interests that they hold.[69]

The war is hard to understand if the only objective was to disarm Saddam or even to remove him from power. Even had the inflated estimates of his WMD capability been accurate, the danger was simply too remote to justify the effort. But if changing the Iraqi regime was expected to bring democracy and stability to the Middle East, discourage tyrants and energize reformers throughout the world, and demonstrate the American willingness to provide a high degree of what it considers world order whether others like it or not, then as part of a larger project, the war makes sense. Those who find both the hopes and the fears excessive if not delusional agree with the great British statesman Lord Salisbury when he tried to bring some perspective to the Eastern Crisis of 1877–1878: "It has generally been acknowledged to be madness to go to war for an idea, but if anything is more unsatisfactory, it is to go to war against a nightmare."[70]

[69] I have discussed how Bush's policy toward Iraq does and does not fit with deterrence thinking in "The Confrontation Between Iraq and the United States: Implications for the Theory and Practice of Deterrence," *European Journal of International Relations* 9 (June 2003): 315–337.

[70] Quoted in R. W. Seton-Watson, *Disraeli, Gladstone, and the Eastern Question* (New York: Norton, 1972), 222.

We can only speculate about the crucial question of whether the Bush doctrine will work. Contrary to the common impression, democracies, especially the United States, do not find it easy to sustain a clear line of policy when the external environment is not compelling. Domestic priorities ordinarily loom large, and few Americans think of their country as having an imperial mission. Wilsonianism may provide a substitute for the older European ideologies of a *mission civilisatrice* and the white man's burden, but since it rests on the assumption that its role will not only be noble but also popular, I am skeptical that it will endure if it meets much indigenous opposition from those who are supposed to benefit from it. Significant casualties will surely be corrosive, and when the going gets tough I think the United States will draw back.

Furthermore, while the United States is the strongest country in the world, its power is still subject to two familiar limitations: it is harder to build than to destroy, and success depends on others' decisions because their cooperation is necessary for the state to reach its goals. Of course, American military capability is not to be ignored, and I doubt whether countries like Iran, Syria, and North Korea will ignore it. They may well reason as Bush expects them to and limit their WMD programs and support for terrorism, if not reform domestically. But the prospects for long-run compliance are less bright. Although a frontal assault on American interests is perhaps unlikely, highly motivated adversaries will not give up the quest to advance their interests as they see them. The war in Iraq has increased the risks of their pursuing nuclear weapons, but it has also increased their incentives to do so. Amid the debate about what these weapons can accomplish, everyone agrees that they can deter invasion, which makes them very attractive to states who fear they might be in the American gun sights. Both Waltz's argument that proliferation will produce stability and the contrary and more common claim that it would make the world more dangerous imply that the spread of nuclear weapons will reduce American influence because others will have less need of its security guarantees and will be able to fend off its threats to their vital interests.[71] The American attempt to minimize the ability of others to resist U.S. pressures is the mark of a country bent, not on maintaining the status quo, but on fashioning a new and better order.

Obviously, U.S. military capabilities matter less in relations with allies and probably with Russia. From them the United States wants wholehearted cooperation on issues such as sharing highly sensitive information on terrorism, rebuilding failed states, preventing proliferation, and, perhaps most importantly, managing the international economy. There is little danger or hope that Europe will form a united counterweight to the United States and try to thwart it by

---

[71] Kenneth Waltz, *The Spread of Nuclear Weapons: More May Be Better* (London: IISS, Adelphi Paper No. 171, 1981); Scott Sagan and Kenneth Waltz, *The Spread of Nuclear Weapons: A Debate Renewed* (New York: Norton, 2003). For a range of views, see Marc Trachtenberg, "Waltzing to Armageddon?" *National Interest* 69 (Fall 2002): 144–155; Eric Herring, ed., *Preventing the Use of Weapons of Mass Destruction*, special issue of *Journal of Strategic Studies* 23 (March 2000); T. V. Paul, Richard Harknett, and James Wirtz, eds., *The Absolute Weapon Revisited: Nuclear Arms and the Emerging International Order* (Ann Arbor: University of Michigan Press, 1998).

active opposition, let alone the use of force. But political resistance is quite possible and, even more than with adversaries, the fate of the American design for world order lies in the hands of its allies.[72] Although the United States governs many of the incentives that Europe and potential supporters face, what it needs from them cannot be coerced. It is possible that they will see themselves better off with the United States as an assertive hegemon, allowing them to gain the benefits of world order while being spared the costs, and they may conclude that any challenge would fail or bring with it dangerous rivalry. Without the war in Iraq, I doubt that the spring of 2003 would have seen the degree of cooperation that the United States obtained from Europe in combatting the Iranian nuclear program and from Japan and the PRC in containing North Korea.

But I suspect that much will depend on the allies' answers to several questions: Can the American domestic political system sustain the Bush doctrine over the long run? Will the United States be open to allied influence and values? Will it put pressure on Israel as well as on the Arabs to reach a settlement? More generally, will it seek to advance the broad interests of the diverse countries and people in the world, or will it exploit its power for its own narrower political, economic, and social interests? Bush's world gives little place for other states—even democracies—except as members of a supporting cast. Conflating broader with narrower interests and believing that one has a monopoly on wisdom are obvious ways that a hegemon can come to be seen as tyrannical.[73] Woodrow Wilson said that both nationalism and internationalism called for the United States to join the League of Nations: "The greatest nationalist is the man who wants his nation to be the greatest nation, and the greatest nation is the nation which penetrates to the heart of its duty and mission among the nations of the world. With every flash of insight into the great politics of mankind, the nation that has that vision is elevated to a place of influence and power which it cannot get by arms."[74] Wilson surely meant what he said, but his great certainty that he knew what was best for the world was troubling. In the presidential campaign, Bush said that the United States needed a "more humble foreign policy."[75] But its objectives and conceptions make the Bush doctrine quite the opposite. Avoiding this imperial temptation will be the greatest challenge that the United States faces.

---

[72] For a discussion of possible forms of nonviolent opposition, see Robert Pape, "Soft Balancing Against the United States" (unpublished paper, University of Chicago, 2003).

[73] See David Calleo, *The German Problem Reconsidered: Germany and the World Order, 1870 to the Present* (New York: Cambridge University Press, 1978) for a summary of relevant laboratory experiments; see Robert Goodin, "How Amoral *Is* Hegemon," *Perspectives on Politics* 1 (March 2003): 123–126.

[74] "A Luncheon Address to the St. Louis Chamber of Commerce," 5 September 1919 in Arthur Link et al., eds., *The Papers of Woodrow Wilson*, vol. 63, *September 4–November 5, 1919* (Princeton: Princeton University Press, 1990), 33.

[75] Quoted in David Sanger, "A New View of Where America Fits in the World," *New York Times*, 18 February 2001.

* I am grateful for comments from Robert Art, Richard Betts, Jim Caraley, Dale Copeland, Peter Gourevitch, Chaim Kaufmann, Robert Lieber, Marc Trachtenberg, and Kenneth Waltz.

Part II:
EXPERIENCES FROM THE FIRST PREVENTIVE WAR

Deciding on War Against Iraq: Institutional Failures

LOUIS FISHER

Following the swift U.S. military victory in Iraq, teams of experts conducted careful searches to discover the weapons of mass destruction that President George W. Bush offered as the principal justification for war. It was his claim that these weapons represented a direct and immediate threat. Months after the president announced victory, little evidence has been found nor is there much reason to expect anything significant to emerge. Stories began to circulate that perhaps the Bush administration had deceived allies, Congress, and the American public.

It is quite late to play the innocent, to express shock at troubling new disclosures. For over a year, the administration supplied a steady stream of unreliable statements. At no time did it make a persuasive, credible, or consistent case for war. Much of its rationale was exploded on a regular basis by the press. The campaign for war was dominated more by fear than facts, more by assertions of what might be, or could be, or used to be, than by what actually existed. Those who now felt duped had not been paying attention.

Month after month, the administration released claims that were unproven. In preparing for war in that manner, it should come as no surprise that plans for a stable, functioning Iraqi civil society seemed to be an afterthought. Having proved itself skilled in military combat, the Bush administration failed to address predictable looting and violence. After Afghanistan, it should have been obvious that a military victory must be followed quickly by a secure environment and visible reconstruction efforts. For its part, Congress seemed incapable of analyzing a presidential proposal and protecting its institutional powers. The decision to go to war cast a dark shadow over the health of U.S. political

LOUIS FISHER is senior specialist in separation of powers at the Congressional Research Service of the Library of Congress. He is the author of many books, including *Presidential War Power* and *Congressional Abdication on War and Spending.*

institutions and the celebrated system of democratic debate and checks and balances.

The dismal performances of the executive and legislative branches raise disturbing questions about the capacity and desire of the United States to function as a republican form of government. Americans are supposed to do more than salute the flag. The pledge of allegiance is to something much more fundamental. Consider the words: "I pledge allegiance to the flag of the United States of America, and to the republic for which it stands." A republic means giving power to the people through their elected representatives, trusting in informed, legislative deliberation rather than monarchical edicts, and keeping the war power in Congress instead of transferring it to the president. Fed unreliable information from the administration, democratic deliberation becomes shallow and vacuous. Lose what it means to be a republic, and the flag stands for nothing.

It is tempting for the Bush administration and its supporters to dismiss opposition to the war in Iraq as primarily leftist and antiwar, inspired by those who insist on international—not unilateral—solutions. That misses the point. After September 11, Americans were united in supporting military action against the terrorist structures in Afghanistan. If no other country had offered us support, Bush could have acted singlehandedly against al Qaeda and the Taliban with full public approval. He would have enjoyed the same public backing had he used military force against any other country or group responsible for September 11. Americans are willing to use force, and use it unilaterally, when necessary to defend the nation. Past and current opposition to the war in Iraq is of the administration's own making, nourished by statements that lacked credibility.

Patriotism is not indiscriminate flag-waving at each and every war. Citizens stand ready to sacrifice lives and fortunes for national security. At the same time, they oppose wars that cause needless deaths, including one's sons and daughters, and regard it a public duty to confront government officials who urge war without justifying it. Military force demands solid evidence that a threat is imminent and war is unavoidable. It is on that ground that the Bush administration and its allies—here and abroad—failed a fundamental democratic test.

A MUDDLED EXPLANATION

David Frum, after a little more than a year as a speechwriter in the Bush White House, offered some insights into the process of policy making at the highest levels. Frum tells us that Bush "hated repetition and redundancy."[1] Frum is convinced that if Bush had read that sentence, he would have deleted the words "and redundancy." Still, Bush never tired of repeating that a link existed between Iraq and al Qaeda, even if the evidence remained tenuous and unpersua-

[1] David Frum, *The Right Man* (New York: Random House, 2003), 48.

sive. Bush said it so often that most of the public came to believe it was true. In this area, he liked both repetition and redundancy.

One of Frum's draft speeches contained the phrase, "I've seen with my own eyes." Bush used his marking pen to add in the margin a sarcastic "DUH." Such experiences convinced Frum that Bush "insisted on strict linear logic."[2] There is much to be said for that. Bush's performance in the 2000 presidential campaign consisted of straight, simple talk, with an impressive ability to connect with an audience. Al Gore's delivery was much more convoluted, leaving listeners uncertain about the destination of his thoughts. Comparatively, Bush was a model of clarity.

Why did Bush, in advocating military action against Iraq, abandon "strict linear logic?" His speeches were filled with strained arguments and dramatic claims that could not be substantiated. Presentations were cloudy, repetitive, and lacking in credibility. It shouldn't have been difficult to make a plausible case for war and stick with it. Bush could have said: "Saddam Hussein has used chemical weapons against his own people. I don't want him in a position to use chemical agents again, possibly along with biological and nuclear weapons. Nor will I give him any potential for transferring such weapons to terrorists from other countries. I will do everything in my power to prevent another attack like September 11. To survive as a nation, we must be willing to act in advance."

Those themes appear in Bush's speeches and statements, but his rationale for war was confused by poorly reasoned statements and claims of Iraqi programs that rested on nonexistent facts. The administration seemed content to throw anything out to see if it would stick. That is the record from August 2002 to the present.

Looking at "All Options"

When the administration first began talking about war against Iraq, White House Spokesman Ari Fleischer cautioned on a number of occasions that President Bush was not rushing into war. Instead, he was described as a deliberate man who carefully studied all options. On 21 August 2002, President Bush called himself "a patient man. And when I say I'm a patient man, I mean I'm a patient man, and that we will look at all options, and we will consider all technologies available to us and diplomacy and intelligence."[3] With such statements Bush seemed to move with great care and circumspection.

A war plan, Americans were told, was not "on the President's desk."[4] At that same press conference on 21 August, Bush noted that "there is this kind of intense speculation that seems to be going on, a kind of a—I don't know how you would describe it. It's kind of a churning—." Secretary of Defense Donald

---

[2] Ibid.

[3] *Weekly Compilation of Presidential Documents*, 38: 1393–1394 (21 August 2002).

[4] Elizabeth Bumiller, "U.S. Must Act First to Battle Terror, Bush Tells Cadets," *New York Times*, 2 June 2002.

Rumsfeld, standing next to him, supplied the missing word: "frenzy." Bush agreed. The country was too preoccupied, he said, with military action against Iraq.

Yet, within five days, the administration switched to a frenzied mode. Vice President Dick Cheney delivered a forceful speech that offered a single option: going to war. He warned that Saddam Hussein would "fairly soon" have nuclear weapons, and that it would be useless to seek a Security Council resolution requiring Iraq to submit to weapons inspectors. Hussein's threat, Cheney said, made preemptive attack against Iraq imperative.[5] The press interpreted his speech as "ruling out anything short of an attack."[6] Newspaper editorials concluded that Cheney's speech "left little room for measures short of the destruction of Saddam Hussein's regime through preemptive military action."[7] On 6 September, two reporters for the *Washington Post* noted the abrupt transition: "this week's frenzy of attention to Iraq was entirely generated by a White House whose occupants returned from the August recess anxious and ready to push the debate to a new level."[8] What happened to the options carefully being weighed by Bush?

In that first month, the administration was not yet walking lock-step. Secretary of State Colin Powell, in a 1 September interview with the BBC, recommended that weapons inspectors should return to Iraq as a "first step" in resolving the dispute with Iraq. Ari Fleischer, asked whether Powell's statement revealed a conflict within the administration, labored to convince reporters that Cheney and Powell agreed on fundamentals: "that arms inspectors in Iraq are a means to an end, and the end is knowledge that Iraq has lived up to its promises that it made to end the Gulf War, that it has in fact disarmed, that it does not possess weapons of mass destruction."[9] However, Cheney had already announced that Iraq *did* possess weapons of mass destruction.

On 3 September, Senate Minority Leader Trent Lott (R-MS) acknowledged the disarray within the administration: "I do think that we're going to have to get a more coherent message together."[10] Asked whether he was comfortable with the White House's presentation of the case for war against Iraq, he responded gamely: "I'd like to have a couple more days before I respond to that."[11] Such frankness must have made it easier for the administration to support Lott's replacement for majority leader, Bill Frist.

[5] Elizabeth Bumiller and James Dao, "Cheney Says Peril of a Nuclear Iraq Justifies Attack," *New York Times*, 27 August 2002.

[6] Dana Milbank, "Cheney Says Iraqi Strike Is Justified," *Washington Post*, 27 August 2002.

[7] "Mr. Cheney on Iraq" (Editorial), *Washington Post*, 27 August 2002.

[8] Dan Balz and Dana Milbank, "Iraq Policy Shift Follows Pattern," *Washington Post*, 6 September 2002.

[9] Dana Milbank, "No Conflict on Iraq Policy, Fleischer Says," *Washington Post*, 3 September 2002.

[10] Alison Mitchell and David E. Sanger, "Bush to Put Case for Action in Iraq to Key Lawmakers," *New York Times*, 4 September 2002.

[11] Helen Dewar and Mike Allen, "Senators Wary About Action Against Iraq," *Washington Post*, 4 September 2002.

"Regime Change"

The meaning of "regime change" changed from week to week. On 4 April 2002, in an interview with a British television network, Bush said: "I made up my mind that Saddam needs to go. . . . The policy of my Government is that he goes. . . . [T]he policy of my Government is that Saddam Hussein not be in power."[12] That was vintage Bush: clear, straight talk. On 1 August, he stated that the "policy of my Government . . . is regime change—for a reason. Saddam Hussein is a man who poisons his own people, who threatens his neighbors, who develops weapons of mass destruction."[13] Without equivocation, Hussein had to go.

The commitment to regime change and offensive war changed abruptly when President Bush addressed the United Nations on 12 September. After cataloguing Saddam Hussein's noncompliance with Security Council resolutions, apparently building a case for regime change and military operations, Bush then laid down five conditions for a peaceful resolution. If Iraq wanted to avoid war, it would have to immediately and unconditionally pledge to remove or destroy all weapons of mass destruction, end all support for terrorism, cease persecution of its civilian population, release or account for all Gulf War personnel, and immediately end all illicit trade outside the oil-for-food program.[14] The underlying message: If Iraq complied with those demands, Saddam Hussein could stay in power.

On 21 October, after Congress had passed the Iraq resolution, Bush again said that Hussein could stay. He announced that if Hussein complied with every UN mandate, "that in itself will signal the regime has changed."[15] An exquisite sentence, with overtones of Bill Clinton, much like a magic trick where you ask: "Could you do that again, only this time more slowly?" Saddam Hussein could now stay in office if he changed.

Belittling Inspections

After the 12 September UN speech, offering peace to Iraq if it complied with the five demands, Iraq agreed four days later to unconditional inspections. Given Iraq's record since 1991, there was good cause to be skeptical of its promises. But the response should have been to test Iraq's sincerity by sending inspection teams there to learn on the ground whether it would give full access to buildings and presidential palaces. Instead, the administration began to make light of inspections. Pentagon spokeswoman Victoria Clarke warned that

---

[12] *Weekly Compilation of Presidential Documents*, 38: 573 (4 April 2002).

[13] Ibid., 1295.

[14] Ibid., 1532.

[15] David E. Sanger, "Bush Declares U.S. Is Using Diplomacy to Disarm Hussein," *New York Times*, 22 October 2002.

inspections would be difficult if not impossible to carry out.[16] If so, why have Bush go to the UN and place that demand on Iraq and the Security Council?

On 26 September, during a campaign speech in Houston, Texas, Bush delivered the standard litany of offenses committed by Saddam Hussein, but added, perhaps carelessly: "this is a guy that tried to kill my dad at one time."[17] The comment made some wonder whether the impulse for war reflected careful considerations of national security or was instead a "family grudge match."[18] The administration offered many reasons for war, often going beyond concerns about weapons of mass destruction. Senator Paul Sarbanes (D-MD) questioned the claims by Secretary Colin Powell that Iraq, to avoid military action, would have to comply with a number of UN resolutions, including one directed against prohibited trade. Sarbanes asked: "Are we prepared to go to war to make sure they comply with U.N. resolutions on illicit trade outside the oil for food program? Will we take military action or go to war in order to make them release or account for all Gulf War personnel whose fate is still unknown? Would we do that?"[19] No answer was forthcoming.

The administration seemed unprepared or unwilling to distinguish between fundamental reasons and less consequential considerations. All became interchangeable, forming a mass here, separating into parts there. Missing throughout this process was integrity. Senator Richard Lugar (R-IN) criticized the undifferentiated laundry list of charges against Saddam Hussein, such as brutality toward his own people. In conversations with top officials of the administration, Lugar was satisfied that they recognized that such conduct could not justify a U.S. war.[20] In public statements, however, the administration—including President Bush—treated all these charges with the same seriousness. Whatever seemed to work was tried.

Why the zigs and zags? Going to war is a serious enterprise and calls for consistency, clarity, and coherence. It is supposed to be reasoned deliberation. In an op-ed piece in the *Washington Post* on 11 October 2002, Michael Kinsley acknowledged that ambiguity can be useful in dealing with other nations. Sending mixed signals can keep an enemy off balance. Yet, Kinsley concluded: "the cloud of confusion that surrounds Bush's Iraq policy is not tactical. It's the real thing. And the dissembling is aimed at the American citizenry, not at Saddam Hussein." Kinsley said that arguments that "stumble into each other like drunks are not serious. Washington is abuzz with the 'real reason' this or that subgroup of the administration wants this war."[21] Even after the military victory in April 2003, people are still asking the same question: "Why did we go to war?"

---

[16] Todd A. Purdum and David Firestone, "Chief U.N. Inspector Backs U.S., Demanding Full Iraq Disclosure," *New York Times*, 5 October 2002.

[17] *Weekly Compilation of Presidential Documents*, 38: 1633 (26 September 2002).

[18] Mike Allen, "Bush's Words Can Go to the Blunt Edge of Trouble," *Washington Post*, 29 September 2002.

[19] Todd S. Purdum, "The U.S. Case Against Iraq; Counting Up the Reasons," *New York Times*, 1 October 2002.

[20] David E. Sanger and Carl Hulse, "Bush Appears to Soften Tone on Iraq Action," *New York Times*, 2 October 2002.

[21] Michael Kinsley, "War for Dummies," *Washington Post*, 11 October 2002.

Legal Authority

Initially the administration concluded that President Bush did not need authority from Congress to mount an offensive war against Iraq. The White House Counsel's office gave a broad reading to the President's power as Commander in Chief and argued that the 1991 Iraq resolution provided continuing military authority to the President, transferring the authority neatly from father to son.[22] In an article for *Legal Times*, I detailed why those arguments were forced and unconvincing.[23] The Framers made the president Commander in Chief, not a monarch.

The White House claimed that Congress, by passing the Iraq Liberation Act of 1998, had already approved U.S. military action against Iraq for violations of Security Council resolutions.[24] That argument was empty. The statute begins by itemizing a number of congressional findings about Iraq: invasion of Iraq and Kuwait, the killing of Kurds, using chemical weapons against civilians, and other offenses. It supported, as a legally nonbinding "sense of Congress," efforts to remove Saddam Hussein from power and replace him with a democratic government. The law states that none of its provisions "shall be construed to authorize or otherwise speak to the use of United States Armed Forces (except as provided in section 4(a)(2)) in carrying out this Act."[25] That section authorized up to $97 million in military supplies to Iraqi opposition groups as part of the transition to democracy in Iraq. By its explicit terms, the statute did not authorize war.

Ari Fleischer announced that Bush "intends to consult with Congress because Congress has an important role to play."[26] Yet, for Bush and his aides to merely "consult" with Congress would not meet the needs of the Constitution. No doubt policy making works better when the president consults with lawmakers, but consultation is not a substitute for receiving statutory authority to go to war. Congress is a legislative body that discharges its constitutional duties by passing statutes to authorize and define national policy. It exists to legislate and legitimate, particularly for military and financial commitments. Only congressional authorization of a war against Iraq would satisfy the Constitution.

BRINGING CONGRESS ON BOARD

For one reason or another, Bush decided in early September 2002 to seek authorization from Congress. On several Sunday talk shows broadcast on 8 September, administration officials abandoned the unilateralist rhetoric and began

---

[22] Mike Allen and Juliet Eilperin, "Bush Aides Say Iraq War Needs No Hill Vote," *Washington Post*, 26 August 2002.

[23] Louis Fisher, "The Road to Iraq," *Legal Times*, 2 September 2002, 34.

[24] "Bush Rejects Hill Limits on Resolution Allowing War," *Washington Post*, 2 October 2002.

[25] 112 Stat. 3181, §8 (1998).

[26] Ron Fournier, "White House Lawyers Give Bush OK on Iraq," *Washington Times*, 26 August 2002.

building a case for a broad coalition. Cheney, having advocated preemptive strikes against Iraq a few weeks earlier, now embraced an entirely different strategy: "We're working together to build support with the American people, with the Congress, as many have suggested we should. And we're also, as many have suggested we should, going to the United Nations."[27]

The Rush to War

Although the administration had debated going to war against Iraq ever since September 11, Congress was expected to act quickly. According to one newspaper story, White House officials "have said that their patience with Congress would not extend much past the current session."[28] The message to Congress was now: Get on board or we'll leave without you. The administration wanted Congress to pass an authorizing resolution before it adjourned for the November elections. National Security Adviser Condoleeza Rice said that President Bush wanted lawmakers to approve the resolution before leaving town, adding that Bush "thinks it's better to do this sooner rather than later."[29]

What was so urgent? Senator Robert C. Byrd (D-WV) deplored "the war fervor, the drums of war, the bugles of war, the clouds of war—this war hysteria has blown in like a hurricane."[30] What could explain the shift from a relaxed policy in August to a "frenzied" demand a month later? White House Chief of Staff Andrew Card gave an interesting reason for waiting until September to advocate military action against Iraq: "from a marketing point of view, you don't introduce new products in August."[31] Was this another careless, flippant remark, or an inadvertent disclosure of the truth?

Bush could not rely on the precedents established by his father. In 1990, after Iraq had invaded Kuwait, the administration did not ask Congress for authority before the November elections. Instead, it first went to the Security Council and requested a resolution to authorize military operations, which passed on 29 November. Only in January 1991, after lawmakers returned, did they debate and pass legislation to authorize war against Iraq.

For reasons that were never explained, Congress in 2002 had to act pell-mell. In an op-ed piece that supported the administration's strategy, former Secretary of State George Shultz argued that the "danger is immediate." Iraq's making of weapons of mass destruction "grows increasingly difficult to counter with each passing day."[32] Thoughtful deliberation was pushed to the side in fa-

---

[27] Mike Allen, "War Cabinet Argues for Iraq Attack," *Washington Post*, 9 September 2002.

[28] David Firestone and David E. Sanger, "Congress Now Promises to Hold Weeks of Hearings About Iraq," *New York Times*, 6 September 2002.

[29] Mike Allen, "War Cabinet Argues for Iraq Attack," *Washington Post*, 9 September 2002.

[30] *Congressional Record*, 148: S8966 (daily edition, 20 September 2002).

[31] Dana Milbank, "Democrats Question Iraq Timing," *Washington Post*, 16 September 2002.

[32] George P. Shultz, "Act Now: The Danger Is Immediate: Saddam Hussein Must Be Removed," *Washington Post*, 6 September 2002.

vor of hyperventilation. Senate Majority Leader Tom Daschle (D-SD) suggested that Bush would have an easier time getting congressional support if he first gained Security Council approval, but the administration would brook no delays.[33] Congress had to act first. There was no constitutional requirement for Congress to wait until the Security Council met and voted, but acting in the months before the November elections placed lawmakers in a subordinate position.

Disarray by Democrats

Democrats, unable to develop a counterstrategy, appeared to favor a prompt vote on the Iraq resolution to get that issue off the table. It was reported that Senator Daschle hoped to expedite action on the Iraq resolution "to focus on his party's core message highlighting economic distress before the November midterm elections."[34] Senator John Edwards (D-NC) counseled quick action: "In a short period of time, Congress will have dealt with Iraq and we'll be on to other issues."[35]

This approach had multiple drawbacks, both moral and practical. Could Democrats credibly authorize a war merely to draw attention to their domestic agenda? That seems unconscionable. As noted by Senator Mark Dayton (D-MN), trying to gain "political advantage in a midterm election is a shameful reason to hurry decisions of this magnitude."[36] Second, voting on the Iraq resolution could never erase the White House's advantage in controlling the headlines, if not through the Iraq resolution then through ongoing, cliffhanging negotiations with the UN Security Council. Third, although these Democrats said they wanted to put the issue of war against Iraq behind them, it would always be in front.

Legislative action before the November elections invited partisan exploitation of the war issue. Several Republican nominees in congressional contests made a political weapon out of Iraq, comparing their "strong stand" on Iraq to "weak" positions by Democratic campaigners. Some of the key races in the nation appeared to turn on what candidates were saying about Iraq.[37] Because of the steady focus on the war, Democrats were unable to redirect the political agenda to corporate crime, the state of the stock market, and the struggling economy.[38]

---

[33] Bradley Graham, "Cheney, Tenet Brief Leaders of Hill on Iraq," *Washington Post*, 6 September 2002.

[34] David Firestone, "Liberals Object to Bush Policy on Iraq Attack," *New York Times*, 28 September 2002.

[35] Dana Milbank, "In President's Speeches, Iraq Dominates, Economy Fades," *Washington Post*, 25 September 2002.

[36] Mark Drayton, "Go Slow on Iraq," *Washington Post*, 28 September 2002.

[37] Jim VandeHei, "GOP Nominees Make Iraq a Political Weapon," *Washington Post*, 18 September 2002.

[38] Dana Milbank, "Democrats Question Iraq Timing," *Washington Post*, 16 September 2002.

The partisan flavor intensified when President Bush, in a speech in Trenton, New Jersey on 23 September, said that the Democratic Senate "is more interested in special interests in Washington and not interested in the security of the American people."[39] That was a stunning charge, invoking national security to brand Democrats as corrupt, if not traitorous. Recognizing that it might have stepped over the line, the administration quickly explained that Bush's remark was delivered in the context of the legislative delay on the Department of Homeland Security, but Democrats faulted Bush for using the war as leverage in the House and Senate races.[40]

After the Trenton speech, Democrats could have announced that Bush had so politicized and poisoned the debate on the Iraq resolution that it could not be considered with the care and seriousness it deserved. Daschle, in particular, could have used his position as Senate Majority Leader to delay a vote until after the elections. Perhaps he lacked the votes in the Senate Democratic Caucus to prevail. If he failed to rally his troops, he would have highlighted his weakness as a leader and advertised the divisions within his own ranks. In the end, however, as evidenced by the vote on the Iraq resolution, Senate Democrats were divided anyway. Several Senate Democrats criticized Daschle for working too closely with Bush on the Iraq resolution and getting nothing in return. Bush's comments on 23 September, they said, made it look like Daschle was being "played for a fool."[41]

UNSUBSTANTIATED EXECUTIVE CLAIMS

Bush and other top officials invited members of Congress to sessions where they would receive confidential information about the threat from Iraq, but the lawmakers said they heard little that was new. After one of the briefings, Senator Bob Graham (D-FL) remarked: "I did not receive any new information."[42] House Minority Whip Nancy Pelosi (D-CA), who also served as ranking Democrat on the House Intelligence Committee, announced that she knew of "no information that the threat is so imminent from Iraq" that Congress could not wait until January to vote on an authorizing resolution.[43] None of the charges against Iraq in Bush's address to the UN was new. After a "top secret" briefing by Defense Secretary Rumsfeld in a secure room in the Capitol, Senator John McCain (R-AZ) soon rose and walked out, saying, "It was a joke."[44]

[39] *Weekly Compilation of Presidential Documents*, 38: 1598 (23 September 2002).

[40] Carl Hulse and Todd S. Purdum, "Daschle Defends Democrats' Stand on Security of U.S.," *New York Times*, 26 September 2002.

[41] Jim VandeHei, "Daschle Angered by Bush Statement," *Washington Post*, 26 September 2002.

[42] Mike Allen and Karen DeYoung, "Bush to Seek Hill Approval on Iraq War," *Washington Post*, 5 September 2002.

[43] Jim VandeHei and Juliet Eilperin, "Democrats Unconvinced on Iraq War," *Washington Post*, 11 September 2002.

[44] Jim VandeHei, "Iraq Briefings: Don't Ask, Don't Tell," *Washington Post*, 15 September 2002.

A Link Between Iraq and al Qaeda?

The administration tried repeatedly to establish a connection between Iraq and al Qaeda, but the reports could never be substantiated. On 25 September, Bush claimed that Saddam Hussein and al Qaeda "work in concert."[45] On the following day, he claimed that the Iraqi regime "has longstanding and continuing ties to terrorist organizations, and there are [al Qaeda] terrorists inside Iraq."[46] Ari Fleischer tried to play down Bush's remark, saying he was talking about what he feared *could* occur.[47] Why weren't Bush and his press secretary able to speak from the same page? Did the ties and links exist, as Bush claimed, or were they merely future possibilities?

Senator Joseph Biden (D-DE), who attended a classified briefing that talked about the relationship between Iraq and al Qaeda, said that credible evidence had not been presented.[48] There was some evidence of possible al Qaeda activity in the northeastern part of Iraq—the community of Ansar al-Islam—but that was Kurdish territory made semiautonomous because of American and British flights over the no-fly zones. Saddam Hussein wasn't in a position to do anything about Ansar. Besides, members of al Qaeda are present in some sixty countries. Presence alone does not justify military force.

Allies in Europe, active in investigating al Qaeda and radical Islamic cells, could find no evidence of links between Iraq and al Qaeda. Interviews with top investigative magistrates, prosecutors, police, and intelligence officials could uncover no information to support the claims by the Bush administration. Investigative officials in Spain, France, and Germany, after dismissing a connection between Iraq and al Qaeda, worried that a war against Iraq would increase the terrorist threat rather than diminish it.[49]

On 27 September, Secretary Rumsfeld announced that the administration had "bulletproof" evidence of Iraq's links to al Qaeda. He said that declassified intelligence reports, showing the presence of senior members of al Qaeda in Baghdad in "recent periods," were "factual" and "exactly accurate." However, when reporters sought to substantiate his claim, officials offered no details to back up the assertions. Having claimed bulletproof support, Rumsfeld admitted that the information was "not beyond a reasonable doubt." That's quite a definition of bulletproof. Senator Chuck Hagel (R-NE) told Secretary of State Powell: "To say, 'Yes, I know there is evidence there, but I don't want to tell you any more about it,' that does not encourage any of us. Nor does it give the American public a heck of a lot of faith that, in fact, what anyone is saying is true."[50]

[45] *Weekly Compilation of Presidential Documents*, 38: 1619 (25 September 2002).

[46] Ibid., 1625.

[47] Mike Allen, "Bush Asserts That Al Qaeda Has Links to Iraq's Hussein," *Washington Post*, 26 September 2002.

[48] Karen De Young, "Unwanted Debate on Iraq-Al Qaeda Links Revived," *Washington Post*, 27 September 2002.

[49] Sebastian Rotella, "Allies Find No Links Between Iraq, Al Qaeda," *Los Angeles Times*, 4 November 2002.

[50] Eric Schmitt, "Rumsfeld Says U.S. Has 'Bulletproof' Evidence of Iraq's Links to Al Qaeda," *New York Times*, 28 September 2002.

In his speech to the nation on 7 October, on the eve of the congressional vote, President Bush said that Iraq "has trained Al Qaida members in bomb-making and poisons and deadly gases."[51] Intelligence officials, however, played down the reliability of those reports.[52] After the vote, the administration promoted a story about Mohamed Atta, the leader of the September 11 attacks, meeting with an Iraqi intelligence officer in Prague in April 2001. Yet, this assertion was also without foundation: Czech President Vaclav Havel and the Czech intelligence service said that there was no evidence that the meeting ever took place. Central Intelligence Agency (CIA) Director George Tenet told Congress that his agency had no information that could confirm the meeting.[53]

On 11 February 2003, Secretary Powell cited an audiotape believed to be of Osama bin Laden as evidence that he was "in partnership with Iraq."[54] The tape contained no such evidence. It specifically criticized "pagan regimes" and the "apostasy" practiced by socialist governments like Iraq. In a military contest between the United States and Iraq, the tape certainly supported Iraq, but that is hardly evidence of partnership. As much as al Qaeda detests Iraq, it detests the United States more. In an op-ed for the *Washington Post* on 13 February, Richard Cohen wondered why Powell had to "gild the lily. The case for war is a good one." He reminded Powell that in the war against Vietnam, the U.S. government's exaggerations and decisions eventually "lost the confidence of the people." The Bush administration, Cohen said, had a habit of tickling the facts and expunging caveats, doubts, and conditional clauses from the record.[55] An editorial in the *New York Times* warned that there was "no need for the administration to jeopardize its own credibility with unproved claims about an alliance between Iraq and Al Qaeda."[56]

Nevertheless, on 1 May 2003, while standing on the deck of the *Abraham Lincoln* carrier to announce military victory over Iraq, Bush announced: "We've removed an ally of Al Qaida."[57] With repetition and redundancy, an unsubstantiated claim has an excellent chance of sticking.

Weapons of Mass Destruction

The administration kept a steady drumbeat for war, releasing various accounts to demonstrate why Iraq was an imminent threat. On 7 September, President

---

[51] *Weekly Compilation of Presidential Documents*, 38: 1717 (7 October 2002).

[52] Karen De Young, "Bush Cites Urgent Iraqi Threat," *Washington Post*, 8 October 2002.

[53] James Risen, "Prague Discounts An Iraqi Meeting," *New York Times*, 21 October 2002; James Risen, "How Politics and Rivalries Fed Suspicions of a Meeting," *New York Times*, 21 October 2002; Peter S. Green, "Havel Denies Telephoning U.S. on Iraq Meeting," *New York Times*, 23 October 2002.

[54] Dan Eggen and Susan Schmidt, "Bin Laden Calls Iraqis to Arms," *Washington Post*, 12 February 2003.

[55] Richard Cohen, "Powellian Propaganda?" *Washington Post*, 13 February 2003.

[56] "Elusive Qaeda Connections" (Editorial), *New York Times*, 14 February 2003.

[57] *Weekly Compilation of Presidential Documents*, 39: 517 (1 May 2003).

Bush cited a report by the International Atomic Energy Agency (IAEA) that the Iraqis were "6 months away from developing a weapon. I don't know what more evidence we need."[58] More evidence was indeed needed because the report Bush referred to didn't exist.[59] It would seem embarrassing for a president to be that far from the truth. Shouldn't some White House aide get kicked out the door for making Bush look ill-informed? There were no such embarrassments and no such casualties.

In his 7 October speech, President Bush claimed that satellite photographs "reveal that Iraq is rebuilding facilities at sites that have been part of his nuclear program in the past."[60] The administration decided to declassify two before-and-after photos of the Al Furat manufacturing facility.[61] This "declassification" was interesting: the administration regularly complained about leaks of sensitive documents to the media, but if classified information seemed to bolster the administration's case, it quickly became public. Five busloads of 200 reporters descended on the site and received a ninety-minute tour by Iraqi generals. The reporters found few clues to indicate a weapons program.[62]

True, a quick visit by reporters meant little. They had neither time nor expertise to explore all the buildings and examine them carefully. But it is equally true that satellite photos are unable to penetrate buildings and analyze their interiors. Only a ground search by experienced inspectors could do that. When the UN inspection teams reached Iraq in November, they could find no evidence of a nuclear weapons program at Al Furat or anywhere else in Iraq.[63]

The Bush administration claimed that Iraq had bought aluminum tubes and planned to use them to enrich uranium to produce nuclear weapons. Specialists from UN inspection teams concluded that the specifications of the tubes were consistent with tubes used for rockets. The tubes could have been modified to serve as centrifuges for enriching uranium, but the modifications would have had to be substantial. Moreover, there was no evidence that Iraq had purchased materials needed for centrifuges, such as motors, metal caps, and special magnets.[64]

On 5 February 2003, in his statement to the UN Security Council, Secretary Powell laid out his case for going to war against Iraq, citing what he considered to be evidence of weapons of mass destruction. With little evidence of a nuclear weapons program, he emphasized that Iraq had mobile production facilities

---

[58] Ibid., 38: 1518.

[59] Dana Milbank, "For Bush, Facts Are Malleable," *Washington Post*, 22 October 2002.

[60] *Weekly Compilation of Presidential Documents*, 38: 1718 (7 October 2002).

[61] "Al Furat Manufacturing Facility, Iraq," *Washington Post*, 8 October 2002.

[62] John Burns, "Iraq Tour of Suspected Sites Gives Few Clues on Weapons," *New York Times*, 13 October 2002.

[63] "Nuclear Inspection Chief Reports Finding No New Weapons," *New York Times*, 28 January 2003.

[64] Michael R. Gordon, "Agency Challenges Evidence Against Iraq Cited by Bush," *New York Times*, 10 January 2003; Joby Warrick, "U.S. Claim on Iraqi Nuclear Program Is Called Into Question," *Washington Post*, 24 January 2003.

"used to make biological agents."[65] In a matter of months, he said, these mobile facilities "can produce a quantity of biological poison equal to the entire amount that Iraq claimed to have produced in the years prior to the Gulf War."[66] After hostilities were over, U.S. forces discovered two mobile labs in Iraq, but it is uncertain what they had been used for.[67] A 28 May 2003 report by the intelligence community found nothing definitive.

Plagiarism and Fabrication

The British government released a nineteen-page report entitled "Iraq: Its Infrastructure of Concealment, Deception and Intimidation," posting it on No. 10 Downing Street's web site. It appeared to be a thorough analysis prepared by the British intelligence agencies. In fact, the report had its own problems with concealment and deception. In February 2003, the British government admitted that much of the report had been lifted from magazines and academic journals, some of it verbatim. Spelling and punctuation errors in the originals were faithfully reproduced in the government's report. Although the government claimed that the report contained "up-to-date details of Iraq's network of intelligence and security," much of it was based on an article by a postgraduate student who focused on events a dozen years old, in the 1990–1991 period.[68] After defending the report, the British government in June 2003 conceded that including the student's article was "regrettable."[69]

In his State of the Union message on 28 January 2003, President Bush said that the British government "has learned that Saddam Hussein recently sought significant quantities of uranium from Africa."[70] Two points deserve mention. First, "sought" is not the same as "bought." More seriously, the British government relied on evidence that its intelligence agencies thought unreliable. The documents turned out to be not only unreliable but actually a fabrication. The forged documents contained crude errors that undermined their credibility.[71] As one U.S. official admitted: "We fell for it."[72] The significant point is not an

---

[65] Michael Dobbs, "Powell Lays Out Case Against Iraq," *Washington Post*, 6 February 2003.

[66] Ibid.

[67] Walter Pincus and Michael Dobbs, "Suspected Bioweapon Mobile Lab Recovered," *Washington Post*, 7 May 2003; "A Suspected Weapons Lab Is Found in Northern Iraq," *New York Times*, 10 May 2003; Judith Miller, "Trailer is a Mobile Lab Capable of Turning Out Bioweapons, a Team Says," *New York Times*, 11 May 2003; Judith Miller and William J. Broad, "U.S. Analysts Link Iraq Labs to Germ Arms," *New York Times*, 21 May 2003.

[68] Sarah Lyall, "Britain Admits That Much of Its Report on Iraq Came From Magazines," *New York Times*, 8 February 2003; Glenn Frankel, "Blair Acknowledges Flaws in Iraq Dossier," *Washington Post*, 8 February 2003.

[69] Jane Wardell, "Blair Aide Concedes Error on Iraq Dossier," *Washington Post*, 26 June 2003.

[70] *Weekly Compilation of Presidential Documents*, 39: 115 (28 January 2003).

[71] Joby Warrick, "Some Evidence on Iraq Called Fake," *Washington Post*, 8 March 2003.

[72] Ibid.

unfortunate mistake but rather the willingness of the administration to exploit and go public with any information no matter how tenuous and suspect.

CONGRESS FOLDS

There was little doubt that President Bush would gain approval for military action in the Republican House. The question was whether the vote would divide along party lines. Some of the partisan issue blurred when House Minority Leader Dick Gephardt (D-MO) broke ranks with many in his party and announced support for a slightly redrafted resolution. He said, "We had to go through this, putting politics aside, so we have a chance to get a consensus that will lead the country in the right direction."[73] Of course, politics could not be put aside. Even when leaders of the two parties and the two branches appealed for nonpartisan or bipartisan conduct, their comments were generally viewed as calculated to have some partisan benefit. Gephardt's interest in running for the presidency was well known, as was Daschle's and several other members of Congress. Democratic Senators John Edwards and Joseph Lieberman, both interested in a 2004 bid for the presidency, endorsed the Iraq resolution. Senator John Kerry, about to announce his bid for the presidency, initially expressed doubts about the resolution but later voted for it.[74] One Democratic lawmaker concluded that Gephardt, by supporting Bush, had "inoculated Democrats against the charge that they are antiwar and obstructionist."[75]

Why were Democrats so anxious about being seen as antiwar? There was no evidence that the public in any broad sense supported immediate war against Iraq. A *New York Times* poll published on 7 October 2002 indicated that 69 percent of Americans believed that Bush should be paying more attention to the economy. Although support was high for military action (with 67 percent approving U.S. military action against Iraq with the goal of removing Hussein from power), when it was asked, "Should the U.S. take military action against Iraq fairly soon or wait and give the U.N. more time to get weapons inspectors into Iraq?" 63 percent preferred to wait. To the question "Is Congress asking enough questions about President Bush's policy toward Iraq?" only 20 percent said too many, while 51 percent said not enough. Asked whether Bush was more interested in removing Hussein than weapons of mass destruction, 53 percent said Hussein and only 29 percent said weapons.[76]

[73] "For Gephardt, Risks and a Crucial Role," *Washington Post*, 3 October 2002.

[74] Dan Balz and Jim VandeHei, "Democratic Hopefuls Back Bush on Iraq," *Washington Post*, 14 September 2002.

[75] David E. Rosenbaum, "United Voice on Iraq Eludes Majority Leader," *New York Times*, 4 October 2002.

[76] Adam Nagourney and Janet Elder, "Public Says Bush Needs to Pay Heed to Weak Economy," *New York Times*, 7 October 2002.

A *Washington Post* story on 8 October described the public's enthusiasm for war against Iraq as "tepid and declining."[77] Americans gave Bush the benefit of the doubt but were not convinced by his arguments. Because of those doubts, "support could fade if the conflict in Iraq becomes bloody and extended."[78] These public attitudes led the *New York Times* to wonder: "Given the cautionary mood of the country, it is puzzling that most members of Congress seem fearful of challenging the hawkish approach to Iraq."[79]

The vote on the Iraq resolution could never be anything other than a political decision, probably the most important congressional vote of the year. Inescapably and legitimately it called for a political judgment. Lawmakers would be voting on whether to commit as much as $100 billion or $200 billion to a war stretching over a period of years. Their actions would stabilize or destabilize the Middle East, strengthen or weaken the war against terrorism, enhance or debase the nation's prestige. Politics would always be present, as would partisan calculations and strategy.

When the House International Relations Committee reported the resolution, it divided thirty-one to eleven. Democrats on the committee split ten to nine in favoring it. Two Republicans, Jim Leach of Iowa and Ron Paul of Texas, opposed it. The forty-seven-page committee report consists of only five pages of text analyzing the resolution.[80] President Bush's speech to the UN occupies another five pages. Twenty-one pages are devoted to an administration document called "A Decade of Deception and Defiance: Saddam Hussein's Defiance of the United Nations" (12 September 2002). It was prepared as a background paper for Bush's speech to the UN. Some of it describes what was supposedly the administration's main concern: the development of weapons of mass destruction. Other sections focused on conditions in Iraq that, while deplorable, could hardly justify war: Iraq's refusal to allow visits by human rights monitors; the expulsion of UN humanitarian relief workers; violence against women; child labor and forced labor; the lack of freedom of speech and press; and refusal to return to Kuwait state archives and museum pieces.

A key section of the report reads: "The Committee hopes that the use of military force can be avoided. It believes, however, that providing the President with the authority he needs to use force is the best way to avoid its use. A signal of our Nation's seriousness of purpose and its willingness to use force may yet persuade Iraq to meet its international obligations, and is the best way to persuade members of the Security Council and others in the international community to join us in bringing pressure on Iraq or, if required, in using armed force against it."[81] Thus, the legislation would decide neither for nor against war. That judgment, which the Constitution places in Congress, would now be left in the hands of the President.

[77] Dana Milbank, "With Congress Aboard, Bush Targets a Doubtful Public," *Washington Post*, 8 October 2002.

[78] Ibid.

[79] "A Nation Wary of War" (Editorial), *New York Times*, 8 October 2002.

[80] H. Rept. No. 107–721, 107th Cong., 2d Sess. (2002).

[81] Ibid., 4–5.

The Tonkin Gulf Precedent

Acting as it did, the House International Relations Committee both authorized military force and hoped it would not be necessary. That kind of straddling reminds one of the Tonkin Gulf resolution of 1964, which Congress passed almost unanimously, with only two dissenting votes in the Senate. Passage of this resolution was not an endorsement of war either. Instead, members of Congress thought that by offering broad, bipartisan support to President Lyndon B. Johnson, war with North Vietnam could be avoided. Like the Iraq resolution, the legislative vote in 1964 was neither for war nor against it.

During Senate debate on the Tonkin Gulf resolution, Gaylord Nelson reviewed the statements by his colleagues and noticed that "every Senator who spoke had his own personal interpretation of what the joint resolution means." He found that "there is no agreement in the Senate on what the joint resolution means."[82] To clarify the intent of the resolution, he offered an amendment to state that President Johnson would seek "no extension of the present military conflict" and that "we should continue to attempt to avoid a direct military involvement in the southeast Asian conflict." Senator J. William Fulbright, floor manager of the resolution, refused to accept the amendment because it would force the two Houses to go to conference to resolve the differences between the versions passed by each chamber. Fulbright didn't want Congress taking another week or so to clarify the resolution. Nevertheless, he felt satisfied that Nelson's amendment expressed "fairly accurately what the President has said would be our policy, and what I stated my understanding was as to our policy." Fulbright believed that the resolution "is calculated to prevent the spread of the war, rather than to spread it."[83] What counts, however, is not what lawmakers say during debate but what the president does with broad statutory authority. The military expansion that began in February 1965 led to the deaths of 58,000 Americans and several million in Southeast Asia.

Congressional debate in 2002 contains some similarities and differences to the Tonkin Gulf resolution. The House passed the Iraq resolution, 296–133, compared to the unanimous House vote in 1964. Yet, the resolutions are virtually identical in transferring to the president the sole decision to go to war and determine its scope and duration. In each case, lawmakers chose to trust in the president, not in themselves. Instead of acting as the people's representatives and preserving the republican form of government, they gave the president unchecked power.

Senate Action

After the House vote in 2002, Senate Majority Leader Daschle announced his support for the resolution. Although he suggested that senators might "go back and tie down the language a little bit more if we can," he insisted that "we have

---

[82] *Congressional Record*, 110: 18458 (1964).
[83] Ibid., 18462.

got to support this effort. We have got to do it in an enthusiastic and bipartisan way."[84] Why the need for enthusiasm and bipartisanship? Why wasn't the argument on the merits? Placing trust in the president or calling for bipartisanship are not proper substitutes for analyzing the need for military force against another country. Senator Kerry, who had earlier raised substantive arguments against going to war against Iraq, now accepted presidential superiority over Congress: "We are affirming a president's right and responsibility to keep the American people safe, and the president must take that grant of responsibility seriously."[85] With that kind of reading of constitutional authority, Congress had little role other than to offer words of encouragement and support to a president who already seemed to possess all the constitutional authority he needed to act singlehandedly. Far from being a coequal branch, Congress was distinctly junior varsity. It no longer functioned as an authorizing body. Its task was simply to endorse what the president had already decided.

A similar position appears in Daschle's statement that "it is important for America to speak with one voice at this critical moment."[86] Comparable statements were made by senators in 1964, when they endorsed the Tonkin Gulf resolution. Why should legislators consider agreement with the president more important than conscientious and individual allegiance to their constitutional duties? The Framers counted on collective judgment, the deliberative process, and checks and balances. All of that is lost when lawmakers decide to join with the president and subordinate their positions to his. A member of Congress takes an oath to support and defend the Constitution, not the president. The experience with the Tonkin Gulf resolution demonstrated that unity and lockstep decision making do not assure wise policy.

This issue played out in other contexts. During debate on the Department of Homeland Security, Senator Daschle said he intended "to give the President the benefit of the doubt." His Democratic colleague, Robert Byrd, took sharp exception: "I will not give the benefit of the doubt to the President. I will give the benefit of the doubt to the Constitution."[87] Byrd watched the congressional debate drift from an initial willingness of lawmakers to analyze issues and weigh the merits to wholesale legislative abdication to the President. To Byrd, the fundamental question of why the United States should go to war was replaced by "the mechanics of how best to wordsmith the President's use-of-force resolution in order to give him virtually unchecked authority to commit the nation's military to an unprovoked attack on a sovereign nation." Having followed the arguments presented by Bush and after questioning the top executive branch

---

[84] John H. Cushman, Jr., "Daschle Predicts Broad Support for Military Action Against Iraq," *New York Times*, 7 October 2002.

[85] Helen Dewar and Juliet Eilperin, "Iraq Resolution Passes Test, Gains Support," *Washington Post*, 10 October 2002.

[86] Jim VandeHei and Juliet Eilperin, "House Passes Iraq War Resolution," *Washington Post*, 11 October 2002.

[87] *Congressional Record*: 148; S9187, S9188 (daily edition, 25 September 2002).

officials responsible for crafting the resolution, Byrd did not find the threat from Iraq "so great that we must be stampeded to provide such authority to this president just weeks before an election."[88]

Republican Senators Lugar, Hagel, and Arlen Specter (PA), after raising serious questions about the Iraq resolution, decided by 7 October to support it.[89] On 10 October, the Senate voted seventy-seven to twenty-three for the resolution. The only Republican voting against the resolution was Lincoln Chafee of Rhode Island. An Independent, James Jeffords of Vermont, also voted No.

A MILITARY, NOT A POLITICAL, VICTORY

The United States triumphed militarily over Iraq in less than a month, but with deep, long-term costs to constitutional government. The euphoria and celebrations at home were strange. No one doubted that U.S. forces would prevail over an Iraq that lacked an air force and had few ground troops willing to fight. It is understandable that great pride would be placed in the American men and women who put their lives at stake in Iraq and accomplished their military mission. But the issue was never whether the United States would win the war. It was whether war was necessary and what would happen in Iraq and the region after military operations had ceased.

Congress failed to discharge its constitutional duties when it passed the Iraq resolution. Instead of making a decision about whether to go to war and spend billions for a multiyear commitment, it transferred those legislative judgments to the President. Legislators washed their hands of the key decisions to go to war and for how long. Congress should not have voted on the resolution before the election, which colored the votes and the political calculations. Voting under that pressure benefited the President.

It would have been better for Congress as an institution and for the country as a whole to first wait for President Bush to request the Security Council to authorize inspections in Iraq. Depending on what the Security Council did or did not do, and on what Iraq agreed or did not agree to do, Congress could then have debated whether to authorize war. Having learned what the Security Council and Iraq actually did, rather than speculate on what they might do, Congress would have been in the position to make an informed choice. Instead, it voted under partisan pressures, with inadequate information, and thereby abdicated its constitutional duties to the President. Congress suffered a loss, as did popular control and the democratic process.

In the end, Congress had two models to choose from. It could have acted after the election, as it did in 1990–1991, or it could have acted in the middle of an election, as in 1964. The first would have maintained the integrity of the legislative institution by minimizing partisan tactics and scheduling legislative

---

[88] Robert C. Byrd, "Congress Must Resist the Rush to War," *New York Times*, 10 October 2002.

[89] Helen Dewar, "Armey, Lugar Reverse Stand on Resolution," *Washington Post*, 8 October 2002.

debate after the Security Council voted. The second would have placed Congress in a position of voting hurriedly without the information it needed and with information it did receive (the two "attacks" in Tonkin Gulf) of dubious quality. In 2002, Congress picked the Tonkin Gulf model. There may be times when Congress might have to authorize war in the middle of an election. The year 2002 wasn't one.

DOCTORING INTELLIGENCE REPORTS

The failure thus far to find weapons of mass destruction in Iraq has raised a serious question: Did the Bush administration deliberately misread or misrepresent intelligence reports to exaggerate the nature of the Iraqi threat? This charge assumes that reports prepared by the intelligence agencies are professionally crafted when presented to administration officials and that distortions begin at that point. Yet, the reports from the intelligence agencies might already have been manipulated.

Consider the CIA report of October 2002, "Iraq's Weapons of Mass Destruction Programs." It was released at a critical time when Congress was considering whether to authorize military operations. On 2 October, President Bush announced a bipartisan agreement on a joint resolution to authorize armed force against Iraq. He stated that Iraq "has stockpiled biological and chemical weapons."[90] In his address to the nation on 7 October, from Cincinnati, he said that Iraq "possesses and produces chemical and biological weapons."[91]

These remarks reflected an analysis prepared by the Central Intelligence Agency. The unclassified version, available on the CIA's web site (www.cia.gov), states unequivocally: "Baghdad has chemical and biological weapons. . . ." The impact of any report depends on its opening line. Readers are apt to skim the rest. Yet, the detailed analytical section that follows contradicts the flat assertion, providing statements that are much more cautious and qualified:

- "Iraq has the ability to produce chemical warfare (CW) agents within its chemical industry. . . ."
- "Iraq probably has concealed precursors, production equipment, documentation, and other items necessary for continuing its CW effort."
- "Baghdad continues to rebuild and expand dual-use infrastructure that it could divert quickly to CW production."
- "Iraq has the capability to convert quickly legitimate vaccine and biopesticide plants to biological warfare (BW) production and already may have done so."

None of the statements in the analytical section support the striking claim in the first paragraph of the CIA report and in Bush's statements to the nation.

---

[90] *Weekly Compilation of Presidential Documents*, 38: 1670 (2 October 2002).
[91] Ibid., 1716.

The same gap between the front material and the internal analysis appears in a 28 May 2003 publication on mobile labs, jointly authored by the CIA and the Defense Intelligence Agency (DIA). Entitled "Iraqi Mobile Biological Warfare Agent Production Plans," the analysis can be found on CIA's web site. The first sentence asserts: "Coalition forces have uncovered the strongest evidence to date that Iraq was hiding a biological warfare program." The analysis within the report offers no evidence for that claim.

The purpose of the mobile labs remains under study. The CIA/DIA report concedes that some of the features of the labs "are consistent with both bioproduction [of BW agents] and hydrogen production" for artillery weather balloons. Clearly, much more analysis is necessary. What is evident now is that intelligence analysts prepared a report, complete with caveats and qualifications, and someone came along and put a screamer up front. Was the classified report more professional and nuanced? When it was decided to put an unclassified version on the web site, did someone think it important—with public consumption in mind—to select a more dramatic, eye-catching lead?

On 18 June 2003, Deputy Defense Secretary Paul Wolfowitz appeared before the House Armed Services Committee, where Rep. Gene Taylor (D-MS) asked whether the intelligence about the threat from Iraq's weapons was wrong. Taylor said he voted for the Iraq resolution because of the administration's warning that Iraq had weapons of mass destruction. He now told Wolfowitz: "A person is only as good as his word. This nation is only as good as its word. And if that's the reason why we did it—and I voted for it—then we need some clarification here." Wolfowitz replied: "If there's a problem with intelligence . . . it doesn't mean that anybody misled anybody. It means that intelligence is an art and not a science."[92]

That modest tone was absent during the debate on the Iraq resolution. The administration treated intelligence as a science, yielding certitude, not doubt. The position was not merely that Iraq had weapons of mass destruction in the past. Bush, Cheney, Rumsfeld, and other top administration officials insisted that Iraq currently had that capability, particularly chemical and biological weapons. According to their analysis, the threat was imminent, not in the future.

Congress should not allow any president to dictate the timing of a vote on war. Democracy depends on laws, but much more on trust. Constitutions and statutes are necessarily general in scope, placing a premium on judgment and discretion. Without confidence in what public officials say and do, laws are easily twisted to satisfy private ends. Leaders who claim to act in the national interest may, instead, pursue personal or partisan agendas. The opportunity for harm is especially great in the field of national security. Approximately $40 billion in secret funds are spent by the U.S. intelligence community. Its mission is to supply reliable analysis for policy makers, both executive and legislative,

[92] Walter Pincus and Dana Priest, "Lawmakers Begin Iraq Intelligence Hearings," *Washington Post*, 19 June 2003.

including whatever caveats and qualifications are appropriate. When those reports are doctored, either before they leave the agency or afterwards, government is likely to blunder. In an age of terrorism, especially after September 11, the public needs full trust in the integrity of its elected leaders and in the intelligence agencies that guide crucial decisions. For all the sophistication of the U.S. political and economic system, if trust is absent, so is popular control. The United States cannot install democracy abroad if it lacks it at home.

CONCLUSIONS

U.S. political institutions failed in their constitutional duties when they authorized war against Iraq. The Bush administration never presented sufficient and credible information to justify statutory action in October 2002 and military operations in March 2003. Statements by executive officials were regularly punctured by press disclosures. The call to war demands a careful marshaling of evidence to build public confidence. The record of the Bush administration on warmaking created distrust of the spoken word and the declassified document. For its part, Congress failed to insist on reliable arguments and evidence before passing the Iraq resolution. There was no need for Congress to act when it did. Instead of passing legislation to authorize war, members of Congress agreed to compromise language that left the decisive judgment with the President. Placing the power to initiate war in the hands of one person was precisely what the Framers hoped to avoid when they drafted the Constitution.

Rather than proceed with deliberation and care, the two branches rushed to war on a claim of imminent threat that lacked credibility. The Bush administration never made a convincing case why the delay of a few months would injure or jeopardize national security. By acting hastily and without just cause, the administration did damage to what President Bush highlighted in his 12 September 2002 address: the relevance of the United Nations. Unwilling to wait an extra month or two to allow UN inspectors to continue their work, the Bush administration missed an opportunity to attract the support of other nations. In place of a multinational effort to remove Saddam Hussein and rebuild Iraq, the United States finds itself six months after the invasion almost solely responsible for an occupation that has uncertain goals, heavy costs, and open-ended duration.

Misperceptions, the Media,
and the Iraq War

STEVEN KULL
CLAY RAMSAY
EVAN LEWIS

The Iraq war and its aftermath have raised compelling questions about the capacity of the executive branch to elicit public consent for the use of military force and about the role the media plays in this process. From the outset, the Bush administration was faced with unique challenges in its effort to legitimate its decision to go to war. Because the war was not prompted by an overt act against the United States or its interests, and was not approved by the UN Security Council, the Bush administration argued that the war was necessary on the basis of a potential threat. Because the evidence for this threat was not fully manifest, the Bush administration led the public to believe that Iraq was developing weapons of mass destruction (WMD) and providing substantial support to the al Qaeda terrorist group. The challenge for the administration was later intensified when the United States occupied Iraq and was unable to find the expected corroborating evidence.

From the outset the public was sympathetic to the idea of removing Saddam Hussein, though only a small minority of Americans was ready to go to war with Iraq without UN Security Council approval.[1] The majority was inclined to believe that Iraq had a WMD program and was supporting al Qaeda. However,

---

[1] Asked in a Chicago Council on Foreign Relations poll in June 2002 about their position on invading Iraq, 65 percent said the United States "should only invade Iraq with UN approval and the support of its allies"; 20 percent said "the US should invade Iraq even if we have to go it alone"; and 13 percent said "the US should not invade Iraq."

STEVEN KULL is the director of the Program on International Policy Attitudes (PIPA), a joint program of the Center on Policy Attitudes and Center for International and Security Studies at Maryland of the School of Public Affairs, University of Maryland.
CLAY RAMSAY is the director of research at PIPA.
EVAN LEWIS is a research associate at PIPA.

most were not persuaded that the case was strong enough to justify taking action unilaterally. The majority preferred to continue looking for more decisive evidence through the UN inspection process and to continue seeking the support of the UN Security Council.[2]

Nevertheless, when the President decided to go to war, the majority of the public expressed support. More significantly, when the United States failed to find the expected evidence that would corroborate the administration's assumptions that prompted the war, the majority continued to support the decision to go to war.[3]

This polling data raises the question of why the public has been so accommodating. Did they simply change their views about the war despite their earlier reservations? Or did they in some way come to have certain false beliefs or misperceptions that would make going to war appear more legitimate, consistent with pre-existing beliefs?

A variety of possible misperceptions could justify going to war with Iraq. If Americans believed that the United States had found WMD in Iraq or had found evidence that Iraq was providing support to al Qaeda, then they may have seen the war as justified as an act of self-defense even without UN approval. If Americans believed that world public opinion backed the United States going to war with Iraq, then they may have seen the war as legitimate even if some members of the UN Security Council obstructed approval.

Of course, people do not develop misperceptions in a vacuum. The administration disseminates information directly and by implication. The press transmits this information and, at least in theory, provides critical analysis. One's source of news or how closely one pays attention to the news may influence whether or how misperceptions may develop.

To find out more about the possible role of misperceptions in public support for the Iraq war, and the role of the media in this process before and during the war, the Program on International Policy Attitudes (PIPA) conducted a series of polls with the polling firm Knowledge Networks (KN). From January through May 2003, a more limited set of questions was asked in four different polls. Later, Knowledge Networks developed a more systematic set of questions that was included in a series of three polls, conducted from June through

---

[2] In August 2002, 55 percent thought Iraq "currently has weapons of mass destruction," and 39 percent thought Iraq is trying to develop these weapons but does not currently have them (CNN/*USA Today*). On al Qaeda, *Newsweek* asked in September 2002, "From what you've seen or heard in the news ... do you believe that Saddam Hussein's regime in Iraq is harboring al Qaeda terrorists and helping them to develop chemical weapons, or not?" Seventy-five percent said yes. Yet, in a 24–25 February 2003 CBS News poll, only 31 percent agreed that "Iraq presents such a clear danger to American interests that the United States needs to act now"; 64 percent agreed that "the US needs to wait for approval of the United Nations before taking action against Iraq," and 62 percent said that "the United States should wait and give the United Nations inspectors more time."

[3] From May through November 2003, the Program on International Policy Attitudes/Knowledge Networks (PIPA/KN) has found a declining majority of 68 percent to 57 percent saying "the US made the right decision ... in going to war with Iraq."

September, with a total of 3,334 respondents. These results were combined with the findings from four other polls, conducted from January through May, for a total data set of 8,634 respondents. In addition, relevant polling data from other organizations were analyzed, including polls that asked questions about possible misperceptions.

The polls were fielded by Knowledge Networks using its nationwide panel. Panel members are recruited through standard telephone interviews with random digit dialing (RDD) samples of the entire adult population and subsequently provided internet access. Questionnaires are then administered over the Internet to a randomly selected sample of the panel.[4]

This article first explores the degree of pervasiveness of misperceptions, particularly the following three: that since the war U.S. forces have found Iraqi WMD in Iraq; that clear evidence has been found that Saddam Hussein was working closely with al Qaeda; and that world public opinion was in favor of the United States going to war with Iraq. Second, it analyzes the relationship between the holding of these misperceptions and support for the Iraq war by using multivariate regression analysis to compare the strength of this factor with a range of other factors. Third, it analyzes the relationship between the holding of misperceptions and the respondent's primary news source. Fourth, it evaluates the relationship between attention to news and the level of misperceptions. Fifth, it analyzes misperceptions as a function of political attitudes, including intention to vote for the President and party identification. A binary logistic regression analysis including misperceptions and eight other factors provides a ranking of factors by power. The article concludes with an analysis of the various factors that could explain the phenomenon of misperceptions, including administration statements and media reporting.

MISPERCEPTIONS RELATED TO THE IRAQ WAR

In the run-up to the war with Iraq and in the postwar period, a significant portion of the American public has held a number of misperceptions[5] relevant to the rationales for going to war with Iraq. While in most cases only a minority has had any particular misperception, a strong majority has had at least one key misperception.

Close Links between Iraq and al Qaeda

Both before and after the war, a substantial portion of Americans have believed that evidence of a link between Iraq and al Qaeda existed. Before the

---

[4] For more information about this methodology, see the Appendix or go to www.knowledgenetworks. com/ganp.

[5] Herein the term "misperceptions" is not used to refer to controversial beliefs about what U.S. intelligence has been able to infer, such as the belief that Saddam Hussein was directly involved in September 11. The term is limited to noncontroversial perceptions such as whether actual weapons or actual evidence have in fact been *found*. The misperception related to world public opinion is established based on polling data discussed later.

TABLE 1

Evidence of Link between Iraq and al Qaeda
(percentages)

Is it your impression that the US has or has not found clear evidence in Iraq that
Saddam Hussein was working closely with the al Qaeda terrorist organization?

	8–9/03	7/03	6/03	(6/03–9/03)
US has	49	45	52	48
US has not	45	49	43	46
(No answer)	6	6	5	6

Source: Program on International Policy Attitudes/Knowledge Networks.

war, in the January PIPA/KN poll, 68 percent expressed the belief that Iraq
played an important role in September 11, with 13 percent even expressing the
belief that "conclusive evidence" of Iraq's involvement had been found. Asked
in June, July, and August-September (Table 1), large percentages (45 to 52 percent) said they believed that the United States had "found clear evidence in
Iraq that Saddam Hussein was working closely with the al-Qaeda [*sic*] terrorist organization."

Harris Interactive in June and August asked, "Do you believe clear evidence that Iraq was supporting al Qaeda has been found in Iraq or not?" In
June, 48 percent said that clear evidence had been found, with just 33 percent
saying that it had not and 19 percent saying they were not sure. Despite inten-
sive discussion of the issue in the press, in August the numbers were essentially
the same: 50 percent believed evidence had been found, 35 percent believed
that it had not been, and 14 percent were unsure.

Weapons of Mass Destruction

Before the war, overwhelming majorities believed that Iraq had WMD.
Though it now appears likely that this belief was incorrect, it does not seem
appropriate to call this a misperception because it was so widespread at the
time, even within the intelligence community.

However, a striking misperception occurred after the war, when the United
States failed to find any WMD or even any solid evidence of a WMD program.
PIPA/KN first asked in May whether respondents thought that the United
States has or has not "found Iraqi weapons of mass destruction" in Iraq, and
34 percent said the United States had (another 7 percent did not know). In
June, Harris Interactive subsequently asked, "Do you believe clear evidence
of weapons of mass destruction has been found in Iraq or not?" and 35 percent
said that it had.

PIPA/KN asked again in late June—during a period with much discussion
in the press about the absence of WMD—and found that the percentage hold-

TABLE 2

Existence of Weapons of Mass Destruction in Iraq
(percentages)

Since the war with Iraq ended, is it your impression that the US has or has not found Iraqi weapons of mass destruction?

	9/03	7/03	6/03	3/03	(6/03–9/03)
US has	24	21	23	34	22
US has not	73	76	73	59	75
(No answer)	3	3	4	7	3

Source: Program on International Policy Attitudes/Knowledge Networks.

ing this belief had dropped to 23 percent. This number then stayed roughly the same in July and early September. In late July, NBC/*Wall Street Journal* asked whether the United States has been successful in "finding evidence of weapons of mass destruction," and 22 percent said that it had. Harris asked again in mid-August and found 27 percent saying that evidence of WMD had been found (Table 2).

Americans have also incorrectly believed that Iraq actually *used* WMD in the recent war with the United States. PIPA/KN asked respondents whether "Iraq did or did not use chemical or biological weapons in the war that had just ended." In May, 22 percent of respondents said that it had. In mid-June, ABC/*Washington Post* presented a slightly adapted version of the question and found 24 percent said that that they thought it had. When asked by PIPA/KN again in August-September, the percentage saying that Iraq had used such weapons slipped only slightly to 20 percent.

World Public Opinion

A key factor in American public support for going to war with Iraq has been its international legitimacy. Right up to the period immediately before the war, a majority favored taking more time to build international support. A key question, then, is how the public perceived world public opinion on going to war with Iraq.

PIPA/KN polls have shown that Americans have misperceived world public opinion on the U.S. decision to go to war and on the way that the United States is generally dealing with the problem of terrorism. This has been true during and after the war and applies to perceptions about world public opinion as a whole, European public opinion, and public opinion in the Muslim world.

In March 2003, shortly after the war started, PIPA/KN asked respondents "how all of the people in the world feel about the US going to war with Iraq." Respondents perceived greater support for the war than existed at the time or has existed since.[6] Only 35 percent perceived correctly that the majority of

[6] Gallup International conducted two international polls (in January and April-May 2003) and Pew Research Center conducted one (in April-May 2003), which included poll questions that directly measured support or opposition to the Iraq war. In the three polls taken together, fifty-six countries were

TABLE 3

World Opinion about the U.S. Decision to Go to War
(percentages)

Thinking about how all the people in the world feel about the US going/having gone to war with Iraq, do you think	9/03	7/03	6/03	3/03	(6/03–9/03)
The majority of people favor it	27	24	25	31	25
The majority of people oppose it	38	42	41	35	41
Views are evenly balanced	33	30	32	31	31
(No answer)	2	4	2	3	3

Source: Program on International Policy Attitudes/Knowledge Network.

people opposed the decision. Thirty-one percent expressed the mistaken assumption that views were evenly balanced on the issue, and another 31 percent expressed the egregious misperception that the majority favored it. Asked again in June, July, and August-September, these views changed very little (Table 3).

Perceptions have been a bit more accurate when it comes to perceiving European public opinion, but still there are widespread misperceptions. Asked in June and August-September, nearly half (48 to 49 percent) correctly said that the "majority of people oppose the United States having gone to war." But 29 to 30 percent believed incorrectly that views are evenly balanced, and 18 percent believed that the majority even favors it.[7]

A substantial number of Americans also misperceive attitudes in the Islamic world toward U.S. efforts to fight terrorism and its policies in the Middle East. Respondents were asked in August-September whether they thought "a majority of people in the Islamic world favor or oppose U.S.-led efforts to fight terrorism." A plurality of 48 percent incorrectly assumed that a majority of Islamic people favors U.S.-led efforts to fight terrorism, while 46 percent assumed that they do not. When asked whether respondents thought "a majority of people in the Islamic world think U.S. policies in the Middle East make the region more or less stable," 35 percent incorrectly assumed that the majority of people

---

surveyed. The January Gallup International poll asked, "Are you in favor of military action against Iraq: under no circumstances; only if sanctioned by the United Nations; unilaterally by America and its allies?" Of the thirty-eight countries polled (including twenty European countries), not a single one showed majority support for unilateral action, and in nearly every case the percentage was very low. When asked, "If military action goes ahead against Iraq, do you think [survey country] should or should not support this action?" in thirty-four of the thirty-eight countries polled (seventeen out of twenty in Europe), a majority opposed having their country support this action. In April-May, the Pew Global Attitudes Survey asked respondents in eighteen countries how they felt about their country's decision to participate or not participate in "us[ing] military force against Iraq." Among the thirteen countries that had not participated, in every case, a large to overwhelming majority approved of the decision. For the three countries that contributed troops, in the United Kingdom and Australia, a majority approved; in Spain, a majority was opposed. For the two countries that had allowed the United States to use bases, in Kuwait, the majority approved; in Turkey, the majority was opposed. For full results, see www.gallup-international.com and www.people-press.org.

[7] Ibid.

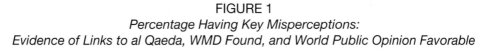

FIGURE 1
Percentage Having Key Misperceptions:
Evidence of Links to al Qaeda, WMD Found, and World Public Opinion Favorable

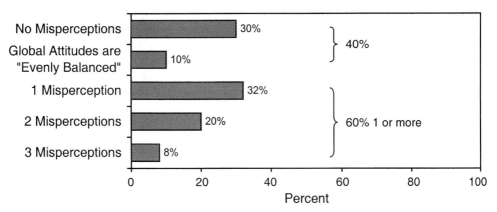

Composite of Polls Conducted June-September 2003

Source: Program on International Policy Attitudes/Knowledge Networks, October 2003.

in the Islamic world feel that U.S. policies make the region more stable, while 60 percent perceived attitudes correctly.[8]

Combined Analysis

Most specific misperceptions are held by a minority of respondents. However, this does not tell us if these misperceptions are held by the same minority or if large percentages have at least one misperception. To find out, we repeated three key perception questions over three polls, conducted in June, July, and August-September with 3,334 respondents.

The three key perception questions used were the ones that found the most egregious misperceptions, and to qualify as a misperception the most extreme form of the misperception was used. These were the beliefs:

- Clear evidence that Saddam Hussein was working closely with al Qaeda has been *found.*
- Weapons of mass destruction have been *found* in Iraq.
- World public opinion *favored* the United States going to war with Iraq.

To determine the pervasiveness of misperceptions, we focused on the 1,362 respondents who heard all three of the perception questions.

Misperceptions were not limited to a small minority that had repeated misperceptions. A majority of 60 percent had at least one of these three unambiguous misperceptions, and only 30 percent had no misperceptions (Figure 1). An-

[8] The Pew Global Attitudes survey in summer 2002 and May 2003 asked in seven countries with primarily Muslim populations (Turkey, Indonesia, Pakistan, Lebanon, Jordan, Kuwait, and Morocco, plus the Palestinian Authority): "Which of the following phrases comes closer to your view? I favor

other 10 percent had the more modest misperception that world public opinion was evenly balanced between support and opposition to the Iraq war.

MISPERCEPTIONS AND SUPPORT FOR WAR

The misperceptions about the war appear to be highly related to attitudes about the decision to go to war, both before and after the war. In every case, those who have the misperception have been more supportive of the war. As the combined analysis of the three key misperceptions will show, those with none of the key misperceptions have opposed the decision while the presence of each additional misperception has gone together with sharply higher support.

Close Links to al Qaeda

Before the war, those who believed that Iraq was directly involved in September 11 showed greater support for going to war even without multilateral approval. In the January PIPA/KN poll, among those who wrongly believed that they had "seen conclusive evidence" that "Iraq played an important role in September 11 attacks," 56 percent said they would agree with a decision by the President to proceed to go to war with Iraq if the UN Security Council refused to endorse such an action. Among those who said they had not seen such evidence but still believed that Iraq was involved in September 11, 42 percent said they would support such a decision. Among those who said they had not seen such evidence and were not convinced that it was true, only 9 percent said they would agree with such a decision.

In the February PIPA/KN poll, support for going to war was high among those who believed that Saddam Hussein was directly involved in September 11 but was progressively lower as the perceived link between Iraq and al Qaeda became more tenuous. Among those who believed that Iraq was directly involved in September 11, 58 percent said they would agree with the President deciding to go to war with Iraq even without UN approval. Among those who believed that Iraq had given al Qaeda substantial support but was not involved in September 11, support dropped to 37 percent. Among those who believed that a few al Qaeda individuals had contact with Iraqi officials, 32 percent were

---

the US-led efforts to fight terrorism, or I oppose the US-led efforts to fight terrorism." In six of the eight cases, strong majorities ranging from 56 to 85 percent in summer 2002, and rising to 67 to 97 percent in May 2003, said they opposed "US-led efforts to fight terrorism." In only one case—Kuwait in May 2003—did a majority say they favored U.S. efforts. In the case of Pakistan, a plurality of 45 percent opposed U.S. efforts in the summer of 2003, rising to 74 percent in May 2003. In May 2003, respondents were asked: "Do you think US policies in the Middle East make the region more stable or less stable?" In six of the eight cases, majorities said that U.S. policies in the Middle East make the region less stable. These majorities ranged from 56 percent in Lebanon to 91 percent in Jordan. In Pakistan, 43 percent said U.S. policies make the Middle East less stable, but another 43 percent said U.S. policies either "made no difference" (12 percent) or that they did not know (31 percent). In Kuwait, a 48 percent plurality said U.S. policies made the Middle East more stable.

FIGURE 2

Support for War and Misperception of Evidence of Iraqi Links to al Qaeda

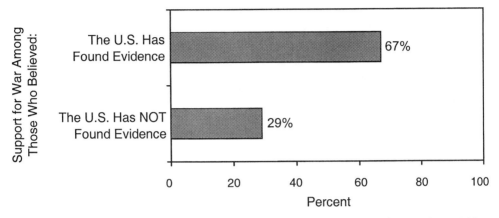

Composite of Polls Conducted June-September 2003

Source: Program on International Policy Attitudes/Knowledge Networks, October 2003.

Note: The question also offered respondents the option of saying that they did not know if going to war was the best thing to do, but that they nonetheless supported the President. Here and in comparisons discussed later, we have limited our analysis to those who took an unequivocal position in favor or against the decision to go to war.

supportive, while just 25 percent expressed support among those who believed that there was no connection.

During the war, Americans who supported the war also said that the supposed link was a major reason for supporting the decision to go to war. An April poll for *Investor's Business Daily* and the *Christian Science Monitor* asked the 72 percent who said they supported the war to rate the importance of a number of reasons for their support. "Iraq's connection with groups like Al-Qaeda" was rated as a major reason by 80 percent.

After the war, nearly half of the respondents mistakenly believed that clear evidence that Saddam Hussein was working closely with al Qaeda had been found. PIPA/KN found a strong relationship between the belief that evidence of such links has been found and support for the decision to go to war. Combining data from June through September, among those with the misperception, 67 percent held the view that going to war was the best thing to do, while only 29 percent expressed support among those who did not have the misperception (Figure 2). Among those without the misperception, 52 percent said it was the wrong decision.

Just as before the war, in the postwar period there was also a strong relationship between beliefs about the nature of the connection between al Qaeda and Iraq and support for the war. Among those who believed that Saddam Hussein was directly involved in September 11, 69 percent said going to war was the best thing to do. Among those who believed that Iraq had given al Qaeda substantial support but was not involved in September 11, approval dropped

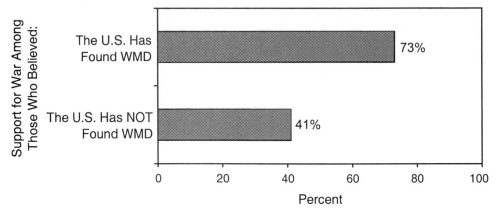

FIGURE 3
Support for the War and Misperception that Iraqi WMD Found

Composite of Polls Conducted May-September 2003

Source: Program on International Policy Attitudes/Knowledge Networks, October 2003.

to 54 percent. Among those who believed that a few al Qaeda individuals had contact with Iraqi officials, 39 percent were supportive, while just 11 percent expressed support among those who believed that there was no connection. Among those who believed that there was no connection, 73 percent thought that going to war was the wrong decision.

Weapons of Mass Destruction

The mistaken beliefs that WMD have been found in Iraq, or that Iraq used WMD in the war, have been highly related to support for the decision to go to war. Consolidating all respondents asked by PIPA/KN in four polls conducted from May through September, among those who believed that WMD have been found, 73 percent thought that going to war was the best decision (Figure 3). Among those who did not have this misperception, only 41 percent held this view.

Similarly, consolidating two polls conducted in May and August-September, among those who believed that Iraq had used chemical and biological weapons in the war, 64 percent said they thought going to war was the best thing to do. Among those who did not have this belief, only 48 percent thought it was the best thing to do.

World Public Opinion

Perceptions of world public opinion on going to war with Iraq have been significantly related to support for the war. This has been true during and after the war.

In the PIPA/KN poll conducted in late March, shortly after the onset of the war, among those who wrongly believed that the majority of the people in the

FIGURE 4

Views of World Public Opinion and Support for War During and After the War

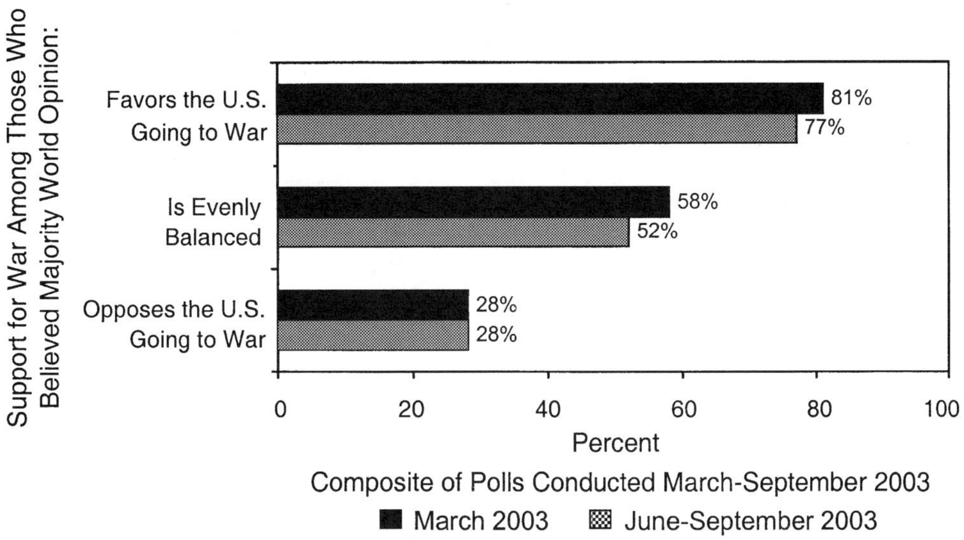

Support for War Among Those Who Believed Majority World Opinion:

Favors the U.S. Going to War	81% / 77%
Is Evenly Balanced	58% / 52%
Opposes the U.S. Going to War	28% / 28%

Percent

Composite of Polls Conducted March-September 2003

■ March 2003 ▨ June-September 2003

Source: Program on International Policy Attitudes/Knowledge Networks, October 2003.

world favored the United States going to war with Iraq, an overwhelming 81 percent said they agreed with the President's decision to go to war with Iraq, despite his failure to garner UN Security Council approval. Among those who—also incorrectly—believed that views were evenly balanced on this question, 58 percent said they agreed. Among those who correctly believed that the majority of people opposed it, only 28 percent said they agreed with the President's decision. When polled after the war (May-September) the pattern was basically the same, though a different question was used to measure support for the war (Figure 4).

Combined Analysis

To determine the cumulative strength of the relationship between various misperceptions and support for the war, we analyzed those who had been asked all of the three key misperception questions—whether evidence of links between Iraq and al Qaeda have been found, whether WMD have been found in Iraq, and whether world public opinion favored the United States going to war with Iraq—in three polls conducted from June through September. These polls revealed a strong cumulative relationship (Figure 5).

Multivariate Analysis

To determine how strong a factor misperceptions are in predicting support for the war as compared to other factors, a binary logistic regression analysis was

FIGURE 5

Cumulative Effect of Having Key Misperceptions on Support for the War

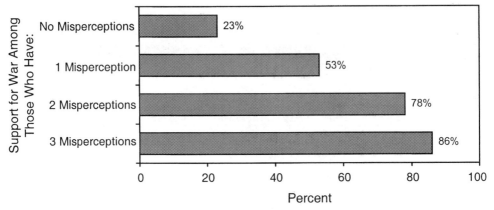

Composite of Polls Conducted June-September 2003

Source: Program on International Policy Attitudes/Knowledge Networks, October 2003.
Note: Misperceptions included were that clear evidence of Iraq-al Qaeda links have been found, WMD have been found, and world public opinion favored the Iraq war.

performed together with eight other factors. Four of the factors were demographic: gender, age, household income, and education. Two other categorical factors were party identification and intention to vote for the President in the next election as opposed to an unnamed Democratic nominee. In addition, there were the factors of how closely people follow events in Iraq and their primary news source. The odds ratio statistic was used to determine the relative likelihood that respondents would support the war. Support for the war was defined as the respondent saying that he or she thought the war was the right decision and the best thing to do, not that he or she was just supporting the President. For this analysis, the number of respondents was 1,219.

When all respondents with one or more of the three key misperceptions were put into one category and compared to those with none of these misperceptions, the presence of misperceptions was the most powerful predictor of support for the war, with those misperceiving being 4.3 times more likely to support the war than those who did not misperceive. The second most powerful predictor was the intention to vote for the President, with those intending to vote for the President being 3 times more likely to support the war than those who planned to vote for the Democratic nominee. Those who intended to vote for the Democratic nominee were 1.8 times less likely to support the war. All other factors were far less influential. Those who followed the news on Iraq very or somewhat closely were 1.2 times more likely to support the war than those who followed it "not very closely" or "not at all." Men were 1.5 times more likely to support the war than women. Those with higher incomes were very slightly more likely to support the war. All other factors were insignificant, including education and age. Party identification by itself would be predictive, but when intention to vote for the President is included, party identification also becomes insignificant.

To determine the cumulative strength of misperceptions as a predictor of war support, the smaller sample that received all of the three key misperceptions questions was analyzed. Respondents were divided into four categories of no misperceptions, exactly one misperception, exactly two misperceptions, and all three misperceptions. Those with just one misperception were 2.9 times more likely to support the war, rising to 8.1 times more likely among those with exactly two misperceptions and to 9.8 times more likely among those with all three misperceptions. In this sample, all other factors remain essentially unchanged, with those intending to vote for the President being 2.8 times and men 1.5 times more likely to support the war. Those intending to vote for the Democratic nominee were 1.6 times less likely to support the war. Attention to news coded as a binary form, however, became insignificant while remaining significant as a continuous variable.

When the three key misperceptions are treated as separate factors, there is wide variation in their power to predict support for the war. By far, the strongest is the perception of world public opinion, with those who perceive the world public opinion as approving of the war being 3.3 times more likely to support the war themselves. Those with the perception that evidence of links to al Qaeda have been found were 2.5 times more likely to support the war, and those who perceived that evidence of WMD have been found were 2.0 times more likely.

MISPERCEPTIONS AS A FUNCTION OF SOURCE OF NEWS

The widespread presence of misperceptions naturally raises the question of whether they are to some extent a function of an individual's source of news. To find out, in three different PIPA/KN polls conducted in June, July, and August-September, an aggregate sample of 3,334 respondents was asked, "Where do you tend to get most of your news?" and offered the options of "newspapers and magazines" or "TV and radio." Overall, 19 percent said their primary news source was print media, while 80 percent said it was electronic. Respondents were then asked, "If one of the networks below is your primary source of news please select it. If you get news from two or more networks about equally, just go on to the next question." The networks offered were ABC, CBS, NBC, CNN, Fox News, PBS, and NPR. Because the PBS and NPR viewers were such a small percentage, we combined them into one category of public networks. In the case of ABC, CBS, and NBC, we do not know how many people primarily got their news from local affiliates and how many from national news shows. Likewise, we do not know if all of those who said that they got their news from

TABLE 4

Frequency of Misperceptions per Respondent: WMD Found, Evidence of al Qaeda Link, and World Majority Support for War
(percentages)

Number of misperceptions per respondent	Fox	CBS	ABC	CNN	NBC	Print Media	NPR/PBS
None of the three	20	30	39	45	45	53	77
One or more misperception	80	71	61	55	55	47	23

Source: Program on International Policy Attitudes/Knowledge Networks.

Fox News primarily got their news from the national cable news network and how many from local Fox affiliates.[9]

The same respondents were also asked about their perceptions, with 1,362 respondents receiving all three key perception questions and 3,334 respondents receiving at least one of them—that is, whether evidence of close links between Iraq and al Qaeda has been found, whether WMD have been found in Iraq, and whether world public opinion approved of the United States going to war with Iraq.

COMBINED ANALYSIS

Because it provides the best overview of the relationship between media sources, this article first analyzes the relationship between media sources and the presence of multiple misperceptions to explore the variation in the level of misperceptions according to the respondents' news source. Afterward, it analyzes the variance for specific misperceptions.

An analysis of those who were asked all of the key three perception questions does reveal a remarkable level of variation in the presence of misperceptions according to news source. Standing out in the analysis are Fox and NPR/PBS, but for opposite reasons. Fox was the news source whose viewers had the most misperceptions. NPR/PBS are notable because their viewers and listeners consistently held fewer misperceptions than respondents who obtained their information from other news sources. Table 4 shows this clearly. Listed are the breakouts of the sample according to the frequency of the three key misperceptions (that is, the beliefs that evidence of links between Iraq and al Qaeda has been found, that WMD have been found in Iraq, and that world public opinion approved of the United States going to war with Iraq) and their primary news source. In the audience for NPR/PBS, there was an overwhelming majority who did not have any of the three misperceptions, and hardly any had all three.

[9] Numbers for those naming a network as their primary news source were as follows: Fox, 520; CBS, 258; CNN, 466; ABC, 315; NBC, 420; NPR/PBS, 91. All findings in this section were statistically significant at the $p<0.05$ level, except where noted.

TABLE 5

*Average of Three Misperception Rates among Viewers and
Listeners: WMD Found, Evidence of al Qaeda Link,
and World Majority Support for War
(percentages)*

News Source	Average Rate per Misperception
Fox	45
CBS	36
CNN	31
ABC	30
NBC	30
Print Media	25
NPR/PBS	11

Source: Program on International Policy Attitudes/Knowledge Networks.

To check these striking findings, the data were analyzed a different way by using the larger sample of 3,334 who had answered at least one of the three questions just mentioned. For each misperception, it was determined how widespread it was in each media audience, and then for each media audience this frequency was averaged for the three misperceptions. Table 5 shows the averages from lowest to highest. Again, the Fox audience showed the highest average rate of misperceptions (45 percent) while the NPR/PBS audience showed the lowest (11 percent).

Close Links to al Qaeda

The same pattern in the distribution of misperceptions among the news sources was obtained in the cases of each specific misperception. When asked whether the United States has found "clear evidence in Iraq that Saddam Hussein was working closely with the al-Qaeda terrorist organization," among the combined sample for the three-month period, 49 percent said that such evidence had been found (Table 6). This misperception was substantially higher among those who get their news primarily from Fox, 67 percent. Once again the NPR/PBS audience was the lowest at 16 percent.

TABLE 6

*Viewers' Beliefs on Whether the United States Has Found
Evidence of an al Qaeda-Iraq Link
(percentages)*

Clear Evidence of al Qaeda Link	NBC	CBS	ABC	Fox	CNN	NPR/PBS	Print Media
US has found	49	56	45	67	48	16	40
US has not found	45	41	49	29	47	85	58

Source: Program on International Policy Attitudes/Knowledge Networks.

TABLE 7

Perception that the United States Has or Has Not Found WMD
(percentages)

Weapons of Mass Destruction	NBC	CBS	ABC	Fox	CNN	NPR/PBS	Print Media
US has found	20	23	19	33	20	11	17
US has not found	79	75	79	64	79	89	82

Source: Program on International Policy Attitudes/Knowledge Networks.

Variations were much more modest on the perception that Iraq was directly involved in September 11. As discussed, the view that Iraq was directly involved in September 11 is not a demonstrable misperception, but it is widely regarded as fallacious by the intelligence community. In this case, the highest level of misperceptions was in the CBS audience (33 percent) followed by Fox (24 percent), ABC (23 percent), NBC (22 percent), and CNN (21 percent). Respondents who got their news primarily from print media (14 percent) and NPR or PBS (10 percent) were less likely to choose this description.

Combining the above group with those who had the less egregious but still unproven belief that Iraq gave substantial support to al Qaeda, the pattern was similar. Among CBS viewers, 68 percent had one of these perceptions, as did 66 percent of Fox viewers, 59 percent of NBC viewers, 55 percent of CNN viewers, and 53 percent of ABC viewers. Print readers were nearly as high at 51 percent, while NPR/PBS audiences were significantly lower at 28 percent.

Weapons of Mass Destruction

When respondents were asked whether the United States has "found Iraqi weapons of mass destruction" since the war had ended, 22 percent of all respondents over June through September mistakenly thought this had happened. Once again, Fox viewers were the highest with 33 percent having this belief. A lower 19 to 23 percent of viewers who watch ABC, NBC, CBS, and CNN had the perception that the United States has found WMD. Seventeen percent of those who primarily get their news from print sources had the misperception, while only 11 percent who watch PBS or listen to NPR had it (Table 7).

World Public Opinion

Respondents were also asked to give their impression of how they think "people in the world feel about the US having gone to war with Iraq." Over the three-month period, 25 percent of all respondents said, incorrectly, "the majority of people favor the US having gone to war" (Table 8). Of Fox watchers, 35 percent said this. Only 5 percent of those who watch PBS or listen to NPR misperceived world opinion in this way. As usual, those who primarily get their

TABLE 8

World Public Opinion on the United States Going to War
(percentages)

Majority of people in world . . .	NBC	CBS	ABC	Fox	CNN	NPR/PBS	Print Media
Favor US going to war in Iraq	20	28	27	35	24	5	17

Source: Program on International Policy Attitudes/Knowledge Networks.

news from print media were the second lowest, with 17 percent having this misperception.

Numerous respondents also chose the option of saying that in world public opinion, views are evenly balanced between favoring and opposing going to war—a misperception, though less egregious. Combining those who said views were evenly balanced with those who assumed that the majority favored the Iraq war—a more inclusive definition of misperception—the same pattern obtained. Fox viewers had the highest level of misperceiving (69 percent) and NPR/PBS the lowest (26 percent). The others also formed a familiar pattern: CBS viewers at 63 percent, ABC at 58 percent, NBC at 56 percent, CNN at 54 percent, and print media at 45 percent.

The same question was asked about European opinion. Perceptions of European views are more accurate among the U.S. public: only 17 percent thought there had been majority support among Europeans for the war. Over the three months, CBS viewers most frequently misperceived European opinion (24 percent); Fox viewers were second (20 percent). The NPR/PBS audience and those relying on printed media were lowest, both at 13 percent.

If one adds together those who thought there was European majority support with those who thought views in Europe were evenly balanced, 47 percent misperceived European opinion; CBS viewers were highest at 56 percent, NBC and Fox viewers were next at 52 percent and 51 percent respectively, while the NPR/PBS audience was lowest at 29 percent. ABC viewers and those using print sources were tied for second lowest at 41 percent.

The Effect of Variations in Audiences

The question thus arises of whether the variation in misperceptions is a function of variations in the demographics or political attitudes of the audience. Some audiences varied according to education, party identification, and support for the President. However, as is evident in the regression analysis, when all of these factors are analyzed together, the respondent's primary source of news is still a strong and significant factor; indeed, it was one of the most powerful factors predicting misperceptions.

MISPERCEPTIONS AS A FUNCTION OF LEVEL OF ATTENTION TO NEWS

It would seem reasonable to assume that misperceptions are due to a failure to pay attention to news and that those who have greater exposure to news would have fewer misperceptions. All respondents were asked, "How closely are you following the news about the situation in Iraq now?" For the summer as a whole (June, July, August-September), 13 percent said they were following the news very closely, 43 percent somewhat closely, 29 percent not very closely, and 14 percent not closely at all.

Strikingly, overall, there was no relation between the reported level of attention to news and the frequency of misperceptions. In the case of those who primarily watched Fox, greater attention to news modestly *increased* the likelihood of misperceptions. Only in the case of those who primarily got their news from print did misperceptions decrease with lower levels of attention, though in some cases this occurred for CNN viewers as well.

The most robust effects were found among those who primarily got their news from Fox. Among those who did not follow the news at all, 42 percent had the misperception that evidence of close links to al Qaeda has been found, rising progressively at higher levels of attention to 80 percent among those who followed the news very closely. For the perception that WMD have been found, those who watched very closely had the highest rate of misperception at 44 percent, while the other levels of attention were lower, though they did not form a clear pattern (not at all, 34 percent; not very, 24 percent; somewhat, 32 percent). Among those who did not follow the news at all, 22 percent believed that world public opinion favored the war, jumping to 34 percent and 32 percent among those who followed the news not very and somewhat closely, respectively, and then jumping even higher to 48 percent among those who followed the news very closely.

With increasing attention, those who got their news from print were less likely to have all three misperceptions. Of those not following the news closely, 49 percent had the misperception that evidence of close links has been found, declining to 32 percent among those who followed the news very closely. Those who did not follow the news at all were far more likely to misperceive (35 percent) that WMD had been found than the other levels (not very, 14 percent; somewhat, 18 percent; very, 13 percent). Twenty-five percent of those who did not follow the news at all had the misperception that world public opinion favored the war, dropping to 16 percent for all other categories.

CNN viewers showed slightly, but significantly, lower levels of misperception on finding WMD and world public opinion at higher levels of attention, though not on evidence of links to al Qaeda.

MISPERCEPTIONS AS A FUNCTION OF POLITICAL ATTITUDES

Not surprisingly, political attitudes did play a role in the frequency of misperceptions. The intention to vote for the President was highly influential. Party

FIGURE 6
Support for President and Frequency of Misperceptions

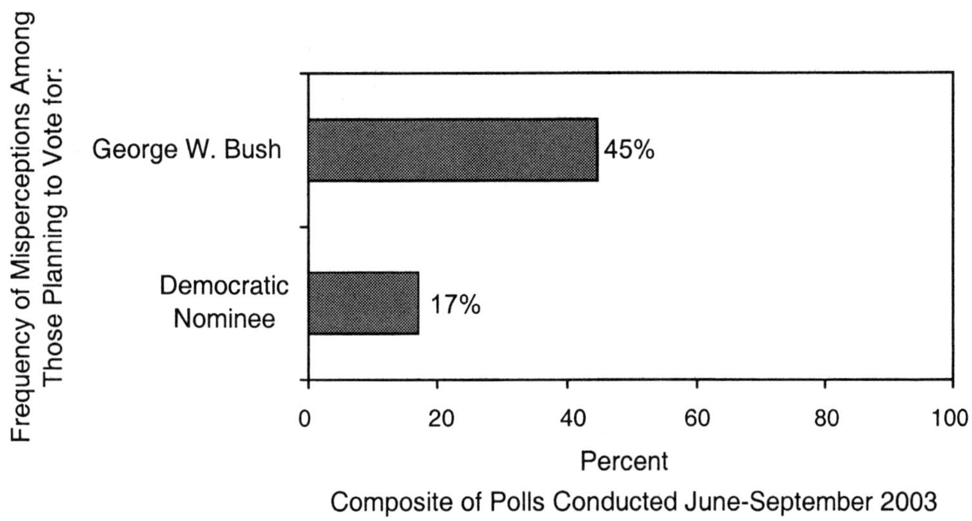

Composite of Polls Conducted June-September 2003

Source: Program on International Policy Attitudes/Knowledge Networks, October 2003.

identification was also influential; however, this effect disappeared after controlling for intention to vote for the President.

Intention to Vote for the President

The polls of June, July, and August-September all included a question, placed near the end, asking whether the respondents thought they would vote for Bush or for the Democratic nominee in the presidential election (Figure 6). In all cases, the responses were very similar to those in numerous other polls at the same time—and showed either a slight edge for Bush or a statistical tie. Only 10 percent did not answer the question. When Bush supporters and supporters of a Democratic nominee are compared, it is clear that supporters of the President are more likely to have misperceptions than are those who oppose him. Multivariate analysis indicates that intention to vote for the President is the single most powerful predictor of misperceptions.

Taking the averages of the percentage that had each of the three key misperceptions—evidence of al Qaeda links found, WMD found, and world public opinion favors war—those who said they would vote for the President were far more likely to misperceive. On average, those who would vote for the President held misperceptions 45 percent of the time, while those who say they will vote for a Democrat held misperceptions, on average, 17 percent of the time (Figure 6).

Looking at the specific cases, in response to the question "Has the US found clear evidence Saddam Hussein was working closely with al-Qaeda?" a strikingly large 68 percent of Bush supporters believed that the United States has found such evidence. On the other side, an equally striking 66 percent of supporters of a Democratic nominee knew that such evidence has not been found. When asked to characterize the relationship between the previous Iraqi government and al Qaeda given four choices, 29 percent of Bush supporters said, "Iraq was directly involved in the 9/11 attacks." Only 15 percent of Democratic supporters chose this description.

Only minorities of either Bush supporters or supporters of a Democratic nominee believe that the United States has found evidence of WMD in Iraq. However, three times as many Bush supporters as Democrat supporters hold this misperception. Thirty-one percent of Bush supporters think the United States has found such evidence, while only 10 percent of Democrat supporters think this.

When asked, "How do you think the people of the world feel about the US having gone to war with Iraq?" Bush supporters were more than three times more likely than supporters of a Democratic nominee to believe that "the majority of people favor the US having gone to war." Thirty-six percent of Bush supporters had this misperception, while only 11 percent of Democratic supporters did.

The PIPA/KN polls asked the same question about Europe, on which misperceptions are less widespread among Americans. Twenty-six percent of Bush supporters mistakenly thought that a majority of Europeans favored the war, while only 7 percent of supporters of a Democratic nominee believed this.

Party Identification

Republicans are also more likely than Democrats or independents to have misperceptions. However, when the analysis controls for support for the President, this party difference largely disappears. For example, among Bush supporters, Republicans, Democrats, and independents were similarly likely to believe that the United States has found clear evidence that Saddam Hussein was working closely with al Qaeda (pro-Bush Republicans, 68 percent; pro-Bush Democrats, 77 percent; pro-Bush independents, 67 percent). On whether the United States has found evidence of WMD, the same pattern among Bush supporters was present (31 percent of pro-Bush Republicans believing such evidence has been found, 29 percent of pro-Bush Democrats believing this, and 29 percent of pro-Bush independents believing this). The same pattern appeared in all cases tested.

RELATIVE STRENGTH OF VARIOUS FACTORS RELATED TO LEVEL OF MISPERCEPTION

To determine which factors had the most power to predict the likelihood of misperceiving, we performed a binary logistic regression analysis, together with eight other factors. Four of the factors were demographic: gender, age, household income, and education. Two other categorical factors were party identification and intention to vote for the President in the next election, as opposed to an unnamed Democratic nominee. In addition, we included the factors of how closely people follow events in Iraq and what their primary news source was. The odds ratio statistic was used to determine the likelihood that respondents would have misperceptions.

In the regression analysis, the most powerful factor was the intention to vote for President Bush. As compared to those who intended to vote for the Democratic nominee or were undecided, those who intended to vote for the President were 2.9 times more likely to believe that close links to al Qaeda have been found, 3.0 times more likely to believe that WMD had been found, and 2.6 times more likely to believe that world public opinion was favorable to the war. Overall, those who intended to vote for the President were 3.7 times more likely to have at least one of these misperceptions.

The second most powerful factor was one's primary source of network news. Analysis shows the factor to be highly significant, but assessing each network is difficult. Though several networks are significant, others are not. To determine the relative importance of each network as a primary source of news, another regression was performed, treating each network as a binary variable and comparing each network's respondents to other respondents. When this analysis is performed, having Fox, CBS, or NPR/PBS as one's primary news source emerges as the most significant predictor of a particular misperception and of misperceptions in general.

To determine the overall importance of one factor to another, a comparison of statistical measures is necessary.[10] Overall, Fox viewing has the greatest and most consistent predictive power in the analysis on a variety of these statistical measures. Table 9 presents the results.

Fox is the most consistently significant predictor of misperceptions. Those who primarily watched Fox were 2.0 times more likely to believe that close links to al Qaeda have been found, 1.6 times more likely to believe that WMD had been found, 1.7 times more likely to believe that world public opinion was favorable to the war, and 2.1 times more likely to have at least one misperception. Interestingly, when asked how the majority of people in the world feel about the war, if the response "views are evenly balanced" is included as a misperception along with "favor," only Fox is a significant predictor of that misperception.

Those who primarily watched CBS were 1.8 times more likely to believe that close links to al Qaeda have been found, 1.9 times more likely to believe that world public opinion was favorable to the war, and 2.3 times more likely to have at least one misperception. However, they were not significantly different on beliefs about the uncovering of WMD.

On the other hand, those who primarily watched PBS or listened to NPR were 3.5 times less likely to believe that close links to al Qaeda have been

---

[10] PIPA compared two statistical measures, the Wald statistic and the difference in the -2 log likelihood if the factor is removed from the analysis.

TABLE 9

Significant Variances in Misperceptions by Primary News Source

	Primary Media Source	Odds/Ratio	N
US has found WMD	Fox	1.6	361
(N = 2,202)	CBS*	1.4	182
	NPR/PBS*	−1.3	53
US has found clear evidence of	Fox	2.0	366
Iraqi link to al Qaeda	CBS	1.8	188
(N = 2,202)	NPR/PBS	−3.5	59
Majority of world favors US	Fox	1.7	294
having gone to war with Iraq	CBS	1.9	168
(N = 1,827)	NPR/PBS	−5.6	55
At least one misperception	Fox	2.1	414
(N = 2,506)	CBS	2.3	213
	NPR/PBS	−3.8	66

Source: Program on International Policy Attitudes/Knowledge Networks.
* Not statistically significant at the 0.05 level. All other media sources did not vary significantly.
For data, please contact the authors.

found, 5.6 times less likely to believe that world public opinion was favorable to the war, and 3.8 times less likely to have at least one misperception. However, they were not significantly different on the issue of WMD.

Level of attention to news was not a significant factor overall, with the exception of those who primarily got their news from Fox. This is consistent with the finding that Fox viewers were more likely to misperceive the more closely they followed events in Iraq. Multiplicative variables were derived for each network by multiplying attention to news by each network dummy variable. A multivariate analysis was performed on misperceptions in which each new combined network-attention level variable was added to the previous model. The results show that Fox viewers are the only ones to be significantly more likely to misperceive with higher levels of attention to news.

The third most powerful factor was intention to vote for the Democratic nominee. As compared to those who intended to vote for President Bush or were undecided, those who intended to vote for the Democratic nominee were 2.0 times less likely to believe that close links to al Qaeda have been found and 1.8 times less likely to believe that world public opinion was favorable to the war. Overall, those who intended to vote for the Democratic nominee were 1.8 times less likely to have at least one of these misperceptions, but did not quite achieve significance on the WMD question.

The fourth most powerful factor was education. Those who had no college, as compared to those had at least some college, were 1.3 times more likely to believe that close links to al Qaeda have been found and 1.4 times more likely to have at least one misperception, but did not quite achieve significance on the other misperceptions.

Age was a very weak factor, with older people being very slightly less likely to misperceive. All other factors—gender, party identification (when intention to vote for the President was included), level of attention to news, and income—were not significant. In a separate analysis, region of the country was included and also not found to be significant.

ANALYSIS

These data lead to the question of why so many Americans have misperceptions that appear to be having a significant impact on attitudes about the Iraq war and why these misperceptions vary according to one's source of news and political attitudes. This analysis starts with possible explanations based on exogenous factors and then moves inward.

The first and most obvious reason that the public had so many of these misperceptions is that the Bush administration made numerous statements that could easily be construed as asserting these falsehoods. On numerous occasions the administration made statements strongly implying that it had intelligence substantiating that Iraq was closely involved with al Qaeda and was even directly involved in the September 11 attacks. For example, in his 18 March 2003 Presidential Letter to Congress, President Bush explained that in going to war with Iraq he was taking "the necessary actions against international terrorists and terrorist organizations, including those nations, organizations, or persons who planned, authorized, committed, or aided the terrorist attacks that occurred on September 11, 2001."[11] When Secretary of State Colin Powell addressed the UN Security Council on 5 February 2003, he presented photographs that were identified as al Qaeda training camps inside Iraq, leaving unclear the fact that the camp in question was in the northern part of Iraq, not under the control of the central Iraqi government.[12] Administration figures continued to refer to the purported meeting between Mohammed Atta and an Iraqi official in Prague even after U.S. intelligence agencies established that Atta was in fact in the United States at the time.[13] More recently, on 14 September 2003, Vice President Richard Cheney made the following ambiguous statement: "If we're successful in Iraq . . . so that it's not a safe haven for terrorists, now we will have struck a major blow right at the heart of the base, if you will, the geographic base of the terrorists who have had us under assault now for many years, but most especially on 9/11."[14] Sometimes the association has been established by inserting a reference to September 11 that is a non sequitur and

[11] President George W. Bush, "Presidential Letter," 18 March 2003, available at http://www.whitehouse.gov/news/releases/2003/03/20030319-1.html.

[12] Secretary Colin L. Powell, "Remarks to the United Nations," New York City, 5 February 2003, available at http://www.state.gov/secretary/rm/2003/17300.htm, 12 October 2003.

[13] Dana Priest and Glenn Kessler, "Iraq, 9/11 Still Linked By Cheney," *Washington Post*, 29 September 2003.

[14] Vice President Richard Cheney, "Meet the Press," 14 September 2003.

then simply moving on, or implying that the connection is so self-evident that it does not require explanation. For example, President Bush's own remarks at his press conference of 28 October 2003 could appear to reinforce multiple misperceptions:

> The intelligence that said he [Saddam Hussein] had a weapon system was intelligence that had been used by a multinational agency, the U.N., to pass resolutions. It's been used by my predecessor to conduct bombing raids. It was intelligence gathered from a variety of sources that clearly said Saddam Hussein was a threat. And given the attacks of September the 11th—it was—you know, we needed to enforce U.N. resolution (sic) for the security of the world, and we did. We took action based upon good, solid intelligence. It was the right thing to do to make America more secure and the world more peaceful.[15]

Here the listener could mistakenly interpret the President's comments as meaning that the same intelligence that determined the United States' policy on war had been accepted as correct by the UN Security Council in its deliberations and that the September 11 attacks, a UN Security Council resolution, and the choice to invade Iraq all followed a logical progression ("given the attacks of September the 11th—it was—you know").

In any case, it is quite clear that the public perceived that the administration was asserting a strong link between Iraq and al Qaeda, even to the point of Iraqi direct involvement in September 11. When PIPA/KN asked in June, "Do you think the Bush administration did or did not imply that Iraq under Saddam Hussein was involved in the September 11th attacks?" 71 percent said that it had.

The administration also made statements that came extremely close to asserting that WMD were found in postwar Iraq. On 30 May 2003, President Bush made the statement, ". . . for those who say we haven't found the banned manufacturing devices or banned weapons, they're wrong. We found them."[16]

Another possible explanation for why the public had such misperceptions is the way that the media reported the news. The large variation in the level of misperceptions does suggest that some media sources may have been making greater efforts than others to disabuse their audiences of misperceptions they may have had so as to avoid feeling conflict about going or having gone to war. Of course, the presence or absence of misperceptions in viewers does not necessarily prove that they were caused by the presence or absence of reliable reporting by a news source. Variations in the level of misperceptions according to news source may be related to variations in the political orientations of the audience. However, when political attitudes were controlled for the variations

---

[15] Full transcript: "Bush Defends Foreign Policy," *Washington Post*, online edition, 28 October 2003, available at http://www.washingtonpost.com/ac2/wp-dyn?pagename=article&node=&contentId=A29127-2003Oct28&notFound=true.

[16] Mike Allen, "Bush: 'We Found' Banned Weapons; President Cites Trailers in Iraq as Proof," *Washington Post*, 31 May 2001.

between the networks and the same attitudes still obtained, it suggests that differences in reporting by media sources were playing a role.

There is also evidence that in the run-up to, during, and for a period after the war, many in the media appeared to feel that it was not their role to challenge the administration or that it was even appropriate to take an active pro-war posture. Fox News' programming on the war included a flag in the left-hand corner and assumed the Defense Department's name for the war: "Operation Iraqi Freedom." When criticized in a letter for taking a pro-war stance, Fox News' Neil Cavuto replied, "So am I slanted and biased? You damn well bet I am. . . . You say I wear my biases on my sleeve? Better that than pretend you have none, but show them clearly in your work."[17] Interestingly, even CBS News, which tends to have a more liberal reputation, seemed to think along these lines. CBS anchor Dan Rather commented in a 14 April 2003 interview with Larry King, "Look, I'm an American. I never tried to kid anybody that I'm some internationalist or something. And when my country is at war, I want my country to win. . . . Now, I can't and don't argue that that is coverage without a prejudice. About that I am prejudiced."[18]

A study of the frequencies of pro-war and anti-war commentators on the major networks found that pro-war views were overwhelmingly more frequent.[19] In such an environment, it would not be surprising that the media would downplay the lack of evidence of links between Iraq and al Qaeda, the fact that WMD were not being found, and that world public opinion was critical of the war. Furthermore, the fact shown in the present study that the audiences of the various networks have varied so widely in the prevalence of misperceptions lends credence to the idea that media outlets had the capacity to play a more critical role, but to varying degrees chose not to.

Reluctant to challenge the administration, the media can simply become a means of transmission for the administration, rather than a critical filter. For example, when President Bush made the assertion that WMD had been found, the 31 May 2003 edition of the *Washington Post* ran a front page headline saying, "Bush: 'We Found' Banned Weapons."[20]

There is also striking evidence that the readiness to challenge the administration is a variable that corresponds to levels of misperception among viewers. The aforementioned study of the frequency of commentary critical of the war found that the two networks notably least likely to present critical commentary were Fox and CBS—the same two networks that in the present study had view-

---

[17] David Folkenflik, "Fox News defends its patriotic coverage: Channel's objectivity is questioned," *Baltimore Sun*, 2 April 2003.

[18] Dan Rather, during the 4 April 2003 *Larry King Show*. Quoted in Steve Rendell and Tara Broughel, "Amplifying Officials, Squelching Dissent: FAIR study finds democracy poorly served by war coverage," *Extra!* (May/June 2003), Fairness and Accuracy in Reporting, available at www.fair. org/extra/0305/warstudy.html.

[19] Steve Rendell and Tara Broughel, "Amplifying Officials, Squelching Dissent."

[20] Allen, "Bush: 'We Found' Banned Weapons," 31 May 2001.

ers most likely to have misperceptions. This is clarified by statistics from Rendell and Broughel's content analysis of network coverage: "The percentage of U.S. sources that were officials varied from network to network, ranging from 75 percent at CBS to 60 percent at NBC. . . . Fox's Special Report with Brit Hume had fewer U.S. officials than CBS (70 percent) and more U.S. anti-war guests (3 percent) than PBS or CBS. Eighty-one percent of Fox's sources were pro-war, however, the highest of any network. CBS was close on the Murdoch network's heels with 77 percent. NBC featured the lowest proportion of pro-war voices with 65 percent."[21]

Another contributing factor may also have been a dynamic in reporting that is not unique to the Iraq war: the absence of something does not constitute a compelling story, while even the prospect of the presence of something does. Thus, shortly after the end of the war, numerous headlines trumpeted even faint prospects that evidence of WMD were about to be found. However, when these prospects failed to materialize, this did not constitute a compelling story and, thus, reporting on it was given a far less prominent position. The cumulative effect of repeatedly hearing the expectation that weapons were about to be found, while hearing little or no disconfirmation, could well contribute to the impression that at least one of these leads was indeed fruitful.

Other more subtle dynamics may also have been at work. The fact that world public opinion was so opposed to the United States going to war with Iraq may have been obscured by giving such high visibility to the U.S. conflict with France in the Security Council. The key story became one of French obstructionism, eclipsing the fact that polls from around the world, as well as the distribution of positions in the UN Security Council, showed widespread opposition to U.S. policy.[22]

One could well argue that this plethora of exogenous factors obviates the need for any explanations based on endogenous factors. Indeed, the fact that no particular misperception studied was found in a clear majority of the public and the fact that 40 percent had none of the key misperceptions buttress confidence in the capacity of the public to sort through misleading stimuli. At the same time, a majority had at least one major misperception, raising the question of why so many people have been susceptible.

The seemingly obvious explanation—that the problem is that people just do not pay enough attention to the news—does not hold up. As discussed,

[21] See footnote 19. Forthcoming studies by Susan Moeller are likely to offer a much more comprehensive view of these dynamics than is available at the time of writing. A report on media coverage of WMD under the aegis of the Center for International and Strategic Studies at the University of Maryland is in preparation for release in early 2004. See also Susan Moeller, "A Moral Imagination: The Media's Response to the War on Terrorism" in Stuart Allen and Barbie Zelizer, eds., *Reporting War* (London: Routledge, forthcoming). On the issue of embedded reporters, see a content analysis by the Project for Excellence in Journalism, "Embedded Reporters: What Are Americans Getting?" at www.journalism.org/resources/research/reports/war/embed/default.asp.

[22] See footnote 6.

higher levels of attention to news did not reduce the likelihood of misperception, and in the case of those who primarily got their news from Fox News, misperceptions increased with greater attention. Furthermore, the presence of misperceptions was not just noise found randomly throughout an inattentive public—the presence of misperceptions formed strong patterns highly related to respondents' primary source of news.

Perhaps the most promising explanation is that the misperceptions have performed an essential psychological function in mitigating doubts about the validity of the war. Polls have shown that Americans are quite resistant to the idea of using military force except in self-defense or as part of a multilateral operation with UN approval.[23] Even if a country is developing nuclear weapons, there is not a consensus in the public that the United States would have the right to use military force to prevent it, though a very strong majority agrees that the UN Security Council would have this prerogative.[24]

Thus, to legitimate the war without UN approval, the President had to make the case that the war would be an act of self-defense. The war against the Taliban had been overwhelmingly approved as legitimate because the Taliban had provided support to al Qaeda and, thus, was a party to the September 11 attack on the United States. Americans showed substantial receptivity to the administration's assertion that Iraq also had links to al Qaeda and that the possibility that Iraq was developing WMD that could be passed to al Qaeda, creating a substantial threat to the United States. But the public also appeared to recognize that the evidence was circumstantial—and this was not a president who commanded so much respect in foreign policy realms that they could simply take his word for it.

The public felt the need for UN approval as an alternate normative basis for war. Early polls showed that a very strong majority was ready to act with UN approval, but less than a third were ready to act unilaterally, and even days before the war a majority was still saying that the United States needed to wait for UN approval.[25] But even months before the war, a clear majority of the pub-

---

[23] Evidence from the 1990s is reviewed in Steven Kull and I.M. Destler, *Misreading the Public: The Myth of a New Isolationism* (Washington, DC: Brookings Institution Press, 1999), 42–57, 67–80, 94–110. The public's views at the outset of the current Iraq experience are documented and analyzed in the report "Iraq Debate 2002," available at www.americans-world.org.

[24] In January 2003, PIPA/KN asked a series of general questions about whether a right existed "to use military force to prevent a country that does not have nuclear weapons from acquiring them." Only 46 percent thought that, without UN approval, a country had the right to use military force on another country in this situation; virtually the same number (48 percent) thought the United States had this right. Seventy-six percent thought the UN Security Council had the right to authorize military force for this purpose. PIPA/Knowledge Networks Poll, "Americans on Iraq and the UN Inspections I," 27 January 2003, available at www.pipa.org/online_reports.html.

[25] For early polls, see footnote 1. Just days before the war in a CBS News poll conducted 4–5 March, only 36 percent agreed that "Iraq presents such a clear danger to American interests that the United States needs to act now," while 59 percent agreed that "The US needs to wait for approval of the United Nations before taking any action against Iraq."

lic said that if the President were to decide to go to war without UN approval they would support him,[26] and when the time came they did. This was a standard rally-round-the-president effect, no doubt intensified by a felt imperative to close ranks in the post-September 11 environment.[27]

Such rally effects, though, are fairly superficial. Even during and after the war, when asked whether they really approve of the decision to go to war as distinguished from just supporting Bush "because he is the president," only about half or less have said they think that going to war was the best thing, while another 15 to 22 percent have said that their approval of the war was just a way to support the president.[28]

Americans had expected that once the United States went into Iraq, they would find evidence that Iraq was linked to al Qaeda and was developing WMD, thus vindicating the decision to go to war as an act of self-defense. Therefore, it is not surprising that many have been receptive when the administration has strongly implied or even asserted that the United States has found evidence that Iraq was working closely with al Qaeda and was developing WMD, and when media outlets—some more than others—have allowed themselves to be passive transmitters of such messages.

Conclusion

From the perspective of democratic process, the findings of this study are cause for concern. They suggest that if the public is opposed to taking military action

[26] In December 2002, January 2003, and February, PIPA/KN presented respondents the following scenario: "Imagine that President Bush moves that the UN approve an invasion of Iraq to overthrow Saddam Hussein, but most of the other members of the UN Security Council want to continue to use threats and diplomatic pressure to get Iraq to comply, and the motion does not pass. President Bush then decides that the US will undertake an invasion of Iraq, even if the US has to do so on its own. Just based on this information, what do you think your attitude would be about this decision?" Respondents were offered the option of agreeing with the President's choice, disagreeing, or choosing "I would not agree with this decision, but I would still support the President." In all cases only a minority of 33 to 43 percent said they would agree, but another 25 to 27 percent said they would support but not agree, thus creating a majority ready to support the President should he decide to proceed.

[27] On the rally effect, see Richard A. Brody, "Crisis, War and Public Opinion: The Media and Public Support for the President" in W. Lance Bennett and David L. Paletz, *Taken by Storm: The Media, Public Opinion, and U.S. Foreign Policy in the Gulf War* (Chicago: University of Chicago Press, 1994); R.A. Brody and C.R. Shapiro, "A Reconsideration of the Rally Phenomenon in Public Opinion" in S. Long, ed., *Political Behavior Annual*, vol. 2 (Boulder, CO: Westview Press, 1989); and John E. Mueller, *War, Presidents and Public Opinion* (New York: Wiley, 1973): 208–213.

[28] Seven times in March and April 2003, Pew Research Center for the People and the Press asked, "Do you think the US made the right decision or the wrong decision in using military force against Iraq?" Those who said it was the right decision were asked whether they supported going to war because they think it was "the best thing for the US to do" or whether they were not sure if it was the best thing to do but they "support Bush's decision, because he is the president." During the war, 69 to 74 percent said the United States made the right decision, of which 48 to 54 percent thought it was the best thing to do, while 15 to 22 percent were unsure of this but supported the President. Each month from May through September, PIPA/KN repeated this question. Over this period, 45 to 53 percent thought that the war was the best thing to do, and 14 to 18 percent were unsure but supported the President.

without UN approval and the President is determined to do so, he has remarkable capacities to move the public to support his decision. This in itself is not worrisome—to the degree it is the product of persuasion, based on the merits of an argument. What is worrisome is that it appears that the President has the capacity to lead members of the public to assume false beliefs in support of his position. In the case of the Iraq war, this dynamic appears to have played a critical role: among those who did not hold the key false beliefs, only a small minority supported the decision to go to war. In a regression analysis, the presence of misperceptions was the most powerful factor predicting support for the war, with intention to vote for the President close behind. This does not prove that the misperceptions alone caused support for the war. It is more likely that it is one key factor that interacted with the desire to rally around the President and the troops. However, it does appear that it would have been significantly more difficult for the President to elicit and maintain support for the decision to go to war if the public had not held such misperceptions.

The President's influence is not limitless. He does not appear to be capable of getting the public to go against their more deeply held value orientations. If he did, then it would not be necessary for the public to develop false beliefs. But he is capable of prompting the public to support him by developing the false beliefs necessary to justify the administration's policies in a way that is consistent with the public's deeper value orientations.

It also appears that the media cannot necessarily be counted on to play the critical role of doggedly challenging the administration. The fact that viewers of some media outlets had far lower levels of misperceptions than did others (even when controlling for political attitudes) suggests that not all were making the maximal effort to counter the potential for misperception.

To some extent, this period may be regarded as unique. We are still living in the aftermath of September 11. With the persisting sense of threat, the public may be more prone to try to accommodate the President, and the media may be more reluctant to challenge the President or to impart news that calls into question the validity of his decisions. And yet, it is also at times of threat that the most critical decisions are likely to be made.

It is likely that with time, public misperceptions will tend to erode. For example, after media coverage of David Kay's interim progress report on the activities of the Iraq Survey Group, the belief that WMD have been found dropped to 15 percent, although the belief that evidence of links to al Qaeda has been found did not drop. At the same time, there was a significant rise in the percentage that said they thought that the President at least stretched the truth when he made the case for war based on Iraq having a WMD program.[29] However, when the mechanisms for informing the public are in some way compromised, the process of the public gradually catching on is a slow one. In the meantime, the administration, by giving incorrect information, can gain sup-

---

[29] See Steven Kull, "Americans Reevaluate Going to War with Iraq," PIPA/Knowledge Networks Poll, 13 November 2003, available at www.pipa.org.

port for policies that might not be consistent with the preferences held by the majority of Americans.

APPENDIX

Methodology

The poll was fielded by Knowledge Networks—a polling, social science, and market research firm in Menlo Park, California—with a randomly selected sample of its large-scale nationwide research panel. This panel is itself randomly selected from the national population of households having telephones and subsequently provided internet access for the completion of surveys (and, thus, is not limited to those who already have internet access). The distribution of the sample in the web-enabled panel closely tracks the distribution of United States Census counts for the U.S. population on such variables as age, race, Hispanic ethnicity, geographical region, employment status, income, and education. The panel is recruited using stratified random digit-dial (RDD) telephone sampling. RDD provides a non-zero probability of selection for every U.S. household having a telephone. Households that agree to participate in the panel are provided with free Web access and an Internet appliance that uses a telephone line to connect to the Internet and uses the television as a monitor. In return, panel members participate in surveys three to four times a month. Survey responses are confidential, and identifying information is never revealed without respondent approval. When a survey is fielded to a panel member, he or she receives an e-mail indicating that the survey is available for completion. Surveys are self-administered. For more information about the methodology, please go to www.knowledgenetworks.com/ganp.

After Saddam:
Regional Insecurity, Weapons of Mass Destruction, and Proliferation Pressures in Postwar Iraq

ANDREW FLIBBERT

The U.S. government's decision to go to war with Iraq was premised on the credible claim that a brutal and unpredictable ruler like Saddam Hussein had to be prevented from developing or retaining weapons of mass destruction (WMD). While some congressional moderates hoped to constrain Iraq's military capability through muscular inspections and close UN supervision, the Bush administration contended that removing Saddam was the best and, ultimately, the only effective course of action. Accordingly, despite global opposition and the UN Security Council's refusal to sanction military intervention, the United States fought a six-week war in March and April 2003, deposing the regime with considerable ease. In the war's aftermath, security has been slow to return to the country, U.S. troops had difficulty locating Saddam and his top advisers, continued guerrilla-style resistance has plagued the American occupation, democracy has proven elusive, and no substantial stockpile of WMD or production facilities have been uncovered. The latter problem, more than any other, has led to new debates over the war's justification, as war supporters and opponents alike continue to question the imminence of the threat to American interests underpinning administration claims and U.S. actions.[1]

[1] The administration's five major public justifications for the war included 1) claims of Iraq's continued possession and development of weapons of mass destruction in violation of UN Security Council resolutions; 2) the regime's purported ties to al Qaeda; 3) Saddam's brutal rule and gross violations of human rights; 4) the promotion of democracy in the Middle East; and 5) the improvement of Arab-Israeli relations.

ANDREW FLIBBERT is visiting professor of political science at Trinity College and an adjunct professor of politics at New York University.

Aside from concern over the politicization and manipulation of intelligence, the major challenge to international security after the war is not simply ascertaining the extent of Iraqi weapons or production facilities. There is little doubt that Iraq once had active nuclear, chemical, and biological programs that would have yielded usable weapons sooner or later. A greater concern is the likelihood that future Iraqi leaders will seek WMD because of the underlying regional pressures for proliferation. U.S. or international efforts to prevent a post-Saddam Iraq from seeking WMD may well prove chimeric, perhaps even impossible in the long run. Removing the Iraqi dictator may have been desirable and even necessary, but it is far from sufficient to end the prospect of a nuclear-armed Iraq. Without a fundamental transformation of the regional security environment, too many incentives will drive any future sovereign Iraqi state to seek nuclear and other WMD. Most of the underlying causes of Iraq's pursuit of WMD remain in place today, and nothing is likely to change this continuing reality. The war launched by the United States could generate the greatest proliferation pressure of all.

The proliferation problem will be only a minor concern in the short and medium term, for it is unlikely that a capacious and independent Iraqi state will re-emerge any time in the coming decade. In fact, there is no reliable guarantee against the long-term disappearance of centralized state authority or Iraq's permanent fragmentation, both of which would preclude a serious weapons program. Even if a new Iraqi government manages to consolidate power and extend its authority beyond Baghdad, it will face the enormous task of reconstructing the country and reconfiguring a viable and supportive social coalition, whether democratic or authoritarian in nature. The United States has a vital, publicly declared interest in preventing the resumption of all prohibited weapons programs. Discoveries of hidden weapons caches or dual-use facilities are possible, but a decade of UN inspections have apparently succeeded in eliminating the lion's share of Iraq's banned programs and will prevent the thousands of Iraqi scientists and engineers from restarting their work any time soon.

In the coming years, however, circumstances are sure to change. This article examines why such change is likely to favor the eventual resumption of Iraqi proliferation efforts. First, the article describes and critiques the decade-long overemphasis on personalistic (first-image) analytical perspectives that have dominated popular, official, and some scholarly thinking about Iraq's drive for WMD.[2] Second, it details the domestic and international incentives propelling Iraqi proliferation and discusses their historical, strategic, and geographic impetus. Third, it shows how Iraq's security dilemma underpins its pursuit of a deterrent capability and how actions by the United States have proven unhelpful and even counterproductive in this domain. Subsequently, it assesses the

---

[2] First-image theorizing focuses analytically on decision making by state leaders and generally leaves aside the domestic and international sources of policy. See Kenneth N. Waltz, *Man, the State, and War* (New York: Columbia University Press, 1959).

major counterarguments: the claim that proliferation in general is either un-problematic or can be stopped militarily, or the alternative claim that democratization, enlightened leadership, or a continued American military presence will eliminate Iraq's quest for weapons. Finally, it concludes that regional conflict resolution is the only viable way to reduce the proliferation pressures that otherwise are sure to affect Iraqi military policies after Saddam.

THE PLACE OF PERSONALITY

Much of the current thinking about Iraq and weapons proliferation reflects a vital legacy of the 1990–1991 Persian Gulf crisis: the personalization of U.S.-Iraqi relations that emerged at the very outset of that crisis. In August 1990, President George H. W. Bush by all accounts was deeply offended by what he saw as a betrayal by Saddam's regime—its invasion of Kuwait—especially after he had sought to fend off congressional critics of Iraq and had worked to maintain good relations with the regime.[3] This anger translated into a domestic political strategy intended to mobilize popular support for the war to "liberate Kuwait" by personalizing the conflict and invoking Saddam's existential threat to American values and interests.[4] President George H. W. Bush was among the first to compare Saddam with Hitler, beginning in Fall 1990. Political analysts, pundits, and government officials thus began to refer to the need to "disarm Saddam," emphasizing his personal idiosyncrasies and psychological attributes as if these qualities were central to regional and global security.[5] In the subsequent decade, this personalistic approach was evident in the perpetuation of the Saddam-as-Hitler analogy, which assumed that Saddam came from a dangerous but rare breed of tyrants and that ousting him in conjunction with minimal democratic reforms would eliminate the threat and start a favorable political chain reaction in the Middle East.

Certainly, analytical attention to state leaders' personalities and decision-making proclivities is essential when explaining their behavior in high-pressure

---

[3] See Bob Woodward, *The Commanders* (New York: Simon & Schuster, 1991) and George Bush and Brent Scowcroft, *A World Transformed* (New York: Vintage Books, 1998).

[4] In building international coalition support, the administration's strategy was less personalistic, emphasizing both *realpolitik* (regional balancing) and Iraq's violation of international law. In President Bush's 29 January 1991 State of the Union address, he highlighted the latter when referring to "the long-held promise of a new world order, where brutality will go unrewarded and aggression will meet collective resistance."

[5] Examples of excessive analytical personalization include Daniel L. Byman and Kenneth M. Pollack, "Let Us Now Praise Great Men: Bringing the Statesman Back In," *International Security* 25 (Spring 2001): 107–146; Efraim Karsh and Inari Rautsi, "Why Saddam Hussein Invaded Kuwait," *Survival* 33 (January/February 1991): 18–30; Laurie Mylroie, "Why Saddam Hussein Invaded Kuwait," *Orbis* 36 (Winter 1993): 123–134; Elaine Sciolino, *The Outlaw State: Saddam Hussein's Quest for Power and the Gulf Crisis* (New York: Wiley, 1991); and Judith Miller and Laurie Mylroie, *Saddam Hussein and the Crisis in the Gulf* (New York: Random House, 1990). See also Andrew Parasiliti's brief response to the Byman and Pollack piece: "The First Image Revisited," *International Security* 26 (Fall 2001): 166–169.

international crises or their making of flagrant blunders in foreign policy. First-image theories of decision making can illuminate those moments when leaders' specific choices have immediate and substantial consequences.[6] Yet, the problems of war and peace reflect more than the choices of a handful of influential personalities, just as ensuring regional security requires more than simply removing a malevolent dictator. Even the most personalistic regimes rest on broader foundations that shape and constrain state action in foreign policy, as second- and third-image theorizing have long acknowledged.[7] In the Iraqi case, U.S. officials' obsession with Saddam all but ignored the domestic pressures and geostrategic imperatives that drive Iraq's actions. They disregarded the fact that Saddam was as much a consequence as a cause of regional insecurity and failed to contend with the more fundamental questions: What were the conditions that created and sustained such an awful regime? Why was Saddam so intent on obtaining WMD? Are his successors likely to do the same thing? International security imperatives suggest that they might.

Domestic and International Incentives

Iraq's incentive to acquire WMD stems from the chronic insecurity of the region and the inherent danger faced by a state that is artificially constructed, ethnically diverse, religiously divided, rich in natural resources, and nearly landlocked. Troubled regional relations affect both domestic and international politics. Domestically, such insecurity often brings out the worst in leaders by creating justifications for despotism, undermining civil society, and distorting the economy. Wartime national security concerns erode civil liberties even in democracies, shifting resources toward defense and permitting previously unthinkable state repression.[8] In international politics, the consequences are much more straightforward: nuclear bombs in a conflict-ridden area lead almost inexorably to the demand for more bombs, no matter who is in charge of any given

---

[6] For a review of psychological approaches to international relations theory, see J.M. Goldgeier and Philip Tetlock, "Psychology and International Relations Theory," *Annual Review of Political Science* 4 (2001): 67–92; and Jerel A. Rosati, "The Power of Human Cognition in the Study of World Politics," *International Studies Review* 2 (2000): 45–75. See also Stanley A. Renshon and Deborah Welch Larson, eds., *Good Judgment in Foreign Policy: Theory and Application* (New York: Rowman & Littlefield, 2002). For an older, important account of decision making and the level-of-analysis problem, see Robert Jervis, *Perception and Misperception in International Politics* (Princeton: Princeton University Press, 1976).

[7] The domestic (second image) and international (third image) influences on foreign policy apply to both democracies and authoritarian regimes and include questions of security and political economy. See Waltz, *Man, the State, and War.*

[8] While focused initially on political economy, the literature on domestic–international interaction began largely with Peter Katzenstein, ed., *Between Power and Plenty: Foreign Economic Policies of Advanced Industrial States* (Ithaca, NY: Cornell University Press, 1978); and Peter Gourevitch, "The Second Image Reversed," *International Organization* 32 (Autumn 1978): 881–911. A valuable contribution to this research agenda for the Middle East is Steven Heydemann, ed., *War, Institutions, and Social Change in the Middle East* (Berkeley and Los Angeles: University of California Press, 2000).

state.[9] Without a higher authority to regulate the behavior of sovereign states, arms races are all but inevitable, especially in tumultuous regions with poorly developed institutional mechanisms to control conflict.[10] There may be additional, domestic-level causes of nuclear proliferation, but regional insecurity can be sufficient in itself.[11]

It is no wonder that Iraq has sought nuclear, chemical, and biological weapons. Carved in a famously arbitrary manner out of the Ottoman Empire, Iraq has clashed with every single one of its six immediate neighbors since gaining independence from Great Britain in 1932.[12] It also has lost multiple confrontations with more powerful adversaries, including two recent wars with the United States in 1991 and 2003, an air strike by Israel on its nuclear facilities in 1981, and military conquest and occupation by Britain in 1919 and 1941. These conflicts were just the latest in a history brimming with both great achievement and periodic military catastrophe for local rulers. The Abbasid Caliph founded Baghdad in 762 and laid the foundations for the Golden Age of classical Islam. But the Caliphate in Baghdad eventually declined, suffered a devastating invasion, and was sacked in 1258 by Mongol forces under Hulagu, the grandson of Genghis Khan. The area between the Tigris and Euphrates rivers, where Iraq lies, is the birthplace of civilization—where writing was invented—but for Iraqis this source of pride comes with an awareness of countless political struggles and military campaigns over several millennia. Its complex society has absorbed an extraordinary range of foreign influences as Arab, Persian, Turkish, Mongol, European, and now American invaders have dominated the region.[13]

[9] This position represents a "defensive" realist view. In general, see Benjamin Frankel, "The Brooding Shadow: Systemic Incentives and Nuclear Weapons Proliferation," *Security Studies* 2 (Spring–Summer 1993): 37–65 and Bradley A. Thayer, "The Causes of Nuclear Proliferation and the Utility of the Nuclear Nonproliferation Regime," *Security Studies* 4 (Spring 1995): 463–519. For an alternative "offensive" realist conceptualization, see John J. Mearsheimer, *The Tragedy of Great Power Politics* (New York: W.W. Norton, 2001). The distinction between offensive and defensive realism is discussed in Glenn H. Snyder, "Mearsheimer's World—Offensive Realism and the Struggle for Security: A Review Essay," *International Security* 27 (Summer 2002): 149–173.

[10] Debates over the consequences of anarchy in international relations are ongoing. For more on the connection between anarchy and arms races, see Charles L. Glaser, "The Causes and Consequences of Arms Races," *Annual Review of Political Science* 3 (2000): 251–276. On the centrality of security institutions under anarchy, see David A. Lake, "Beyond Anarchy: The Importance of Security Institutions," *International Security* 26 (Summer 2001): 129–160.

[11] I do not claim that domestic-level (institutional, bureaucratic, political economy) or individual-level explanations for nuclear proliferation are untenable. To the contrary, a state's decision to go nuclear may have international or domestic sources, depending on the particular circumstances. We may not have enough cases to make solid generalizations, but the realist paradigm suggests at least one certainty about the likelihood of proliferation. Other certainties remain to be determined.

[12] Charles Tripp, *A History of Iraq*, 2nd ed. (Cambridge: Cambridge University Press, 2002); Marion Farouk-Sluglett and Peter Sluglett, *Iraq Since 1958* (London: I.B. Taurus, 1990); and Phebe Marr, *The Modern History of Iraq* (Boulder, CO: Westview, 1985).

[13] For an overview of the region's history, see Arthur Goldschmidt, *A Concise History of the Middle East*, 7th ed. (Boulder, CO: Westview, 2002).

If Iraqis today have a long historical memory for such events, this is not due to an inherent cultural inclination to dwell on the past. It is the result of decades of state policy in which the Baathist regime and its predecessors have tried to construct a uniquely Iraqi national identity by highlighting the region's epic struggles with foreign invaders. In the 1980s, for example, this strategy included frequent reference to the Iran–Iraq war as "Saddam's *Qadisiyya*," invoking the well-known Arab victory over the Persians in 637. For more than three decades, the state also used Iraq's Mesopotamian heritage to tap into the country's celebrated ancient past, cultivating a narrower, patriotic identity to complement the broader currents of Arab nationalism.[14] After 1990, the regime shifted away from secular leftist rhetoric and toward Islamic discourse, selecting bellicose passages from the *Qur'an* and *Hadith* to frame Iraq's confrontation with foreign powers.[15] This use of the past represents a typical legitimation and mobilizational strategy for building national identities, similar to any other political actor's cultivation of historical myth to further contemporary objectives. Such efforts certainly are not exclusive to authoritarian regimes; it does not take a dictator to realize their benefits in any realm requiring communal or national solidarity.[16]

This use of history, however, will leave a legacy long after Saddam is gone. Combined with the stark realities of Iraq's geopolitical position, it will affect how Iraqis understand the international dangers they are likely to face in the coming decades. National myths can be learned and unlearned over time, but they retain a certain discursive hegemony until replaced with something else.[17] This is a slow and complicated process; it is not simply a matter of informing Iraqis about the distortions in the state-propagated worldview. Most Iraqis already understand the politicized nature of the information environment they have inhabited, but many lack a trusted reference point with which to form an alternative perspective. The abrupt, war-induced termination of decades of state propaganda will not change popular or elite threat perceptions in the short term, nor will it lead to an informed citizenry that embraces the views of its

[14] For more on Baathist cultural policy with reference to ancient Mesopotamia, see Amatzia Baram, "Mesopotamian Identity in Ba'thi Iraq," *Middle Eastern Studies* 19 (October 1983): 427–449 and Baram, *Culture, History, and Ideology in the Formation of Ba'thist Iraq, 1968–1989* (New York: St. Martin's Press, 1991). For an account of Iraqi public art under Saddam, see Kanan Makiya, *The Monument: Art, Vulgarity, and Responsibility in Iraq* (Berkeley: University of California Press, 1991).

[15] The regime's appropriation of Islam is discussed in Ofra Bengio, *Saddam's Words: Political Discourse in Iraq* (New York: Oxford University Press, 1998).

[16] Debate continues on the origins and nature of nationalism as well as the role of state power in constructing and manipulating social identities. See Benedict Anderson, *Imagined Communities* (London: Verso, 1989). More state-centric views include Ernest Gellner, *Nations and Nationalism* (Ithaca, NY: Cornell University Press, 1983) and John Breuilly, *Nationalism and the State* (Chicago: University of Chicago Press, 1982).

[17] State-sanctioned identities like race have provided a basis for political mobilization long after their creation for other purposes. See Anthony W. Marx, *Making Race and Nation: A Comparison of the United States, South Africa, and Brazil* (Cambridge: Cambridge University Press, 1998).

conquerors. Given Iraq's experience with both the United States and the sanctions-supporting international community, many years will pass before most Iraqis abandon the idea that the country is vulnerable to external threats and foreign invaders. Recent reality has done nothing to dispel the notion and may even reinforce it. While future Iraqi leaders may believe that Saddam bore responsibility for incurring the wrath of the United States, they still will seek to guard Iraqi sovereignty in the face of threats from the outside world.

Outsiders may claim that none of Iraq's present-day neighbors poses a grave and immediate threat, but the view from Baghdad is quite different.[18] Iran, to the east, is a potential nuclear power with almost triple Iraq's population, geographic advantages like open access to the sea, religious ties to the Iraqi Shia majority, and nearly quadruple the land mass. And while Iraq is roughly the size of California, Iran is larger than Alaska.[19] Turkey, a major military power and NATO member to the north, is double Iraq's size and has triple its population.[20] Iraq and Turkey have had recurring disputes over everything from Kurdish militants to water rights because Iraq's freshwater lifelines—the Tigris and Euphrates rivers—flow from Turkey.[21] Israel, just over the horizon to the west, is much smaller and acutely vulnerable, but for precisely this reason, it has become the strongest military power in the region and perhaps ranks fourth in the world.[22] Israel has undeclared nuclear, chemical, and biological weapons of its own—an open secret of sorts.[23] Finally, Saudi Arabia, a wealthy power with strategic depth on Iraq's southern flank, has a rapidly growing population and a latent military potential that no future leadership in Baghdad will ignore given Saudi acquiescence to American military intervention in Iraq. Already possessing a small but modern air force and Chinese CSS-2 ballistic missiles with a range of 2800 kilometers, Saudi power may increase in response to either

[18] Stephen Walt defines threat in terms of both the distribution of power and "geographic proximity, offensive capabilities, and perceived intentions." See *The Origins of Alliances* (Ithaca, NY: Cornell University Press, 1987), 5.

[19] See R.K. Ramazani, *Revolutionary Iran: Challenge and Response in the Middle East* (Baltimore: The Johns-Hopkins University Press, 1988).

[20] American nuclear weapons reportedly remain in Turkey at Incirlik. See the National Security Archive at http://www.gwu.edu/~nsarchiv/news/19991020/, 29 May 2003.

[21] The Turkish-Iraqi water conflict is expected to get worse as a result of Turkey's ongoing Greater Anatolia Project (GAP), which includes the Ataturk Dam and dozens of hydroelectric power plants in the Kurdish southeast.

[22] Ordinal military rankings are subjective and limited in usefulness. Of the eight nuclear powers, the Israel Defense Forces have important qualitative and quantitative advantages over all but the United States, Russia, and China.

[23] On Israeli nuclear programs and policy, see Shai Feldman, *Israeli Nuclear Deterrence: A Strategy for the 1980s* (New York: Columbia University Press, 1982) and his follow-up work, *Nuclear Weapons and Arms Control in the Middle East* (Cambridge, MA: MIT Press, 1997). On Israel's chemical and biological programs, see Richard A. Falkenrath, Robert D. Newman, and Bradley A. Thayer, *America's Achilles Heel: Nuclear, Biological, and Chemical Terrorism and Covert Attack* (Cambridge, MA: MIT Press, 1998), 64. On reported Israeli progress in completing the strategic triad, see "Israel Can Launch Nuclear Weapons from Subs–Report," *New York Times*, 11 October 2003.

troubles with its longtime ally, the United States, or the growth of Iranian power.[24]

Just as unnervingly from an Iraqi standpoint, some of its regional rivals have been allied with each other in recent years, or at least they have cooperated extensively on the political, economic, and military fronts. An important Turkish-Israeli strategic relationship began with the establishment of diplomatic relations in 1991 and has expanded to include joint military exercises, intelligence cooperation, and arms sales, with Jordan participating on a low-profile occasional basis.[25] Syria and Iran have had significant ties, most notably during the Iran–Iraq war of the 1980s, but continuing to this day in their support for Hezbollah in southern Lebanon. Nine Arab states, including Saudi Arabia, Egypt, and Syria sent tens of thousands of troops to help drive Iraq from Kuwait in 1991.[26] Three weeks before Iraq's invasion in 1990, Kuwait held its first high-level talks with Iran since the revolution in 1979, signaling a return to its traditional foreign policy of regional balancing.[27] Even Israel and Iran, closely aligned until the latter's revolution, still managed to cooperate militarily during the infamous Iran-Contra scandal in the early 1980s, with some observers noting their ongoing potential for strategic alliance.[28]

Although Iraqi aggression prompted much of its neighbors' cooperation, shifting Middle Eastern alignments in a post-Saddam era may not prove reassuring to Baghdad.[29] Some regional partnerships will persist indefinitely, such as a Turkish-Israeli relationship now devoted to countering Syria and Iran. Moreover, no Iraqi regime will be indifferent to technological changes affecting the regional military balance, such as Iran's development of the Shihab-4 missile, with a 2000-kilometer range, and its apparent rapid progress on a nuclear

[24] Saudi annual defense expenditures have risen to approximately $27 billion since 2001. They are the eighth largest in the world, greater than all the other states in the Middle East combined except Israel. SIPRI Military Expenditure Database at http://projects.sipri.se/milex/mex_database1.html. Data on ballistic missile development and proliferation is found at the website of Lancaster University's Centre for Defence and International Security Studies: http://www.cdiss.org/btablea.htm.

[25] See Wolfango Piccoli, "Turkish-Israeli Military Agreements and Regional Security in the Gulf" in Bjorn Moller, ed., *Oil and Water: Cooperative Security in the Persian Gulf* (New York: I.B. Taurus, 2001) and William Hale, *Turkish Foreign Policy: 1774–2000* (Portland, OR: Frank Cass, 2001). See also Sabri Sayari, "Turkey: The Changing European Security Environment and the Gulf Crisis," *Middle East Journal* 46 (Winter 1992): 183–198.

[26] For a Saudi perspective on the 1991 Arab coalition, see HRH General Khalid Bin Sultan, *Desert Warrior: A Personal View of the Gulf War by the Joint Forces Commander* (New York: HarperCollins, 1995). For a broader perspective written by an influential Egyptian journalist, see Mohamed Heikal, *Illusions of Triumph: An Arab View of the Gulf War* (New York: HarperCollins, 1992).

[27] On Iranian Foreign Minister Velayati's trip to Kuwait, see *Middle East Economic Digest*, 20 July 1990, 4. A preinvasion interpretation of Kuwaiti foreign policy is found in Abdul-Reda Assiri, *Kuwait's Foreign Policy: City-State in World Politics* (Boulder, CO: Westview Press, 1990).

[28] For more on the Tehran-Tel Aviv Alignment and a broader perspective on Iranian-Israeli relations, see Ramazani, *Revolutionary Iran*, 147–161.

[29] Details of earlier Middle Eastern alliance patterns are found in Walt, *The Origins of Alliances*.

deterrent of its own, favored even by reformist factions.[30] A defensive all-Arab counteralliance centered on Baghdad is highly unlikely in the short term given the fears and resentments generated by nearly thirteen years of intra-Arab conflict over Iraq. Arab states like Kuwait would find such an alliance unnecessary at best and untenable at worst, having staked their security to a close relationship with the United States. Even an implausible new arrangement combining the six Gulf Cooperation Council states with Egypt, Syria, and Iraq could not provide substantial long-term reassurance to Iraq if it becomes situated between two regional nuclear powers. Iraq is bound to feel acute existential threats no matter what relationships it forms with local or international actors, and alliances alone are unlikely to deliver the American will or the Arab capacity to counter these threats.

Few states in the world today face a comparable combination of potential military threat and geographic constraint while also having substantial human and financial resources with which to overcome such circumstances. Geography alone dictates that Iraq under any future leadership will be exceptionally vulnerable to its neighbors.[31] Very few countries are comparably surrounded and confined—none in the Western hemisphere, only one in Asia, and a mere handful in Africa and Central Europe.[32] Perhaps none has had such troubled relations with neighbors on which it must rely so heavily. With only nineteen kilometers of coastline, no deepwater port facilities, and no unimpeded access to the high seas, Iraq's economic growth will always depend on the willingness of other states to permit the passage of its commercial traffic and oil exports via pipelines, overland trucking, and shipping through the choke points of the Persian Gulf.[33] Even if this vulnerability is unlikely to be exploited under most circumstances, all Iraqis will remember the devastating effects of more than a decade of sanctions, enforceable largely because of the country's particular

[30] Missile ranges are found at the Centre for Defence and International Security Studies: http://www.cdiss.org/btablea.htm.

[31] Iraq's geographic dilemmas are discussed in Ahmad Yousef Ahmad, "The Dialectics of Domestic Environment and Role Performance: The Foreign Policy of Iraq" in Bahgat Korany and Ali E. Hillal Dessouki, eds., *The Foreign Policies of Arab States: The Challenge of Change*, 2nd ed. (Boulder, CO: Westview, 1991). See also Charles Tripp, "The Foreign Policy of Iraq" in Raymond Hinnebusch and Anoushiravan Ehteshami, eds., *The Foreign Policies of Middle East States* (Boulder, CO: Lynne Rienner, 2002). See also the extensive discussion of geostrategic imperatives of the region from a great power perspective found in Geoffrey Kemp and Robert E. Harkavy, *Strategic Geography and the Changing Middle East* (Washington, DC: Brookings Institution Press and Carnegie Endowment for International Peace, 1997).

[32] Only eight other countries have six or more adjacent neighbors and poor (or no) access to the sea: Afghanistan (6), Austria (8), Hungary (7), Burkina Faso (6), Chad (6), Mali (7), Niger (7), and Zambia (7).

[33] A dated but still useful account of Iraq's geostrategic dilemma in the Persian Gulf is found in Gerald Blake, *Maritime Aspects of Arabian Geopolitics* (London: Arab Research Center, 1982). In 1992, pursuant to UN Security Council Resolution 687, the UN Boundary Demarcation Commission further reduced Iraq's access to the sea by moving the Kuwaiti border northward by 1,870 feet, putting part of Umm Qasr Naval Base in Kuwaiti territory.

physical location. It is not excessive geographic determinism to observe that neither changing alliance patterns nor global partnerships can transform the physical constraints limiting Iraqi independence.

DETERRENCE AND THE SECURITY DILEMMA

In managing all of Iraq's relationships and vulnerabilities in a post-Saddam world, WMD represent a potent means of deterrence.[34] This remains true even if their use would constitute an egregious violation of evolving international norms. States under military duress tend to arm themselves to the teeth even if doing so undermines their security in the long run by eliciting dramatic, escalatory responses from powerful potential rivals. This security dilemma has been evident to students of international politics at least since John Herz and Robert Jervis.[35] Most importantly, the security dilemma applies to Iraq with or without Saddam in power, for its logic operates even in the absence of dictators with much-vaunted nuclear ambitions. The militarily counterproductive, politically damaging, or morally repugnant nature of such weapons does not reduce the likelihood of state efforts to obtain them even if other factors limit the success of such efforts. And with both an educated population and the second largest proven oil reserves in the world, Iraq will have the intellectual and financial capacity to do what its leaders deem necessary and appropriate. The realities of geography, economics, technology and, most importantly, a fundamental political impulse will conspire against all long-term efforts to stop Iraq.[36]

Worse yet, arguments from the international community to stop the proliferation of WMD fall on deaf ears when they seem wholly self-interested or

---

[34] Thomas Schelling's concept of "passive deterrence"—letting adversaries know of a nuclear arsenal without declaring what conditions would prompt their use—is relevant here. See Schelling, *The Strategy of Conflict* (New York: Oxford University Press, 1963), 207–229. Also possible is McGeorge Bundy's "existential deterrence"—the general fear-inducing capacity that counters threats to a state's survival. See Bundy, "Existential Deterrence and its Consequences" in Douglas MacLean, ed., *The Security Gamble: Deterrence Dilemmas in the Nuclear Age* (Totowa, NJ: Rowman and Allanheld, 1984), 8–9. See also Robert Jervis, *The Meaning of the Nuclear Revolution: Statecraft and the Prospect of Armageddon* (Ithaca, NY: Cornell University Press, 1989); and Bernard Brodie, *War and Politics* (New York: Macmillan 1973).

[35] John H. Herz, "Idealist Internationalism and the Security Dilemma," *World Politics* 2 (January 1950): 157–180 and Robert Jervis, "Cooperation Under the Security Dilemma," *World Politics* 30 (January 1978): 186–214. More recently, see Charles L. Glaser, "The Security Dilemma Revisited," *World Politics* 50 (October 1997): 171–201. Others in the Realist tradition who have written on the security dilemma range from Thucydides to Herbert Butterfield, Hans Morgenthau, Arnold Wolfers, and Kenneth Waltz.

[36] For a revealing, if speculative, account of the regime-preserving function of Iraqi WMD, see the 22 February 2002 testimony of Charles A. Duelfer, United Nations Special Commission deputy director, before the U.S. Senate Armed Services Committee, Subcommittee on Emerging Threats and Capabilities. It is reprinted as "Why Saddam Wants Weapons of Mass Destruction" in Micah L. Sifry and Christopher Cerf, eds., *The Iraq War Reader: History, Documents, Opinions* (New York: Simon & Schuster, 2003): 412–413.

hypocritical. The United States only began to abandon its offensive biological arsenal in 1969 during the Nixon administration. It acceded to the Biological Weapons Convention in 1972, but it did not ratify the agreement until late 1974. The Central Intelligence Agency kept its own, unauthorized cache of biological weapons until sometime after the Church committee revelations in 1975.[37] As for chemical weapons, the United States did not relinquish its stockpile until joining the Chemical Weapons Convention in 1992, pledging to destroy the many thousands of tons of chemical agents it had accumulated since World War II.[38] For decades, the United States maintained a chemical weapons capability while working assiduously to prevent its local adversaries in the Middle East from developing their own. In the 1980s, for example, a weak regional nemesis in Libya was the object of American military threats, public denunciations, and a concerted diplomatic campaign. In this same period, however, the Reagan and Bush administrations considered Iraq a counterweight to Iran and gave it vastly more lenient treatment, even after Iraq used chemical weapons on Iranian troops and its own Kurdish population.[39]

Most dramatically, the United States has maintained a nuclear deterrent for nearly six decades and remains the only country in the world to have used nuclear weapons in wartime. While the American strategic stockpile has been reduced considerably from its Cold War peak, U.S. officials have barely paid lip service to the American obligation under the 1968 nuclear Non-Proliferation Treaty to rid the country eventually of all nuclear weapons. Even if understandable given the magnitude of the Soviet threat and the reluctance of other nuclear powers to disarm, such a position is bound to elicit a skeptical response from critics. To this day, moreover, the United States retains scientific research programs in nuclear, chemical, and biological weapons.[40] This continued research, in part, is to contend with the very real danger of their future use against American interests. But as a matter of political reality, probably all sovereign states question the U.S. arrogation to itself of the right to limit their possession of WMD while continuing to expand American capability and knowledge in

---

[37] Jonathan B. Tucker, "A Farewell to Germs: The U.S. Renunciation of Biological and Toxin Warfare, 1969–70," *International Security* 27 (Summer 2002), 144. In mid-September 2001, Pentagon planners reportedly considered poisoning the Afghan food supply—an act of biological warfare—and very nearly presented the idea to President Bush, who that same day made public comments about Osama bin Laden being "wanted dead or alive." See Woodward, *Bush at War* (New York: Simon & Schuster, 2002), 99–101.

[38] Richard M. Price, *The Chemical Weapons Taboo* (Ithaca, NY: Cornell University Press, 1997).

[39] On U.S. concerns over the Libyan chemical weapons program and facility at Rabta, see the statement before the Committee on Governmental Affairs, Hearings on the Global Spread of Chemical and Biological Weapons, by William H. Webster, Director, Central Intelligence Agency, 10 February 1989. Iraq's 1987 use of chemical weapons against the Kurds at Halabja is documented in Human Rights Watch/Middle East, *Iraq's Crime of Genocide: The Anfal Campaign against the Kurds* (New Haven, CT: Yale University Press, 1995).

[40] Some U.S. research programs today may even violate the Biological Weapons Convention. See Tucker, "A Farewell to Germs," 144–148.

this domain. Even defensive American efforts can therefore prompt seemingly offensive responses from states like Iraq, its neighbors, and all others unconvinced of the benevolence of American power.

The phrase "weapons of mass destruction" itself is an odd antieuphemism designed to sound especially threatening, distasteful, and offensive. Its use is reasonable, since nuclear, chemical, and biological weapons are horrific in immeasurable ways. But most contemporary observers in American political discourse deploy the phrase as if it were a term of art or a technical term. In fact, it is a distinctly political term and a rhetorical device used with the clear purpose of describing the kinds of weapons that American adversaries may seek and that the United States and the international community does not want them to have. Its political function is apparent in the fact that American policy makers never refer to the U.S. military's development, possession, and potential use of WMD. Their statements on America's nuclear arsenal oscillate between cold claims of *raisons d'état* and warm reassurances of likely American restraint in the event of a crisis. Nowhere outside of the United States is this phrase used with a comparably disingenuous mix of innocence and arrogance.[41]

Those who believe that the United States alone can put the genie of WMD technology and know-how back in its early twentieth-century bottle will be disappointed.[42] The proliferation pressures on states like Iraq are too intense, and they will assure the continued flow of weapons-making knowledge, materials, and hardware to the region. Persistent demand will be met by a ready combination of footloose firms competing in the global weapons marketplace, states in desperate need of revenue, and scientists with valuable but increasingly commonplace skills. Broader trends in the history of military technology and weapons diffusion show that obtaining WMD in all their endless variety can only get easier over time.[43] Close international scrutiny of any given state might suffice for a while, but this pressure just increases the incentive to abstain from the direct international procurement of complete weapons systems in favor of embedding production in domestic civilian infrastructure. The removal of Saddam will not change any of these dynamics because it was not simply Saddam or any individual state decision maker that drove Iraqi proliferation efforts.[44]

[41] The U.S. government includes ballistic missiles in its official definition of WMD. Falkenrath et al., *America's Achilles Heel*, 13.

[42] For an argument about the difficulties of stopping proliferation through arms control, see Jonathan Schell, "The Folly of Arms Control," *Foreign Affairs* 79 (September–October 2000): 22–46.

[43] Basic nuclear weapons science no longer requires someone like Einstein. An overview of the technological aspects of nuclear weapons proliferation is found in Robert F. Mozley, *The Politics and Technology of Nuclear Proliferation* (Seattle: University of Washington Press, 1998). For another perspective on proliferation problems, see Brad Roberts, ed., *Weapons Proliferation in the 1990s* (Cambridge, MA: MIT Press, 1995).

[44] This may contradict Shai Feldman's assertion that "Iraq's massive effort to build nuclear weapons could not have been undertaken and implemented without the initiation, push, guidance, and leadership of Saddam Hussein, the country's sole leader." See Feldman, *Nuclear Weapons and Arms Control in the Middle East*, 53–54. This claim is true but tautological. Saddam certainly was the linchpin to the Iraqi program, but it does not follow that a future Iraqi effort could only be made under his leadership. There is no support for the contention that weapons programs require the patronage of individual dictators.

THE PROLIFERATION PROBLEM

Some analysts say that proliferation itself is not inherently disastrous. Deterrence even worked with the likes of Stalin because it hangs on nothing more than the fear of punishment for bad behavior. This argument of the "proliferation optimists" includes the leading neorealist of our day, Kenneth Waltz.[45] With even a minimal desire to survive, nuclear powers tend to avoid provocative gambits in foreign policy when facing rivals possessing a credible deterrent. After moving to the brink of annihilation during the Cuban missile crisis in 1962, the United States and the Soviet Union settled into a reasonably stable deterrent relationship. Similarly, Iraq's decision in 1991 not to use chemical or biological warheads against Israel or the U.S.-led coalition lends credence to the claim that Saddam was rational enough to have been deterred.[46] Likewise, no sensible Iraqi leader would ever transfer WMD to small, independent-minded nonstate actors like al Qaeda for fear of retaliation from the states these groups target. Only a weak rationality is necessary for deterrence to function; it is less a product of rationally calculated certainty and more the result of simple-to-achieve uncertainty. A wounded nuclear power might strike back with utterly devastating effect.[47]

The problem with this position is that a truly stable system of deterrence requires all potential antagonists to possess reasonably secure second-strike capabilities. In other words, all parties must have weapons that probably can survive a preemptive attack and be used to strike back at their enemies. Second-strike capabilities create both technical challenges and political problems for state leaders. These capabilities are not easy to build and maintain, as evidenced by ongoing global concern over the stability of the Indian-Pakistani deterrent relationship. One consequence of accepting proliferation, moreover, is that states like Iran and Saudi Arabia—at a bare minimum—would feel the need to acquire WMD to assure their own security. A ripple effect would be inevitable throughout the entire Middle East, North Africa, and conceivably much farther. And as critics of Waltz have pointed out, the likelihood that such weapons could be used accidentally rises with each new nuclear power.[48] Military organizations pursuing their own bureaucratic interests might even pro-

---

[45] See Scott D. Sagan and Kenneth N. Waltz, *The Spread of Nuclear Weapons: A Debate Renewed* (New York: W.W. Norton, 2003). A review of the broader literature on deterrence is Paul K. Huth, "Deterrence and International Conflict: Empirical Findings and Theoretical Debates," *Annual Review of Political Science* 2 (1999): 25–48.

[46] Shai Feldman, "Israeli Deterrence During the Gulf War" in Joseph Alpher, ed., *War in the Gulf: Implications for Israel* (Tel Aviv: Jaffee Center for Strategic Studies, 1992), 184–209.

[47] The role of rationality in deterrence has been the subject of great debate and a voluminous literature. For a recent discussion of deterrence theory and proliferation, see Robert Powell, "Nuclear Deterrence Theory, Nuclear Proliferation, and National Missile Defense," *International Security* 27 (Spring 2003): 86–118.

[48] Bruce G. Blair, *The Logic of Accidental Nuclear War* (Washington, DC: Brookings, 1993); and Scott D. Sagan, *The Limits of Safety: Organizations, Accidents, and Nuclear Weapons* (Princeton: Princeton University Press, 1993).

voke unintended deterrence failures that lead to the deliberate use of nuclear weapons.[49] The cost of high-intensity warfare in a nuclear Middle East is unthinkable, so proliferation gives us little cause for genuine optimism.[50]

If proliferation represents a real danger, the counterproliferation posture currently in vogue at the Pentagon may be correct in recognizing the obsolescence of traditional arms control measures and the Cold War security architecture.[51] But the end of the Cold War did not herald the end of the security dilemma. An aggressively interventionist stance, therefore, is flawed in its emphasis on rogue states as the most profound threat to U.S., regional, and global security.[52] By reducing the challenge facing the world to the purported nuclear ambitions of a handful of dictators, this approach ignores the structural sources of instability and paints a Manichean picture of international politics. The world never has been divided neatly into two contending camps with authoritarian regimes led by deposable tyrants on one side and law-abiding states amenable to arms control on the other. As a practical matter, moreover, a military assault on all potential threats to American security is simply beyond U.S. capacity. In the Iraqi case, attacks on its nuclear facilities in 1981 by Israel and 1991 by the international coalition failed to end the regime's pursuit of WMD, not simply because they left the evil of Saddam in place, but because they left Iraq itself in place, an acutely vulnerable state with the wherewithal to continue taking matters into its own hands in an era when this is increasingly possible.

THE DEMOCRATIC SOLUTION

The leading counterargument to this grim cautionary tale is that democracy is the solution. This claim comes in a few varieties. The most common notion, implicit in Bush administration rhetoric, is that democracies are more moder-

[49] On the possibility of accidents, the difficulty of preserving second-strike capabilities, and other direct critiques of Waltz's position, see Sagan and Waltz, *The Spread of Nuclear Weapons*, 46–87; 156–184.

[50] Left- and right-leaning accounts of deterrence and proliferation, written for wider audiences, include Jonathan Schell, "The Case Against the War," *The Nation*, 3 March 2003 and reprinted as "Pre-Emptive Defeat, or How Not to Fight Proliferation" in Sifry and Cerf, eds, *The Iraqi War Reader*, 506–526; and Kenneth Pollack, *The Threatening Storm: The Case for Invading Iraq*, excerpted as "Can We Really Deter a Nuclear-Armed Saddam?" in Sifry and Cerf, eds., 403–411.

[51] For more on U.S. counterproliferation policy, imminent threat, and rogue states, see Section V, "The National Security Strategy of the United States," September 2002, 8–10. See also the administration's "National Security Strategy to Combat Weapons of Mass Destruction," December 2002.

[52] As stated in "The National Security Strategy of the United States," "But new deadly challenges have emerged from rogue states and terrorists. . . . Rogue regimes seek nuclear, biological, and chemical weapons as well. These states' pursuit of, and global trade in, such weapons has become a looming threat to all nations. . . . It has taken almost a decade for us to comprehend the true nature of this new threat. Given the goals of rogue states and terrorists, the United States can no longer solely rely on a reactive posture as we have in the past. The inability to deter a potential attacker, the immediacy of today's threats, and the magnitude of potential harm that could be caused by our adversaries' choice of weapons, do not permit that option," 9.

ate, reasonable, and cautious than authoritarian regimes.[53] By this logic, a democratic Iraq would never waste its considerable resources on dangerous and destructive weapons programs. But even democracy does not constitute a cure for the malady of proliferation pressure, and a democratic Iraq will not be inoculated against the temptation to go nuclear someday. Why would future Iraqi voters not want a potent and compelling deterrent? Why would they be any different from the Indian, Israeli, and Pakistani publics? After all, for more than two decades, average Iraqis have suffered the brunt of the burden for the country's ill-conceived and catastrophic foreign adventures. Regime type simply does not eliminate the external threats to national security—whether real or imagined—that lead states to pursue these weapons. If the perceived threats are high, Iraq is likely to seek WMD no matter what kind of regime governs or who rules in Baghdad.

Some observers also note that democracies are less inclined to launch wars of aggression, especially against other democracies. This particular claim points to democratic West Germany and Japan as exemplary reformed aggressors because their expansionism ended decisively with their defeat in World War II.[54] Although theories of democratic peace may have some validity, even liberal democracies are compelled to defend themselves in whatever ways they see fit. Democracies may not fight, but they do arm. Few liberal democracies exist without either their own nuclear deterrent or a rock-solid security arrangement underwritten by a powerful ally. Japan currently has the world's fourth largest defense budget, but its security pact with the United States is more likely to keep it non-nuclear than any of its constitutional provisions.[55] Iraq will have little reason to believe that its ultimate security will be assured by even a close relationship with the United States unless it has the kind of nuclear umbrella extended to postwar West Germany and Japan.[56] Just as the creation of NATO

[53] The administration took this position to promote the war in February and March 2003. See, for example, President Bush's 26 February speech at the American Enterprise Institute, in which he declared, "The nation of Iraq, with its proud heritage, abundant resources and skilled and educated people is fully capable of moving toward democracy and living in freedom. The world has a clear interest in the spread of democratic values, because stable and free nations do not breed the ideologies of murder. *They encourage the peaceful pursuit of a better life.*" (Emphasis added.)

[54] The vast "democratic peace" literature is reviewed in detail in James Lee Ray, "Does Democracy Cause Peace?" *Annual Review of Political Science* 1 (June 1998): 27–46. See also Michael E. Brown, Sean M. Lynn-Jones, and Steven E. Miller, eds., *Debating the Democratic Peace* (Cambridge, MA: MIT Press, 1996) and Bruce Russett, ed., *Triangulating Peace: Democracy, Interdependence, and International Organizations* (New York: W.W. Norton, 2001).

[55] Japan actually may have the second or third largest defense budget. U.S. assurances may become inadequate in the minds of Japanese voters and political leaders if North Korean saber rattling continues. Data on defense spending can be found at the SIPRI Military Expenditure Database, http://projects.sipri.se/milex/mex_major_spenders.html.

[56] American nuclear weapons actually were kept in Japan and twenty-six other countries and territories, according to a recently declassified Pentagon study, "History of the Custody and Deployment of Nuclear Weapons: July 1945 through September 1977," accessed at http://www.gwu.edu/~nsarchiv/news/19991020/. The study was first reported in Robert S. Norris, William M. Arkin, and William Burr, "Where They Were," *Bulletin of the Atomic Scientists* 55 (November–December 1999): 26–35.

in 1949 was not sufficiently reassuring for Great Britain and France to forgo their own arsenals, a future Iraq is unlikely to abstain from seeking the deadliest weapons available.

A final, similar counterargument is that any degree of democracy in Iraq will make proliferation less likely by having a transformative effect on the regional security environment. This assertion is intuitively appealing, but probably incorrect. One cannot improve regional security without changing regional relationships. This is a structural or relational factor, not a consequence of one regime's tendencies or attributes. Since democracies in Iraq, Iran, and Israel would not necessarily have amicable relations, one cannot assume that democratization will produce better regional relations. Even if these states signed peace treaties, each would still calculate that friendship might not last forever. Fears of the future, reinforced by memories of the past, create powerful incentives to build or retain a deterrent capability. In Europe, it took two world wars, tens of millions of deaths, a common external threat, and decades of institution building for the European Union and NATO to create the political and security community that exists there today. This outcome is not likely to be replicated in the Middle East anytime soon, even under hegemonic American tutelage.

THE LIMITS OF LEADERSHIP

One further hope of the Bush administration may be that good leadership will prevent bad things from happening, easing the transition to an inherently more peaceful democratic regime. But even the most enlightened leadership is not sufficient. If George W. Bush—better yet, George Washington—were at Iraq's helm under likely future circumstances, surely he would find himself looking for ways to defend the country against its nuclear-armed rivals near and far. If someone like Nelson Mandela or Vaclav Havel governed Iraq, the country still would have acute security concerns. F.W. de Klerk's decision to scrap South Africa's nuclear program in February 1990 and accede to the nuclear Non-Proliferation Treaty in July 1991 was only possible because of the increasingly benign regional security environment.[57] The single most important variable for determining a state's defense spending, weapons profile, and its likelihood of seeking WMD is not whether the country is run by a thuggish dictator. Nor is

---

[57] It probably was desirable because of the increasingly hostile international economic environment that apartheid South Africa faced by the late 1980s. See William J. Long and Suzette R. Grillot, "Ideas, Beliefs, and Nuclear Policies: The Cases of South Africa and Ukraine," *Nonproliferation Review* 7 (Spring 2000): 24–40 and Waldo Stumpf, "South Africa's Nuclear Weapons Program: From Deterrence to Dismantlement," *Arms Control Today* 25 (December 1995–January 1996): 3–8. Stumpf was the deputy head of South Africa's Atomic Energy Corporation. For a discussion of competing theoretical explanations for South Africa's nuclear weapons policies, see Peter Liberman, "The Rise and Fall of the South African Bomb," *International Security* 26 (Fall 2001): 45–86.

it a domestic-level variable like regime type, whether democratic or authoritarian. It is the external security environment in which a given state exists.[58]

The 1968 Treaty on the Non-Proliferation of Nuclear Weapons (NPT), which now has over 180 signatories, locked in place a nuclear apartheid of haves and have-nots that succeeded in controlling proliferation for more than two decades.[59] Yet, it probably worked because much of the world had joined a Cold War alliance system that afforded most states relative security. Critics of all political stripes now question its long-term viability.[60] Those states that declined to join the NPT, including India, Pakistan, and Israel, did so because they felt genuine insecurity despite the alliance system. Cuba, not surprisingly, did not accede until 2002 because Soviet assurances proved inadequate in the aftermath of the Bay of Pigs invasion and the Cuban missile crisis. States such as Australia, South Korea, Sweden, Taiwan, Brazil, and Argentina have reversed or abandoned nuclear programs, but only because their security situations allowed or demanded such forbearance.[61] Similarly, a transformed European security environment enabled the George W. Bush and Bill Clinton administrations to elicit the Ukraine's 1994 agreement to relinquish the weapons it had inherited from the Soviet era. Even Switzerland stockpiled hundreds of tons of uranium ore until 1989 because it wanted to be able to develop nuclear weapons if its security environment deteriorated significantly.[62]

Ironically, an American military invasion of Iraq to disarm the regime could make Iraq's future leaders more likely to seek WMD. Even a friendly regime in Baghdad may be quietly encouraged by North Korea's open defiance of the United States, thus far unpunished because of its unmistakable capacity to retaliate with both conventional and unconventional weapons against American intervention. As the revolution in military affairs widens the conventional military gap between the United States and the rest of the world, more state leaders will conclude that a minimal nuclear deterrent is essential to their political autonomy and perhaps their personal survival. In the current climate, any leader-

[58] American defense spending since the founding of the republic has waxed and waned, not in conjunction with the quality of American democracy, but as a function of external threats. This pattern began with John Adams's decision to expand the U.S. navy in response to concerns about French and British power, and it continued through both world wars, the Cold War, and contemporary concerns about terrorism.

[59] Indian Foreign Minister Jaswant Singh used this provocative formulation in justifying his country's May 1998 nuclear tests. See Jaswant Singh, "Against Nuclear Apartheid," *Foreign Affairs* 77 (September–October 1998): 41–52.

[60] See Jonathan Schell, "The Folly of Arms Control." For critiques by William Kristol and other prominent neoconservatives, see "Rebuilding America's Defenses: Strategy, Forces and Resources For a New Century," A Report of the Project for the New American Century, September 2000. This report and related items are available at http://www.newamericancentury.org/publicationsreports.htm.

[61] American diplomatic pressure on Taiwan to forgo nuclear weapons probably would have failed if the government of Taiwan had concluded that its security would be better served with nuclear weapons. American nuclear weapons were placed in Taiwan from 1960 to 1974. See Robert S. Norris, William M. Arkin, and William Burr, "Where They Were," *Bulletin of the Atomic Scientists*, 26–35.

[62] Falkenrath et al., 65–66.

ship at odds with the Bush administration will have a greater incentive to explore all the options. The Bush administration itself has begun to undermine the normative taboo against the use of nuclear weapons by calling for a new generation of "bunker buster" weapons that kill on a supposedly more reasonable scale, only decapitating leadership. Any potential leadership targets are sure to notice this, along with the administration's pursuit of missile defense and the Bush doctrine's substitution of preventive war for deterrence as the cornerstone of American security policy.[63]

Occupation and Outpost

Under the present circumstances, the only sure way to keep Iraq from seeking WMD will be an open-ended U.S. military occupation–too costly in human, material, and political terms. In such a scenario, American soldiers would die in Iraq on a regular basis. Perhaps this would occur only in small numbers, but it would be unavoidable if they continue to occupy much of Baghdad and other cities, just as American police officers die on duty in large cities in the United States. Nor can occupation itself be done cheaply in financial terms because Iraqi oil revenues would be insufficient to pay for both the country's domestic needs and the maintenance of tens of thousands of U.S. forces. The international diplomatic costs of a long-term American presence would not be insignificant, especially if the United States goes it alone and Iraqi domestic instability continues. On a popular political level, a permanent American occupation of Iraq would be disastrous for U.S. relations with the Arab and Muslim worlds, relations that will mean success or failure in confronting the most implacable American enemies. A similar but genuinely multinational occupation force could include only those few countries with both the political will and military capacity to contribute.[64]

A seemingly more palatable alternative to full-blown occupation would be to establish a low-profile but capable U.S. military presence at a handful of relatively isolated bases, perhaps at the international airport near Baghdad, the H2 and H3 airfields in the western desert, Tallil air base near al-Nasiriyya in the south, and at Bashur in the Kurdish north.[65] With troops and aircraft at these

[63] Essential statements of the Bush doctrine include President Bush's 1 June 2002 speech at West Point, where he declared that "new threats require new thinking," and "The National Security Strategy of the United States" (Washington, DC: September 2002). On the doctrine itself, see Robert Jervis, "Understanding the Bush Doctrine," *Political Science Quarterly* 118 (Fall 2003): 365–388. For an analysis of missile defense, written early in the Bush administration, see Charles L. Glaser and Steve Fetter, "National Missile Defense and the Future of U.S. Nuclear Weapons Policy," *International Security* 26 (Summer 2001): 40–92.

[64] Other contributors may step forward, but allied troop commitments in Afghanistan—an effort with wider international support—may combine with instability in Iraq to leave American forces with most of the burden of occupation.

[65] Bush administration officials reportedly first disclosed this possibility in April 2003. See Thom Shanker and Eric Schmitt, "Pentagon Expects Long-Term Access to Key Iraqi Bases," *New York Times*, 20 April 2003.

locales alone, the threat of direct American military intervention could underpin subtler means of economic and political control, ranging from economic aid and trade relations to security assurances and eventual arms sales. All this might induce the new regime—whether democratic or not—to make the desired choices in both domestic and foreign policy. Such an alternative promises to accommodate Iraq's security needs by delegating substantial decision-making authority to the United States, and it provides a guaranteed source of leverage against the over-development of Iraqi military power. Since the United States will have an interest in maintaining regional stability and supporting at least some aspects of Iraqi national development, this arrangement appears to cut the Gordian knot of Iraq's complex political and strategic dilemmas.

Nonetheless, Iraq's distribution of social and political forces does not predict a favorable national consensus on any form of permanent U.S. military presence.[66] Such a consensus is the only contingency that would allow domestic opponents of this arrangement to be reined in. Unlike their relative acquiescence to a temporary occupation today, many ordinary Iraqis will be leery of their country becoming an enduring American military outpost. This scenario is too reminiscent of Britain's military intervention during World War II after which most Iraqis rejected decisively a continued British presence. Even though the outpost was reduced to two Royal Air Force detachments in 1947, an Iraqi-British treaty providing for the retention of troops could not be ratified the next year because of intense popular opposition that culminated in bloody rioting in January 1948 and November 1952.[67] The present-day context may not be so different, but even if it is, the political interests of many Iraqis will differ from an Iraqi national interest that is ostensibly well-served by American protectors. This divergence will assure their resistance. Some political elites, moreover, will take advantage of nationalist sentiment to excoriate an American neocolonial role in the region. A majority of Iraqis will view it at best as an unwarranted constraint on Iraqi sovereignty and at worst as a Praetorian Guard for an illegitimate regime. The larger the U.S. force, the more likely it will provoke a political response; the smaller the force, the less capacity it will have to monitor and control Iraqi military development.

Even virtual invisibility will not prevent the issue from becoming a rallying cry of nationalist discontent, just as Britain's lingering military presence in Egypt's Suez Canal Zone energized the Muslim Brothers in 1950s Egypt.[68] A host of domestic, regional, and even global political actors will reject any long-term U.S. role that is sufficiently large to change the course of Iraqi politics, perhaps

[66] For historical perspective on Iraqi social cleavages, see Hanna Batatu, *The Old Social Classes and the Revolutionary Movements of Iraq* (Princeton: Princeton University Press, 1979).

[67] The demonstrations of 1948 and 1952, known respectively as *al-wathba* (the Leap) and *al-intifada* (the Upheaval) became part of the mythology of the 1958 Iraqi revolution. Tripp, *A History of Iraq*, 118–131.

[68] For an insider account of Nasser and the Anglo-Egyptian treaty ending Britain's Canal Zone garrisons, see Anthony Nutting, *Nasser* (New York: E.P. Dutton, 1972), 68–73.

delighting quietly in the political traction it will give them with their constituents. Legal Iraqi opposition groups, antisystem parties, underground terrorist organizations, and American foes worldwide will resent and resist such a presence. There will be plenty of opponents in a country of nearly twenty-five million people: hundreds of thousands of Iraqis have lost family members to American military power, and not all of them blame Saddam for their losses. Iraq's particular geography and porous borders will make it difficult to interdict foreign activists and agitators from all over, some of whom will arrive quite openly via Baghdad international airport. American attempts to use subtler diplomatic and economic means of control will meet international resistance from states resentful of U.S. domination. Some Iraqis will welcome an American force, maybe in large numbers if the presence facilitates other aspects of the country's political, economic, and social life. But a permanent foreign military outpost has never been sustained in the heart of the region, least of all one designed expressly to limit Iraqi sovereignty and hold the country in check.

REGIONAL SOLUTIONS

Only regional conflict resolution, or at least its mitigation, can reduce to a manageable level one of the most certain sources of proliferation pressure: intense regional insecurity. Even if the security dilemma cannot be eliminated in a world of sovereign states, recognition of its continued dynamics may help to reduce its worst consequences. Ultimately, states seek the deadliest weapons whenever they are caught up in intractable conflict, whether of their own making or as a legacy of past political failures. To put it more optimistically, no state has ever sought and obtained nuclear weapons in the absence of a serious external threat.[69] The very invention of nuclear weapons in the United States was driven by war and insecurity: the fear that Nazi Germany would get the bomb first.[70] No doubt, other political factors were at play in the American case, but regional and global insecurity are among the few sure-fire causes of arms proliferation, all but guaranteeing determined and even imprudent state efforts to counter seeming threats to national existence.

Saddam may have passed from the scene, but peace, security, and stability will elude the Middle East until its most serious disputes are resolved. A resolution to the Palestinian-Israeli conflict is a sensible starting point because it remains the linchpin to Arab-Israeli antagonism and its elimination would give new momentum to regional arms control initiatives that are otherwise untena-

[69] The South African experience contradicts this claim only if entirely domestic political and economic factors gave birth to its nuclear program. This scenario is plausible but unlikely. See Peter Liberman, "The Rise and Fall of the South African Bomb."

[70] The Soviets followed suit, not necessarily because Stalin had nuclear ambitions or was bent on world domination. To do otherwise would have permitted a vulnerability that few state leaders will accept.

ble.[71] This alone would be insufficient, however, because Iraqi insecurity is not a result of Palestinian-Israeli enmity. A durable regional order cannot be built and maintained while states like Iraq, Iran, and Israel fear for their existence, even if such fears are unfounded and elicit self-destructive behavior. Under these circumstances, proliferation pressures are sure to undo any momentary stability achieved by a dominant party, leading to new cycles of confrontation and crisis. Iraq's future leaders will respond predictably to the regional security environment they face, regardless of their political loyalties and the hopes and wishes of the international community. While the evolution and diffusion of weapons technology creates dangerous vulnerabilities for all states, it also provides a constructive political opportunity for those seeking to change an unstable and risk-filled status quo. Conflict resolution may not eliminate all the dangers and uncertainties of international life, but it is a clear and necessary first step toward regional transformation.

A lasting regional order, like its domestic counterpart, cannot be imposed on the Middle East from the outside, especially if local political actors see it as unjust and self-interested. Even the United States lacks the capacity to remake the Middle East entirely as it wishes. These limitations notwithstanding, a durable order would benefit from both the committed leadership of the most powerful international actors and the development of strong and resilient international institutions.[72] Having taken possession of Iraq by force, America now has a responsibility and an interest in expanding the number of parties involved in determining the country's future and creating a transparent process for restoring Iraqi sovereignty without abandoning it in the face of inevitable difficulties. This process might start with the Iraqis themselves, rather than with American interlopers assuming to know best the interests and aspirations of one of the oldest settled communities in the world. It might also benefit from closer cooperation with an international community that Washington seems to have shunned since the debacle at the UN Security Council before the war. Either way, the United States needs to move beyond simple-minded notions of a post-Saddam paradise and the false promise of a hegemonic peace.

---

[71] For details on the Arms Control and Regional Security talks in the Middle East, see Feldman, *Nuclear Weapons and Arms Control in the Middle East.*

[72] For more on the construction of postwar order, focusing on great-power conflict but relevant here also, see G. John Ikenberry, *After Victory: Institutions, Strategic Restraint, and the Rebuilding of Order after Major Wars* (Princeton: Princeton University Press, 2001).

Part III:
AMERICAN POWER AND THE IMPLICATIONS FOR DEMOCRACY

Limits of American Power

JOSEPH S. NYE, JR.

Not since Rome has one nation loomed so large above the others. In the words of *The Economist*, "the United States bestrides the globe like a colossus. It dominates business, commerce and communications; its economy is the world's most successful, its military might second to none."[1] French foreign minister Hubert Védrine argued in 1999 that the United States had gone beyond its superpower status of the twentieth century. "U.S. supremacy today extends to the economy, currency, military areas, lifestyle, language and the products of mass culture that inundate the world, forming thought and fascinating even the enemies of the United States."[2] Or as two American triumphalists put it, "Today's international system is built not around a balance of power but around American hegemony."[3] As global interdependence has increased, many have argued that globalization is simply a disguise for American imperialism. The German newsmagazine *Der Spiegel* reported that "American idols and icons are shaping the world from Katmandu to Kinshasa, from Cairo to Caracas. Globalization wears a 'Made in USA' label."[4]

The United States is undoubtedly the world's number one power, but how long can this situation last, and what should we do with it? Some pundits and

[1] "America's World," *The Economist*, 23 October 1999.

[2] Lara Marlowe, "French Minister Urges Greater UN Role to Counter US Hyperpower," *The Irish Times*, 4 November 1999. In 1998, Védrine coined the term "hyperpower" to describe the United States because "the word 'superpower' seems to me too closely linked to the cold war and military issues." Hubert Védrine with Dominique Moisi, *France in an Age of Globalization* (Washington, DC: Brookings Institution Press, 2001), 2.

[3] Robert Kagan and William Kristol, "The Present Danger," *The National Interest* (Spring 2000).

[4] William Drozdiak, "Even Allies Resent U.S. Dominance," *Washington Post*, 4 November 1997.

JOSEPH S. NYE, JR., is dean of the Kennedy School of Government at Harvard University and was chairman of the National Intelligence Council and an assistant secretary of defense in the Clinton administration. A frequent contributor to the *New York Times*, *Washington Post*, and *Wall Street Journal*, he is the author of several books, including *Governance in a Globalizing World* and *Bound to Lead: The Changing Nature of American Power*. This article is adapted from his most recent book, *The Paradox of American Power*.

scholars argue that U.S. preeminence is simply the result of the collapse of the Soviet Union and that this "unipolar moment" will be brief.[5] American strategy should be to husband strength and engage the world only selectively. Others argue that America's power is so great that it will last for decades, and the unipolar moment can become a unipolar era.[6] Charles Krauthammer argued in early 2001 that "after a decade of Prometheus playing pygmy, the first task of the new administration is to reassert American freedom of action." We should refuse to play "the docile international citizen. . . . The new unilateralism recognizes the uniqueness of the unipolar world we now inhabit and thus marks the real beginning of American post-Cold War foreign policy."[7]

Even before September 2001, this prescription was challenged by many, both liberals and conservatives, who consider themselves realists and consider it almost a law of nature in international politics that if one nation becomes too strong, others will team up to balance its power. In their eyes, America's current predominance is ephemeral.[8] As evidence, they might cite an Indian journalist who urges a strategic triangle linking Russia, India, and China "to provide a counterweight in what now looks like a dangerously unipolar world,"[9] or the president of Venezuela telling a conference of oil producers that "the 21st century should be multipolar, and we all ought to push for the development of such a world."[10] Even friendly sources such as *The Economist* agree that "the one-superpower world will not last. Within the next couple of decades a China with up to 1½ billion people, a strongly growing economy and probably a still authoritarian government will almost certainly be trying to push its interests. . . . Sooner or later some strong and honest man will pull post-Yeltsin Russia together, and another contender for global influence will have reappeared."[11] In my view, terrorism notwithstanding, American preponderance will last well into this century—but only if the United States learns to use power wisely.

Predicting the rise and fall of nations is notoriously difficult. In February 1941, publishing magnate Henry Luce boldly proclaimed the "American cen-

---

[5] See Charles Krauthammer, "The Unipolar Moment," *Foreign Affairs* (Winter 1990–1991): 23–33; Christopher Lane, "The Unipolar Illusion: Why New Great Powers Will Arise," *International Security* (Spring 1993): 5–51; Charles Kupchan, "After Pax Americana: Benign Power, Regional Integration and the Sources of Stable Multipolarity," *International Security* (Fall 1998).

[6] William Wohlforth, "The Stability of a Unipolar World" in Michael Brown et al., *America's Strategic Choices*, rev. ed. (Cambridge, MA: MIT Press, 2000), 305, 309; also from a liberal perspective, G. John Ikenberry, "Institutions, Strategic Restraint, and the Persistence of American Postwar Order," *International Security* (Winter 1998–99): 43–78.

[7] Charles Krauthammer, "The New Unilateralism," *Washington Post*, 8 June 2001.

[8] Kenneth Waltz, "Globalization and Governance," *Political Science and Politics* (December 1999): 700.

[9] Sunanda K. Datta-Ray, "Will Dream Partnership Become Reality?" *The Straits Times* (Singapore), 25 December 1998.

[10] Hugo Chavez quoted in Larry Rohter, "A Man with Big Ideas, a Small Country . . . and Oil," *New York Times*, 24 September 2000.

[11] "When the Snarling's Over," *The Economist*, 13 March 1999.

tury." Yet by the 1980s, many analysts thought Luce's vision had run its course, the victim of such culprits as Vietnam, a slowing economy, and imperial overstretch. In 1985, economist Lester Thurow asked why, when Rome had lasted a thousand years as a republic and an empire, we were slipping after only fifty.[12] Polls showed that half the public agreed that the nation was contracting in power and prestige.[13]

The declinists who filled American bestseller lists a decade ago were not the first to go wrong. After Britain lost its American colonies in the eighteenth century, Horace Walpole lamented Britain's reduction to "a miserable little island" as insignificant as Denmark or Sardinia.[14] His prediction was colored by the then current view of colonial commerce and failed to foresee the coming industrial revolution that would give Britain a second century with even greater preeminence. Similarly, the American declinists failed to understand that a "third industrial revolution" was about to give the United States a "second century."[15] The United States has certainly been the leader in the global information revolution.

On the other hand, nothing lasts forever in world politics. A century ago, economic globalization was as high by some measures as it is today. World finance rested on a gold standard, immigration was at unparalleled levels, trade was increasing, and Britain had an empire on which the sun never set. As author William Pfaff put it, "Responsible political and economic scholars in 1900 would undoubtedly have described the twentieth-century prospect as continuing imperial rivalries within a Europe-dominated world, lasting paternalistic tutelage by Europeans of their Asian and African colonies, solid constitutional government in Western Europe, steadily growing prosperity, increasing scientific knowledge turned to human benefit, etc. All would have been wrong."[16] What followed, of course, were two world wars, the great social disease of totalitarian fascism and communism, the end of European empires, and the end of Europe as the arbiter of world power. Economic globalization was reversed and did not again reach its 1914 levels until the 1970s. Conceivably, it could happen again.

Can we do better as we enter the twenty-first century? The apocrypha of Yogi Berra warns us not to make predictions, particularly about the future. Yet we have no choice. We walk around with pictures of the future in our heads as

[12] Paul Kennedy, *The Rise and Fall of the Great Powers: Economic Change and Military Conflict from 1500–2000* (New York: Random House, 1987); Lester Thurow, *The Zero Sum Solution* (New York: Simon and Schuster, 1985).

[13] Martilla and Kiley, Inc. (Boston, MA), *Americans Talk Security*, no. 6, May 1988, and no. 8, August 1988.

[14] Quoted in Barbara Tuchman, *The March of Folly: From Troy to Vietnam* (New York: Knopf, 1984), 221.

[15] Daniel Bell, *The Coming of Post-Industrial Society: A Venture in Social Forecasting* (New York: Basic Books, 1999 [1973]), new introduction.

[16] William Pfaff, *Barbarian Sentiments: America in the New Century*, rev. ed. (New York: Hill and Wang, 2000), 280.

a necessary condition of planning our actions. At the national level, we need such pictures to guide policy and tell us how to use our unprecedented power. There is, of course, no single future; there are multiple possible futures, and the quality of our foreign policy can make some more likely than others. When systems involve complex interactions and feedbacks, small causes can have large effects. And when people are involved, human reaction to the prediction itself may make it fail to come true.

We cannot hope to predict the future, but we can draw our pictures carefully so as to avoid some common mistakes.[17] A decade ago, a more careful analysis of American power could have saved us from the mistaken portrait of American decline. More recently, accurate predictions of catastrophic terrorism failed to avert a tragedy that leads some again to foresee decline. It is important to prevent the errors of both declinism and triumphalism. Declinism tends to produce overly cautious behavior that could undercut influence; triumphalism could beget a potentially dangerous absence of restraint, as well as an arrogance that would also squander influence. With careful analysis, the United States can make better decisions about how to protect its people, promote values, and lead toward a better world over the next few decades. I begin this analysis with an examination of the sources of U.S. power.

THE SOURCES OF AMERICAN POWER

We hear a lot about how powerful America has become in recent years, but what do we mean by power? Simply put, power is the ability to effect the outcomes you want and, if necessary, to change the behavior of others to make this happen. For example, NATO's military power reversed Slobodan Milosevic's ethnic cleansing of Kosovo, and the promise of economic aid to Serbia's devastated economy reversed the Serbian government's initial disinclination to hand Milosevic over to the Hague tribunal.

The ability to obtain the outcomes one wants is often associated with the possession of certain resources, and so we commonly use shorthand and define power as possession of relatively large amounts of such elements as population, territory, natural resources, economic strength, military force, and political stability. Power in this sense means holding the high cards in the international poker game. If you show high cards, others are likely to fold their hands. Of course, if you play your hand poorly or fall victim to bluff and deception, you can still lose, or at least fail to get the outcome you want. For example, the United States was the largest power after World War I, but it failed to prevent the rise of Hitler or Pearl Harbor. Converting America's potential power resources into realized power requires well-designed policy and skillful leadership. But it helps to start by holding the high cards.

[17] On the complexities of projections, see Joseph S. Nye, Jr., "Peering into the Future," *Foreign Affairs* (July-August 1994); see also Robert Jervis, "The Future of World Politics: Will It Resemble the Past?" *International Security* (Winter 1991–1992).

Traditionally, the test of a great power was "strength for war."[18] War was the ultimate game in which the cards of international politics were played and estimates of relative power were proven. Over the centuries, as technologies evolved, the sources of power have changed. In the agrarian economies of seventeenth- and eighteenth-century Europe, population was a critical power resource because it provided a base for taxes and the recruitment of infantry (who were mostly mercenaries), and this combination of men and money gave the edge to France. But in the nineteenth century, the growing importance of industry benefited first Britain, which ruled the waves with a navy that had no peer, and later Germany, which used efficient administration and railways to transport armies for quick victories on the Continent (though Russia had a larger population and army). By the middle of the twentieth century, with the advent of the nuclear age, the United States and the Soviet Union possessed not only industrial might but nuclear arsenals and intercontinental missiles.

Today the foundations of power have been moving away from the emphasis on military force and conquest. Paradoxically, nuclear weapons were one of the causes. As we know from the history of the cold war, nuclear weapons proved so awesome and destructive that they became muscle bound—too costly to use except, theoretically, in the most extreme circumstances.[19] A second important change was the rise of nationalism, which has made it more difficult for empires to rule over awakened populations. In the nineteenth century, a few adventurers conquered most of Africa with a handful of soldiers, and Britain ruled India with a colonial force that was a tiny fraction of the indigenous population. Today, colonial rule is not only widely condemned but far too costly, as both cold war superpowers discovered in Vietnam and Afghanistan. The collapse of the Soviet empire followed the end of European empires by a matter of decades.

A third important cause is societal change inside great powers. Postindustrial societies are focused on welfare rather than glory, and they loathe high casualties except when survival is at stake. This does not mean that they will not use force, even when casualties are expected—witness the 1991 Gulf War or Afghanistan today. But the absence of a warrior ethic in modern democracies means that the use of force requires an elaborate moral justification to ensure popular support (except in cases where survival is at stake). Roughly speaking, there are three types of countries in the world today: poor, weak preindustrial states, which are often the chaotic remnants of collapsed empires; modernizing industrial states such as India or China; and the postindustrial societies that prevail in Europe, North America, and Japan. The use of force is common in the first type of country, still accepted in the second, but less toler-

---

[18] A. J. Taylor, *The Struggle for Mastery in Europe, 1848–1918* (Oxford, UK: Oxford University Press, 1954), xxix.

[19] Whether this would change with the proliferation of nuclear weapons to more states is hotly debated among theorists. Deterrence should work with most states, but the prospects of accident and loss of control would increase. For my views, see Joseph S. Nye, Jr., *Nuclear Ethics* (New York: Free Press, 1986).

ated in the third. In the words of British diplomat Robert Cooper, "A large number of the most powerful states no longer want to fight or to conquer."[20] War remains possible, but it is much less acceptable now than it was a century or even half a century ago.[21]

Finally, for most of today's great powers, the use of force would jeopardize their economic objectives. Even nondemocratic countries that feel fewer popular moral constraints on the use of force have to consider its effects on their economic objectives. As Thomas Friedman has put it, countries are disciplined by an "electronic herd" of investors who control their access to capital in a globalized economy.[22] And Richard Rosecrance writes, "In the past, it was cheaper to seize another state's territory by force than to develop the sophisticated economic and trading apparatus needed to derive benefit from commercial exchange with it."[23] Imperial Japan used the former approach when it created the Greater East Asia Co-prosperity Sphere in the 1930s, but Japan's post-World War II role as a trading state turned out to be far more successful, leading it to become the second largest national economy in the world. It is difficult now to imagine a scenario in which Japan would try to colonize its neighbors, or succeed in doing so.

As mentioned above, none of this is to suggest that military force plays no role in international politics today. For one thing, the information revolution has yet to transform most of the world. Many states are unconstrained by democratic societal forces, as Kuwait learned from its neighbor Iraq, and terrorist groups pay little heed to the normal constraints of liberal societies. Civil wars are rife in many parts of the world where collapsed empires left power vacuums. Moreover, throughout history, the rise of new great powers has been accompanied by anxieties that have sometimes precipitated military crises. In Thucydides' immortal description, the Peloponnesian War in ancient Greece was caused by the rise to power of Athens and the fear it created in Sparta.[24] World War I owed much to the rise of the kaiser's Germany and the fear that it created in Britain.[25] Some foretell a similar dynamic in this century arising from the rise of China and the fear it creates in the United States.

Geoeconomics has not replaced geopolitics, although in the early twenty-first century there has clearly been a blurring of the traditional boundaries between the two. To ignore the role of force and the centrality of security would

---

[20] Robert Cooper, *The Postmodern State and the World Order* (London: Demos, 2000), 22.

[21] John Mueller, *Retreat from Doomsday: The Obsolescence of Major War* (New York: Basic Books, 1989).

[22] Thomas Friedman, *The Lexus and the Olive Tree: Understanding Globalization* (New York: Farrar, Straus and Giroux, 1999), chap. 6.

[23] Richard N. Rosecrance, *The Rise of the Trading State* (New York: Basic Books, 1986), 16, 160.

[24] Thucydides, *History of the Peloponnesian War*, trans. Rex Warner (London: Penguin, 1972), book I, chapter 1.

[25] And in turn, as industrialization progressed and railroads were built, Germany feared the rise of Russia.

be like ignoring oxygen. Under normal circumstances, oxygen is plentiful and we pay it little attention. But once those conditions change and we begin to miss it, we can focus on nothing else.[26] Even in those areas where the direct employment of force falls out of use among countries—for instance, within Western Europe or between the United States and Japan—nonstate actors such as terrorists may use force. Moreover, military force can still play an important political role among advanced nations. For example, most countries in East Asia welcome the presence of American troops as an insurance policy against uncertain neighbors. Moreover, deterring threats or ensuring access to a crucial resource such as oil in the Persian Gulf increases America's influence with its allies. Sometimes the linkages may be direct; more often they are present in the back of statesmen's minds. As the Defense Department describes it, one of the missions of American troops based overseas is to "shape the environment."

With that said, economic power *has* become more important than in the past, both because of the relative increase in the costliness of force and because economic objectives loom large in the values of postindustrial societies.[27] In a world of economic globalization, all countries are to some extent dependent on market forces beyond their direct control. When President Clinton was struggling to balance the federal budget in 1993, one of his advisers stated in exasperation that if he were to be reborn, he would like to come back as "the market" because that was clearly the most powerful player.[28] But markets constrain different countries to different degrees. Because the United States constitutes such a large part of the market in trade and finance, it is better placed to set its own terms than are Argentina or Thailand. And if small countries are willing to pay the price of opting out of the market, they can reduce the power that other countries have over them. Thus American economic sanctions have had little effect, for example, on improving human rights in isolated Myanmar. Saddam Hussein's strong preference for his own survival rather than the welfare of the Iraqi people meant that crippling sanctions failed for more than a decade to remove him from power. And economic sanctions may disrupt but not deter nonstate terrorists. But the exceptions prove the rule. Military power remains crucial in certain situations, but it is a mistake to focus too narrowly on the military dimensions of American power.

---

[26] Henry Kissinger portrays four international systems existing side by side: the West (and Western Hemisphere), marked by democratic peace; Asia, where strategic conflict is possible; the Middle East, marked by religious conflict; and Africa, where civil wars threaten weak postcolonial states. "America at the Apex," *The National Interest* (Summer 2001).

[27] Robert O. Keohane and Joseph S. Nye, Jr., *Power and Interdependence*, 3rd ed. (New York: Longman, 2000), chap. 1.

[28] James Carville quoted in Bob Woodward, *The Agenda: Inside the Clinton White House* (New York: Simon and Schuster, 1994), 302.

SOFT POWER

In my view, if the United States wants to remain strong, Americans need also to pay attention to our soft power. What precisely do I mean by soft power? Military power and economic power are both examples of hard command power that can be used to induce others to change their position. Hard power can rest on inducements (carrots) or threats (sticks). But there is also an indirect way to exercise power. A country may obtain the outcomes it wants in world politics because other countries want to follow it, admiring its values, emulating its example, aspiring to its level of prosperity and openness. In this sense, it is just as important to set the agenda in world politics and attract others as it is to force them to change through the threat or use of military or economic weapons. This aspect of power—getting others to want what you want—I call soft power.[29] It coopts people rather than coerces them.

Soft power rests on the ability to set the political agenda in a way that shapes the preferences of others. At the personal level, wise parents know that if they have brought up their children with the right beliefs and values, their power will be greater and will last longer than if they have relied only on spankings, cutting off allowances, or taking away the car keys. Similarly, political leaders and thinkers such as Antonio Gramsci have long understood the power that comes from setting the agenda and determining the framework of a debate. The ability to establish preferences tends to be associated with intangible power resources such as an attractive culture, ideology, and institutions. If I can get you to *want* to do what I want, then I do not have to force you to do what you do *not* want to do. If the United States represents values that others want to follow, it will cost us less to lead. Soft power is not merely the same as influence, though it is one source of influence. After all, I can also influence you by threats or rewards. Soft power is also more than persuasion or the ability to move people by argument. It is the ability to entice and attract. And attraction often leads to acquiescence or imitation.

Soft power arises in large part from our values. These values are expressed in our culture, in the policies we follow inside our country, and in the way we handle ourselves internationally. The government sometimes finds it difficult to control and employ soft power. Like love, it is hard to measure and to handle, and does not touch everyone, but that does not diminish its importance. As Hubert Védrine laments, Americans are so powerful because they can "inspire the dreams and desires of others, thanks to the mastery of global images through film and television and because, for these same reasons, large numbers of students from other countries come to the United States to finish their studies."[30] Soft power is an important reality.

[29] For a more detailed discussion, see Joseph S. Nye, Jr., *Bound to Lead: The Changing Nature of American Power* (New York: Basic Books, 1990), chap. 2. This builds on what Peter Bachrach and Morton Baratz called the "second face of power" in "Decisions and Nondecisions: An Analytical Framework," *American Political Science Review* (September 1963): 632–42.

[30] Védrine, *France in an Age of Globalization*, 3.

Of course, hard and soft power are related and can reinforce each other. Both are aspects of the ability to achieve our purposes by affecting the behavior of others. Sometimes the same power resources can affect the entire spectrum of behavior from coercion to attraction.[31] A country that suffers economic and military decline is likely to lose its ability to shape the international agenda as well as its attractiveness. And some countries may be attracted to others with hard power by the myth of invincibility or inevitability. Both Hitler and Stalin tried to develop such myths. Hard power can also be used to establish empires and institutions that set the agenda for smaller states—witness Soviet rule over the countries of Eastern Europe. But soft power is not simply the reflection of hard power. The Vatican did not lose its soft power when it lost the Papal States in Italy in the nineteenth century. Conversely, the Soviet Union lost much of its soft power after it invaded Hungary and Czechoslovakia, even though its economic and military resources continued to grow. Imperious policies that utilized Soviet hard power actually undercut its soft power. And some countries such as Canada, the Netherlands, and the Scandinavian states have political clout that is greater than their military and economic weight, because of the incorporation of attractive causes such as economic aid or peacekeeping into their definitions of national interest. These are lessons that the unilateralists forget at their and our peril.

Britain in the nineteenth century and America in the second half of the twentieth century enhanced their power by creating liberal international economic rules and institutions that were consistent with the liberal and democratic structures of British and American capitalism—free trade and the gold standard in the case of Britain, the International Monetary Fund, World Trade Organization, and other institutions in the case of the United States. If a country can make its power legitimate in the eyes of others, it will encounter less resistance to its wishes. If its culture and ideology are attractive, others more willingly follow. If it can establish international rules that are consistent with its society, it will be less likely to have to change. If it can help support institutions that encourage other countries to channel or limit their activities in ways it prefers, it may not need as many costly carrots and sticks.

---

[31] The distinction between hard and soft power is one of degree, both in the nature of the behavior and in the tangibility of the resources. Both are aspects of the ability to achieve one's purposes by affecting the behavior of others. Command power—the ability to change what others do—can rest on coercion or inducement. Co-optive power—the ability to shape what others want—can rest on the attractiveness of one's culture and ideology or the ability to manipulate the agenda of political choices in a manner that makes actors fail to express some preferences because they seem to be too unrealistic. The forms of behavior between command and co-optive power range along a continuum: command power, coercion, inducement, agenda setting, attraction, co-optive power. Soft power resources tend to be associated with co-optive power behavior, whereas hard power resources are usually associated with command behavior. But the relationship is imperfect. For example, countries may be attracted to others with command power by myths of invincibility, and command power may sometimes be used to establish institutions that later become regarded as legitimate. But the general association is strong enough to allow the useful shorthand reference to hard and soft power.

In short, the universality of a country's culture and its ability to establish a set of favorable rules and institutions that govern areas of international activity are critical sources of power. The values of democracy, personal freedom, upward mobility, and openness that are often expressed in American popular culture, higher education, and foreign policy contribute to American power in many areas. In the view of German journalist Josef Joffe, America's soft power "looms even larger than its economic and military assets. U.S. culture, lowbrow or high, radiates outward with an intensity last seen in the days of the Roman Empire—but with a novel twist. Rome's and Soviet Russia's cultural sway stopped exactly at their military borders. America's soft power, though, rules over an empire on which the sun never sets."[32]

Of course, soft power is more than just cultural power. The values the U.S. government champions in its behavior at home (for example, democracy), in international institutions (listening to others), and in foreign policy (promoting peace and human rights) also affect the preferences of others. America can attract (or repel) others by the influence of its example. But soft power does not belong to the government in the same degree that hard power does. Some hard power assets (such as armed forces) are strictly governmental, others are inherently national (such as our oil and gas reserves), and many can be transferred to collective control (such as industrial assets that can be mobilized in an emergency). In contrast, many soft power resources are separate from American government and only partly responsive to its purposes. In the Vietnam era, for example, American government policy and popular culture worked at crosspurposes. Today popular U.S. firms or nongovernmental groups develop soft power of their own that may coincide or be at odds with official foreign policy goals. That is all the more reason for the government to make sure that its own actions reinforce rather than undercut American soft power. All these sources of soft power are likely to become increasingly important in the global information age of this new century. And, at the same time, the arrogance, indifference to the opinions of others, and narrow approach to our national interests advocated by the new unilateralists are a sure way to undermine American soft power.

Power in the global information age is becoming less tangible and less coercive, particularly among the advanced countries, but most of the world does not consist of postindustrial societies, and that limits the transformation of power. Much of Africa and the Middle East remains locked in preindustrial agricultural societies with weak institutions and authoritarian rulers. Other countries, such as China, India, and Brazil, are industrial economies analogous to parts of the West in the mid-twentieth century.[33] In such a variegated world, all three sources of power—military, economic, and soft—remain relevant, although to different degrees in different relationships. However, if current economic and social trends continue, leadership in the information revolution and

---

[32] Josef Joffe, "Who's Afraid of Mr. Big?" *The National Interest* (Summer 2001): 43.

[33] See Cooper, *Postmodern State*; Bell, *The Coming of Post-Industrial Society*.

TABLE 1

Leading States and Their Power Resources, 1500–2000

Period	State	Major Resources
Sixteenth century	Spain	Gold bullion, colonial trade, mercenary armies, dynastic ties
Seventeenth century	Netherlands	Trade, capital markets, navy
Eighteenth century	France	Population, rural industry, public administration, army, culture (soft power)
Nineteenth century	Britain	Industry, political cohesion, finance and credit, navy, liberal norms (soft power), island location (easy to defend)
Twentieth century	United States	Economic scale, scientific and technical leadership, location, military forces and alliances, universalistic culture and liberal international regimes (soft power)
Twenty-first century	United States	Technological leadership, military and economic scale, soft power, hub of transnational communications

soft power will become more important in the mix. Table 1 provides a simplified description of the evolution of power resources over the past few centuries.

Power in the twenty-first century will rest on a mix of hard and soft resources. No country is better endowed than the United States in all three dimensions—military, economic, and soft power. Its greatest mistake in such a world would be to fall into one-dimensional analysis and to believe that investing in military power alone will ensure its strength.

Balance or Hegemony?

America's power—hard and soft—is only part of the story. How others react to American power is equally important to the question of stability and governance in this global information age. Many realists extol the virtues of the classic nineteenth-century European balance of power, in which constantly shifting coalitions contained the ambitions of any especially aggressive power. They urge the United States to rediscover the virtues of a balance of power at the global level today. Already in the 1970s, Richard Nixon argued that "the only time in the history of the world that we have had any extended periods of peace is when there has been a balance of power. It is when one nation becomes infinitely more powerful in relation to its potential competitors that the danger of war arises."[34] But whether such multipolarity would be good or bad for the United States and for the world is debatable. I am skeptical.

War was the constant companion and crucial instrument of the multipolar balance of power. The classic European balance provided stability in the sense of maintaining the independence of most countries, but there were wars among the great powers for 60 percent of the years since 1500.[35] Rote adherence to the balance of power and multipolarity may prove to be a dangerous approach to global governance in a world where war could turn nuclear.

Many regions of the world and periods in history have seen stability under hegemony—when one power has been preeminent. Margaret Thatcher warned against drifting toward "an Orwellian future of Oceania, Eurasia, and Eastasia—three mercantilist world empires on increasingly hostile terms. . . . In other words, 2095 might look like 1914 played on a somewhat larger stage."[36] Both the Nixon and Thatcher views are too mechanical because they ignore soft power. America is an exception, says Josef Joffe, "because the 'hyperpower' is also the most alluring and seductive society in history. Napoleon had to rely on bayonets to spread France's revolutionary creed. In the American case, Munichers and Muscovites *want* what the avatar of ultra-modernity has to offer."[37]

The term "balance of power" is sometimes used in contradictory ways. The most interesting use of the term is as a predictor about how countries will behave; that is, will they pursue policies that will prevent any other country from developing power that could threaten their independence? By the evidence of history, many believe, the current preponderance of the United States will call forth a countervailing coalition that will eventually limit American power. In the words of the self-styled realist political scientist Kenneth Waltz, "both friends and foes will react as countries always have to threatened or real predominance of one among them: they will work to right the balance. The present condition of international politics is unnatural."[38]

In my view, such a mechanical prediction misses the mark. For one thing, countries sometimes react to the rise of a single power by "bandwagoning"—that is, joining the seemingly stronger rather than weaker side—much as Mussolini did when he decided, after several years of hesitation, to ally with Hitler. Proximity to and perceptions of threat also affect the way in which countries react.[39] The United States benefits from its geographical separation from Eu-

---

[34] Nixon quoted in James Chace and Nicholas X. Rizopoulos, "Towards a New Concert of Nations: An American Perspective," *World Policy Journal* (Fall 1999): 9.

[35] Jack S. Levy, *War in the Modern Great Power System, 1495–1975* (Lexington: University Press of Kentucky, 1983), 97.

[36] Margaret Thatcher, "Why America Must Remain Number One," *National Review*, 31 July 1995, 25.

[37] Josef Joffe, "Envy," *The New Republic*, 17 January 2000, 6.

[38] Kenneth Waltz, "Globalization and American Power," *The National Interest* (Spring 2000): 55–56.

[39] Stephen Walt, "Alliance Formation and the Balance of Power," *International Security* (Spring 1985).

rope and Asia in that it often appears as a less proximate threat than neighboring countries inside those regions. Indeed, in 1945, the United States was by far the strongest nation on earth, and a mechanical application of balancing theory would have predicted an alliance against it. Instead, Europe and Japan allied with the Americans because the Soviet Union, while weaker in overall power, posed a greater military threat because of its geographical proximity and its lingering revolutionary ambitions. Today, Iraq and Iran both dislike the United States and might be expected to work together to balance American power in the Persian Gulf, but they worry even more about each other. Nationalism can also complicate predictions. For example, if North Korea and South Korea are reunited, they should have a strong incentive to maintain an alliance with a distant power such as the United States in order to balance their two giant neighbors, China and Japan. But intense nationalism resulting in opposition to an American presence could change this if American diplomacy is heavy-handed. Nonstate actors can also have an effect, as witnessed by the way cooperation against terrorists changed some states' behavior after September 2001.

A good case can be made that inequality of power can be a source of peace and stability. No matter how power is measured, some theorists argue, an equal distribution of power among major states has been relatively rare in history, and efforts to maintain a balance have often led to war. On the other hand, inequality of power has often led to peace and stability because there was little point in declaring war on a dominant state. The political scientist Robert Gilpin has argued that "*Pax Britannica* and *Pax Americana*, like the *Pax Romana*, ensured an international system of relative peace and security." And the economist Charles Kindleberger claimed that "for the world economy to be stabilized, there has to be a stabilizer, one stabilizer."[40] Global governance requires a large state to take the lead. But how much and what kind of inequality of power is necessary—or tolerable—and for how long? If the leading country possesses soft power and behaves in a manner that benefits others, effective countercoalitions may be slow to arise. If, on the other hand, the leading country defines its interests narrowly and uses its weight arrogantly, it increases the incentives for others to coordinate to escape its hegemony.

Some countries chafe under the weight of American power more than others. *Hegemony* is sometimes used as a term of opprobrium by political leaders in Russia, China, the Middle East, France, and others. The term is used less often or less negatively in countries where American soft power is strong. If hegemony means being able to dictate, or at least dominate, the rules and arrangements by which international relations are conducted, as Joshua Goldstein argues, then the United States is hardly a hegemon today.[41] It does have

[40] Robert Gilpin, *War and Change in World Politics* (New York: Cambridge University Press, 1981), 144–45; Charles Kindleberger, *The World in Depression, 1929–1939* (Berkeley: University of California Press, 1973), 305.

[41] Joshua S. Goldstein, *Long Cycles: Prosperity and War in the Modern Age* (New Haven: Yale University Press, 1988), 281.

a predominant voice and vote in the International Monetary Fund, but it cannot alone choose the director. It has not been able to prevail over Europe and Japan in the World Trade Organization. It opposed the Land Mines Treaty but could not prevent it from coming into existence. Saddam Hussein remained in power for more than a decade despite American efforts to drive him out. The U.S. opposed Russia's war in Chechnya and civil war in Colombia, but to no avail. If hegemony is defined more modestly as a situation where one country has significantly more power resources or capabilities than others, then it simply signifies American preponderance, not necessarily dominance or control.[42] Even after World War II, when the United States controlled half the world's economic production (because all other countries had been devastated by the war), it was not able to prevail in all of its objectives.[43]

Pax Britannica in the nineteenth century is often cited as an example of successful hegemony, even though Britain ranked behind the United States and Russia in GNP. Britain was never as superior in productivity to the rest of the world as the United States has been since 1945, but Britain also had a degree of soft power. Victorian culture was influential around the globe, and Britain gained in reputation when it defined its interests in ways that benefited other nations (for example, opening its markets to imports or eradicating piracy). America lacks a global territorial empire like Britain's, but instead possesses a large, continental-scale home economy and has greater soft power. These differences between Britain and America suggest a greater staying power for American hegemony. Political scientist William Wohlforth argues that the United States is so far ahead that potential rivals find it dangerous to invite America's focused enmity, and allied states can feel confident that they can continue to rely on American protection.[44] Thus the usual balancing forces are weakened.

Nonetheless, if American diplomacy is unilateral and arrogant, our preponderance would not prevent other states and nonstate actors from taking actions

[42] See Robert O. Keohane, *After Hegemony: Cooperation and Discord in the World Political Economy* (Princeton: Princeton University Press, 1984), 235.

[43] Over the years, a number of scholars have tried to predict the rise and fall of nations by developing a general historical theory of hegemonic transition. Some have tried to generalize from the experience of Portugal, Spain, the Netherlands, France, and Britain. Others have focused more closely on Britain's decline in the twentieth century as a predictor for the fate for the United States. None of these approaches has been successful. Most of the theories have predicted that America would decline long before now. Vague definitions and arbitrary schematizations alert us to the inadequacies of such grand theories. Most try to squeeze history into procrustean theoretical beds by focusing on particular power resources while ignoring others that are equally important. Hegemony can be used as a descriptive term (though it is sometimes fraught with emotional overtones), but grand hegemonic theories are weak in predicting future events. See Immanuel Wallerstein, *The Politics of the World Economy: The States, the Movements, and the Civilizations: Essays* (New York: Cambridge University Press, 1984), 38, 41; George Modelski, "The Long Cycle of Global Politics and the Nation-State," *Comparative Studies in Society and History* (April 1978); George Modelski, *Long Cycles in World Politics* (Seattle: University of Washington Press, 1987). For a detailed discussion, see Nye, *Bound to Lead*, chap. 2.

[44] Wohlforth, "The Stability of a Unipolar World."

that complicate American calculations and constrain its freedom of action.[45] For example, some allies may follow the American bandwagon on the largest security issues but form coalitions to balance American behavior in other areas such as trade or the environment. And diplomatic maneuvering short of alliance can have political effects. As William Safire observed when Presidents Vladimir Putin and George W. Bush first met, "Well aware of the weakness of his hand, Putin is emulating Nixon's strategy by playing the China card. Pointedly, just before meeting with Bush, Putin traveled to Shanghai to set up a regional cooperation semi-alliance with Jiang Zemin and some of his Asian fellow travelers."[46] Putin's tactics, according to one reporter, "put Mr. Bush on the defensive, and Mr. Bush was at pains to assert that America is not about to go it alone in international affairs."[47]

Pax Americana is likely to last not only because of unmatched American hard power but also to the extent that the United States "is uniquely capable of engaging in 'strategic restraint,' reassuring partners and facilitating cooperation."[48] The open and pluralistic way in which U.S, foreign policy is made can often reduce surprises, allow others to have a voice, and contribute to soft power. Moreover, the impact of American preponderance is softened when it is embodied in a web of multilateral institutions that allow others to participate in decisions and that act as a sort of world constitution to limit the capriciousness of American power. That was the lesson the United States learned as it struggled to create an antiterrorist coalition in the wake of the September 2001 attacks. When the society and culture of the hegemon are attractive, the sense of threat and need to balance it are reduced.[49] Whether other countries will unite to balance American power will depend on how the United States behaves as well as the power resources of potential challengers.

[45] Stephen Walt, "Keeping the World 'Off-Balance': Self-Restraint and US Foreign Policy," *Kennedy School Research Working Paper Series 00–013*, October 2000.

[46] William Safire, "Putin's China Card," *New York Times*, 18 June 2001.

[47] Patrick Tyler, "Bush and Putin Look Each Other in the Eye," *New York Times*, 17 June 2001.

[48] Ikenberry, "Institutions, Strategic Restraint," 47; also Ikenberry, "Getting Hegemony Right," *The National Interest* (Spring 2001): 17–24.

[49] Josef Joffe, "How America Does It," *Foreign Affairs* (September-October 1997).

The Rise of Europe,
America's Changing Internationalism,
and the End of U.S. Primacy

CHARLES A. KUPCHAN

America today arguably has greater ability to shape the future of world politics than any other power in history. The military, economic, technological, and cultural dominance of the United States is unprecedented. The opportunity that America has before it also stems from the geopolitical opening afforded by the cold war's end. Postwar periods are moments of extraordinary prospect, usually accompanied by searching debate and institutional innovation. It is no accident that the Concert of Europe was erected after the end of the Napoleonic Wars, that the League of Nations came into being at the close of World War I, and that the founding of the United Nations followed the end of World War II.

Despite the opportunities afforded by its dominance and by the end of the cold war, America is squandering the moment. From the fall of the Berlin Wall until September 11, 2001, the United States had no grand strategy, no design to guide the ship of state. The first Bush administration did an admirable job of presiding over the end of the cold war but did little to shape what came next. The Clinton team managed reasonably well the international challenges that it faced but never articulated a conceptual foundation or overarching set of guiding principles. The early months of the George W. Bush administration were characterized primarily by inconsistency, with the ambitious unilateralism of the neoconservatives clashing head-on with the neoisolationist instincts of the president and his fellow heartland conservatives.

CHARLES A. KUPCHAN is an associate professor of government in the School of Foreign Service and Government Department of Georgetown University, and senior fellow at the Council on Foreign Relations. He has just published *The End of the American Era: U.S. Foreign Policy and the Geopolitics of the Twenty-first Century* from which this article is partially drawn.

Since September 11, the United States has had a grand strategy—one based on the principles of preeminence and preemption. But it is a manifestly inappropriate grand strategy. Washington's swaggering brand of global leadership and its dismissive attitude toward international institutions have succeeded in alienating much of the world and straining to the breaking point many of America's key partnerships.

Rather than rallying behind the United States, countries around the world are distancing themselves from Washington and locking arms to resist a wayward America. France, Germany, and Russia did their best to block America's rush to war against Iraq; the Western alliance is unlikely to survive the transatlantic rift that has opened. After North Korea restarted its nuclear weapons program, South Korea, China, and Japan all made clear they would not back Washington's refusal to negotiate bilaterally with Pyongyang. Anti-American sentiment has been on the rise in just about every quarter of the globe.[1] Even in countries that have for decades been close U.S. allies—such as Germany and South Korea—politicians are winning office by running on platforms calling for independence from Washington. America seems well on its way to compromising perhaps its most precious asset—its international legitimacy.

The failure of the United States to manage more successfully the post-cold war international order is a direct by-product of Washington's misperception of the world's geopolitical landscape. Backed up by repeated scholarly pronouncements about the longevity of unipolarity, successive administrations have operated under the assumption that U.S. primacy is here to stay. As William Wohlforth sums up the prevailing wisdom, "the current unipolarity is not only peaceful but durable. . . . For many decades, no state is likely to be in a position to take on the United States in any of the underlying elements of power."[2] Such confidence in the durability of U.S. preponderance bred the complacency of the 1990s. Washington believed that order would devolve naturally from hierarchy; there was no pressing need for institutional innovation. The blustery policies of the Bush administration have similarly been based on the presumption that a combination of preeminence and uncompromising leadership will induce the rest of the world to get in line.

This confidence about the longevity of the American era is not only misplaced but also dangerous. America appears to be committing the same error as most other great nations that have come before it—mistaking for a more permanent peace the temporary great-power quiescence that usually follows resolution of a major geopolitical divide. The decade that followed the cold war's end was admittedly one of bounty and peace for America. The current

---

[1] See Richard Morin, "World Image of U.S. Declines: Poll Says Countries Suspicious of Iraq Motives, Global Role," *Washington Post*, 5 December 2002.

[2] See William C. Wohlforth, "The Stability of a Unipolar World," *International Security* 24 (Summer 1999): 8, 10–22; Stephen G. Brooks and William C. Wohlforth, "American Primacy in Perspective," *Foreign Affairs* 81 (July/August 2002); and Charles Krauthammer, "The Unipolar Moment Revisited," *The National Interest* 70 (Winter 2002/2003).

dominance of the United States is no illusion; by any measure, America is in a class by itself. The events of September 11 certainly left the United States with a new-found vulnerability, but they also fostered confidence that the threat of terrorism would further unite the world's major players.

The international system, however, is fickle and fragile, and can come apart with remarkable speed. In 1910, Europeans were confident of the peace-causing benefits of economic interdependence and the irrationality of armed conflict. By the late summer of 1914, Europe's great powers were at war. The United States enjoyed prosperity and optimism during the second half of the 1920s. By 1933, the world was well into a painful depression, Hitler was in control of Germany, and the century was fast headed toward its darkest moments. In early 1945, the United States was busy building a postwar partnership with the Soviet Union, U.S. forces were rapidly demobilizing, and the American people were looking to the United Nations to preserve world peace. Within a few short years, the cold war was under way, and the United States and Soviet Union were threatening each other with nuclear annihilation.

The reemergence of rivalry and conflict among the world's major states is by no means foreordained. But there is no better way to ensure its return than for America to set its sights on terrorism and presume that great-power peace is here to stay. Instead, America should realize that its preponderance and the stability it breeds are already beginning to slip away. Europe is in the midst of a revolutionary process of political and economic integration that is gradually eliminating the importance of its internal borders and centralizing authority in Brussels. The European Union's collective wealth will soon rival that of the United States. As the diplomatic standoff over Iraq made clear, the continent's main powers are increasingly ready to act as a collective counterweight to U.S. power. Russia, which joined France and Germany in trying to prevent the war, will ultimately rebound and may well take its place in an integrating Europe. Asia is not far behind. China is already a regional presence, and its economy is growing apace. And Japan, the world's second-largest economy, will eventually climb out of recession and gradually expand its political and military influence.

At the same time that challengers to its dominance are on the rise, the United States is fast abandoning its embrace of a liberal brand of internationalism—one committed to multilateral action and international institutions. Instead, America is veering toward unilateralist and neoisolationist extremes, a change of course that will both alienate rising centers of power and encourage their autonomy. President George W. Bush early on made known his unilateralist proclivities. Within six months of taking office, Bush had pulled out of the Kyoto Protocol on Climate Change, made clear his intention to withdraw from the Anti-Ballistic Missile (ABM) Treaty, stated his opposition to the Comprehensive Test Ban Treaty and the pact establishing the International Criminal Court, backed away from establishing a body to verify the 1972 Biological Weapons Convention, and watered down a UN agreement aimed at controlling the proliferation of small arms. Bush also revealed his neoisolationist instincts, making clear that he intended to rein in the country's commitments, back away from mediating peace efforts in troubled regions, and focus on matters closer to home.

For many, the events of September 2001 arrested this trend, convincing the Bush administration and the American public of the need for wide-ranging, multilateral engagement. As Andrew Sullivan, the former editor of *The New Republic*, wrote only a few days after the attack, "We have been put on notice that every major Western city is now vulnerable. . . . For the United States itself," Sullivan continued, "this means one central thing. Isolationism is dead."[3] Others asserted that the attack would encourage Washington to rediscover multilateralism. G. John Ikenberry claimed that terrorism would push the United States "back toward a more centrist foreign policy" that "stresses alliances [and] multilateral cooperation," thereby providing "new sinews of cohesion among the great powers."[4]

It is by no means clear, however, that terrorism inoculates the United States against the allure of either isolationism or unilateralism. In the long run, America's leaders may well find the country's security better served by reducing its overseas commitments and raising protective barriers than by chasing terrorists through the mountains of Afghanistan or toppling Saddam Hussein. The United States has a strong tradition dating back to the Founding Fathers of seeking to cordon itself off from foreign troubles, an impulse that could well be reawakened by the rising costs of global engagement. America's initial response to the attacks of September 11, after all, was to close its borders with Mexico and Canada, ground the nation's air traffic, and patrol the country's coasts with warships and jet fighters. And when the United States does act, it may well do so without the support of the international community—as in Iraq—undermining both the spirit and the form of multilateral engagement.

The American era is alive and well, but the rise of alternative centers of power and a difficult and diffident U.S. internationalism will ensure that it comes undone as this new century progresses—with profound geopolitical consequences. The stability and order that devolve from American preponderance will gradually be replaced by renewed competition for primacy. The unstoppable locomotive of globalization will run off its tracks as soon as Washington is no longer behind the controls. Pax Americana is poised to give way to a much more unpredictable and dangerous global environment. And the chief threat will come not from the likes of Osama bin Laden, but from the return of traditional geopolitical rivalry.

As a matter of urgency, America needs to begin to prepare itself and the rest of the world for this more uncertain future. To wait until American preponderance is already gone would be to squander the enormous opportunity that comes with primacy. America must devise a grand strategy for the transition to a world of multiple power centers now, while it still has the luxury of doing so. This is the central challenge of this article.

---

[3] "Why Did It Have to be a Perfect Morning?" *The Sunday Times*, 15 September 2001.

[4] G. John Ikenberry, "American Grand Strategy in the Age of Terror," *Survival* 43 (Winter 2001–2002): 19–20.

THE WANING OF UNIPOLARITY

Most scholars of international politics trace change in the distribution of power to two sources: the secular diffusion over time and space of productive capabilities and material resources; and balancing against concentrations of power motivated by fear of exploitation. Today's great powers will become tomorrow's has-beens as nodes of innovation and efficiency move from the core to the periphery of the international system. In addition, reigning hegemons threaten secondary states, causing them to form countervailing coalitions and take other steps to offset their material disadvantage. Taken together, these dynamics drive the cyclical pattern of the rise and fall of great powers.[5]

The contemporary era departs from this historical pattern; neither the diffusion of power nor traditional military balancing against the United States will be decisive factors driving the coming transition in the international system. It will be decades before any single state can match the United States in terms of either military or economic capability. Nor is explicit balancing against American power likely to provoke a countervailing coalition. The United States is separated from both Europe and Asia by large expanses of water, making American power less threatening. Anti-American sentiment may be on the rise in many parts of the world. But it is hard to imagine that the United States would engage in behavior sufficiently aggressive to provoke an opposing alliance of industrialized countries. Europeans, South Koreans, and others may not welcome U.S. troops in their neighborhoods as they have for decades, but there are no signs that countries in Europe or Asia are contemplating balancing against the United States in military terms.

In contrast to the past, the waning of today's unipolarity will be driven by two unusual suspects: regional amalgamation in Europe and the erosion of liberal internationalism in the United States. Europe is gradually emerging as a counterweight to the United States. It will not challenge America militarily, but it will increasingly constitute an alternative center of power in economic and political terms. At the same time, America's changing internationalism will compromise the international order that the United States itself took the lead role in constructing, expediting the transition to a more divided and unruly global system. Fittingly enough, the end of American primacy may be made in America.

The Rise of Europe

Europe is in the midst of a long-term process of political and economic integration that is gradually eliminating the importance of borders and is centralizing authority and resources. To be sure, the European Union (EU) is not an amal-

---

[5] See Robert Gilpin, *War and Change in World Politics* (Cambridge, UK: Cambridge University Press, 1981); Paul Kennedy, *The Rise and Fall of the Great Powers* (New York: Random House, 1987); and Christopher Layne, "The Unipolar Illusion: Why New Great Powers Will Rise," *International Security* 17 (Spring 1993).

gamated polity with a single center of authority. Nor does Europe have a military capability commensurate with its economic resources. But trend lines do indicate that Europe is heading in the direction of becoming a new center of power. Now that its single market has been accompanied by a single currency, Europe has a collective weight on matters of trade and finance rivaling that of the United States. The aggregate wealth of the EU's fifteen members is already approaching that of America, and the coming entry of a host of new members will strengthen Europe's hand.

In addition, Europe has recently embarked on efforts to forge a common defense policy and to acquire the military wherewithal to operate independently of U.S. forces.[6] The EU has appointed a high representative for foreign and security policy, created the bodies necessary to provide political oversight, and started to revamp its forces. After parting company with the United States over the war against Iraq, France, Germany, Belgium, and Luxembourg announced that they were taking further steps to deepen defense cooperation. And Germany moved closer to ending military conscription in favor of a more capable professional force.[7] Even under the most optimistic of scenarios, the EU's military capability will certainly remain quite limited compared to that of the United States. And it will be decades, if ever, before the EU becomes a unitary state, especially in light of its impending enlargement to the east. But as its resources grow and its decision making becomes more centralized, power and influence will become more equally distributed between the two sides of the Atlantic.

Skeptics counter that the EU is unlikely to cohere as an effective actor in the global arena; the national states remain too strong and the union too decentralized and divided by cultural and linguistic boundaries. But Europe has repeatedly defied the skeptics as it has successfully moved from a free trade area to a single market and to a single currency. Eastward enlargement does risk the dilution of the union, threatening to make its decision-making bodies more unwieldy. But precisely because of this risk, it is also likely to trigger institutional reform, inducing a core group of states to pursue deeper integration. Important in both practical and symbolic terms, EU member states are now considering the drafting and ratification of a constitution, the appointment of a single foreign minister, and the establishment of a directly-elected chief executive.

A changing political discourse within Europe is also fueling the EU's geopolitical ambition. For most of its history, national leaders have justified European integration to their electorates by arguing that it is needed to help Europe escape its past. Union was the only way out of great-power rivalry. But World War II has by now receded sufficiently far into history that escaping the past no longer resonates as a pressing cause for many Europeans. The younger gen-

---

[6] The EU has set a goal of being able by 2003 to deploy a force of roughly 60,000 troops within 60 days of notification and to sustain the deployment for one year.

[7] Tony Paterson, "Schroder to End Conscription in Push for EU Rapid Reaction Force," *Daily Telegraph*, 13 April 2003.

erations who lived through neither the war nor Europe's rebuilding have no past from which they seek escape. The dominant political discourse that has for decades given the EU its meaning and momentum is rapidly losing its salience.

In its place is emerging a new discourse, which emphasizes Europe's future rather than its past. Instead of justifying integration as a way to check the power and geopolitical ambition of the national state, it portrays integration as a way to acquire power and project geopolitical ambition for Europe as a whole. French President Jacques Chirac, in a speech delivered in Paris in November 1999, could hardly have been clearer: "The European Union itself [must] become a major pole of international equilibrium, endowing itself with the instruments of a true power."[8] Even the British, who for decades kept their distance from the EU, have changed their minds. In the words of Prime Minister Tony Blair, "Europe's citizens need Europe to be strong and united. They need it to be a power in the world. Whatever its origin, Europe today is no longer just about peace. It is about projecting collective power."[9]

Such sentiments only intensified after the election of George W. Bush because of the unilateralist substance and tone of his foreign policy. In the wake of Bush's call to widen the war against terrorism to Iraq, Iran, and North Korea, French Foreign Minster Hubert Vedrine called for Europe to speak out against a United States that acted "unilaterally, without consulting others, making decisions based on its own view of the world and its own interests." When asked about how to deal with American preponderance, German Chancellor Gerhard Schröder replied that "the answer or remedy is easy: a more integrated and enlarged Europe" that has "more clout." Valery Giscard d'Estaing opened the EU's constitutional convention in March 2002 by noting that successful reform of the union's institutions would ensure that "Europe will have changed its role in the world. . . . It will be respected and listened to," he continued, "not only as the economic power it already is, but as a political power that will speak as an equal with the largest existing and future powers on the planet." Romano Prodi, president of the commission, agreed that one of the EU's chief goals is to create "a superpower on the European continent that stands equal to the United States."[10]

Integration is thus being relegitimated among European electorates, but paradoxically through a new brand of pan-European nationalism. Europe's states may have rid themselves for good of their individual claims to great-

---

[8] Speech on the occasion of the 20th Anniversary of the Institute Francais des Relations Internationales, Elysee Palace, 4 November 1999. Text distributed by the French Embassy in Washington, DC.

[9] Speech to the Polish Stock Exchange, 6 October 2000, available at http://www.number-10.gov.uk/news.asp?NewsId=1341&SectionId=32.

[10] Suzanne Daley, "French Minister Calls U.S. Policy 'Simplistic,'" *New York Times*, 7 February 2002; Alan Friedman, "Schroeder Assails EU Deficit Critics," *International Herald Tribune*, 2 February 2002; Steven Erlanger, "Europe Opens Convention to Set Future of Its Union," *New York Times*, 1 March 2002; T. R. Reid, "EU Summit Ends with a Bang and a Whimper," *Washington Post*, 17 March 2002.

power status, but such aspirations are returning at the level of a collective Europe. As these new political currents gather momentum, so will Europe's geopolitical ambition. Europe need not emerge as a superpower with a global range of interests and commitments, if its rise is to alter the effective polarity of the international system. As Europe's wealth, military capacity, and collective character increase, so will its appetite for greater international influence. Just as America's will to extend its primacy stems not just from self-interest, but also from an emotional satisfaction derived from its leadership position—call it nationalism—so will Europe's rise provoke a yearning for greater status. As the United States currently sits atop the international pecking order, the EU's search for greater autonomy will, at least initially, take the form of resisting U.S. influence and ending its decades of deference to Washington.

An EU that becomes less dependent on the United States for its security and more often stands its ground on the major issues of the day will be sufficient to alter the structural dynamics of the transatlantic relationship. Increasing rivalry between the United States and Europe promises to deal a serious blow to the effectiveness of international organizations. Most multilateral institutions have relied on a combination of U.S. leadership and European back-stopping to produce consensus and joint action. The United States and Europe have often voted as a bloc, leading to a winning coalition in the UN, the International Monetary Fund, the World Bank, and many other bodies. When Europe resists rather than backs up American leadership in multilateral institutions, those institutions are likely to become far less effective instruments.

Early signs of such resistance have already been quite visible. In May 2001, EU member states took the lead in voting the United States off the UN Commission on Human Rights, the first time Washington had been absent from the body since its formation in 1947. The apparent rationale was to deliver a payback for America's increasing unilateralism and to express disapproval of America's death penalty. The same day, in a separate vote of the UN's Economic and Social Council, the United States lost its seat on the International Narcotics Control Board. Early in 2003, America again found itself outflanked at the UN, with France and Germany taking the lead in denying Washington the Security Council's approval of war against Iraq.

The United States and Europe are also likely to engage in more intense competition over trade and finance. America and Europe today enjoy a remarkably healthy economic relationship, with both parties benefiting from strong flows of trade and investment. A more assertive Europe and a less competitive American economy do, however, increase the likelihood that trade disputes will become more politicized. When the Bush administration announced new tariffs on imported steel in March 2002, the EU vowed to contest the move at the World Trade Organization (WTO). Pascal Lamy, the EU's top trade official, commented that "the U.S. decision to go down the route of protectionism

is a major setback for the world trading system."[11] In May 2003, the EU announced that it intended to impose duties on imports of U.S. goods unless
Washington repealed a law giving tax breaks to U.S. exporters.

Europe's restriction on imports of genetically modified foods, a ban that
could cost U.S. companies billions of dollars, has particular potential to trigger
a major dispute and polarize global trade talks. The emergence of the euro as
an alternative reserve currency also creates the potential for diverging views
about management of the international financial system. The competitive de-
valuations and monetary instability of the interwar period made amply clear
that the absence of a dominant economic power can provoke considerable financial turmoil and go-it-alone foreign policies—even among like-minded allies.

Looking beyond the coming decade, economic growth in East Asia will further the onset of a new distribution of global power. Japan already has a world-
class economy and will eventually climb out of recession. During the last decade, China enjoyed an economic growth rate of about 10 percent per year. The
World Bank estimates that by 2020, "China could be the world's second largest
exporter and importer. Its consumers may have purchasing power larger than
all of Europe's. China's involvement with world financial markets, as a user and
supplier of capital, will rival that of most industrialized countries."[12] The rise
of Japan and China will ultimately contribute to the return of a multipolar
global landscape.

America's Reluctant and Unilateralist Internationalism

The second trend that will bring the unipolar moment to an end sooner rather
than later is the changing character of internationalism in the United States.
Unipolarity rests on the existence of a polity that not only enjoys preponderance but also is prepared to underwrite order in a manner that affirms its international legitimacy and benign character. If the United States were to tire of
being the global protector of last resort or behave in a way that induced other
nations to rally against rather than with U.S. power, unipolarity would still
come undone even if American resources were to remain supreme. This hypo-
thetical is in the midst of turning into reality.

America's diminishing appetite for liberal internationalism is a direct product of the changing international environment. America refused to embrace liberal internationalism until World War II, when the prospect of Germany and
Japan becoming aggressors with global reach necessitated its multilateral
involvement in shaping the balance of power in both Europe and East Asia.
The Soviet threat then ensured that the United States would maintain extensive
overseas commitments and institutional entanglements for the rest of the twentieth century.

[11] Edmund Andrews, "Angry Europeans to Challenge U.S. Steel Tariffs at WTO," *New York Times*, 6 March 2002.

[12] World Bank, *China 2020: Development Challenges in the New Century* (Washington, DC: World Bank, 1997), 103.

The cold war is now over and the fault line between two hostile blocs gone. America faces the threat of terrorism, but this is an elusive and sporadic threat, one that appears more likely to push the United States to the extremes of unilateralism and neoisolationism than to a centrist internationalism. In this new strategic environment, many of the same considerations that constrained the country's appetite for multilateral engagement from its founding in the eighteenth century until the attack on Pearl Harbor in 1941 are again coming to the fore.

America has from its early days been remarkably ambivalent about taking on international responsibilities. The Founding Fathers were quite explicit in their conviction that the security of the United States would be best served by reining in its external ambition and avoiding entangling alliances. They felt that the United States could fulfill the need for expanding commerce without getting embroiled in distant lands. As a rising power during the nineteenth century, the United States waited decades before translating its world-class economic power into military strength and external ambition. And even then, it attempted to avoid major strategic commitments abroad until World War II and the cold war left it with little choice.[13]

This potent strain of isolationism is the product of two factors. First, the United States is blessed with wide oceans to its east and west and nonthreatening countries to its north and south. Because of its enviable geopolitical location, America is justified in calculating that its security is at certain times and under certain circumstances best served by less, rather than more, engagement abroad. International terrorism, the ballistic missile, and fiber optics no doubt diminish the extent to which America can afford to cordon itself off from threats in distant quarters. But proximity still matters, and the distance of the United States from other areas continues to afford it a natural security and sense of isolation.

Second, the political culture and constitutional structure of the United States have checked the scope of the country's external ambition. During the early years of the republic, the individual states were loath to give up their rights to maintain independent militias and armed forces. They were also fearful of giving too much coercive capacity to the federal government, creating a network of constitutional checks and balances to decentralize power.[14] Times have obviously changed, but such internal checking mechanisms continue to constrain the conduct of U.S. foreign policy. The Senate's rejection of U.S. participation in the League of Nations, the War Powers Act, and the more recent efforts of Congress to mandate the withdrawal of U.S. troops from the Balkans are all manifestations of the continuing institutional constraints on American internationalism.

---

[13] On the rise of the United States as a great power, see Fareed Zakaria, *From Wealth to Power* (Princeton: Princeton University Press, 1998).

[14] See Daniel Deudney, "The Philadelphian System: Sovereignty, Arms Control, and Balance of Power in the American States-Union, circa 1787–1861," *International Organization* 49 (Spring 1995): 191–228.

The domestic politics of foreign policy also promises to grow more complicated in the coming years. Diplomacy is no longer the preserve of an internationalist Ivy League elite that shuttles between Foggy Bottom, Wall Street, and foreign capitals. What happens inside the beltway still matters, but, more than ever before, so do decisions and attitudes in Atlanta, Dallas, Seattle, Silicon Valley, and Los Angeles, each of which has its unique interests and brand of internationalism. Regional divides hardly evoke the passions that they did during America's early decades. But political, economic, and cultural differences that fall along regional lines are again coming to play an important role in shaping the country's foreign relations.

Consider the demographic makeup of the American population. An electorate with ancestral allegiances primarily to Europe is being transformed by the ongoing influx of immigrants from Latin America and by higher birthrates within the Latino community. By the second half of this century, Caucasians of European background will represent less than 50 percent of the U.S. population, with Latino Americans representing between one-fourth and one-third of the country. Latinos tend to concentrate in the Southwest, opening up the prospect of increasing regional differences.[15] This growing diversity could make it more difficult for America to generate a common internationalism and could lead to a country much more focused on the Western Hemishere.

America's unilateralist bent also has deep roots in the country's politics and culture. Since the republic's early days, Americans have viewed international institutions with suspicion, fearful that they will encroach upon the nation's sovereignty and room for maneuver. Avoiding entangling alliances and restricting the power of the federal government are enterprises that hit a populist chord and run deep within the American creed. After World War II, Americans of necessity shed some of their aversion to multilateral engagement; building a cohesive community of liberal democracies and managing the Western world required an elaborate network of institutions. But even during the cold war, unilateral urges often prevailed. On issues ranging from the tenor of diplomacy with the Soviet Union, to the Arab-Israeli conflict, to arms control, to international trade, the Western allies frequently complained of a wayward America all too often acting alone.

Absent the constraints of the cold war, America's unilateralist impulse has strengthened considerably. The vulnerability associated with the threat of terrorism has also played a role, as has electoral politics. A populist unilateralism runs strongest in the South and Mountain West, the fastest growing regions in the country, which are George W. Bush's main constituency.[16] America has also gravitated toward unilateralism out of frustration with its inability to get its way as often as in the past. Accustomed to calling the shots, the United States is

---

[15] U.S. Census Bureau, Census 1990. Available at: http://www.census.gov/population/projections/nation/summary.

[16] Walter Russell Meade, "The Jacksonian Tradition," *The National Interest* 58 (Winter 1999/2000): 5–29.

likely to go off on its own when others refuse to follow Washington's lead, which the Europeans have been doing with greater frequency as their strength and self-confidence grow.

It is admittedly puzzling that isolationism and unilateralism are making a comeback at the same time. At least on the surface, they represent contradictory impulses, with isolationists calling for disengagement and unilateralists favoring unfettered global leadership. But they are in reality opposite sides of the same coin. They share common ideological origins in America's fear of entanglements that may compromise its liberty and sovereignty. The country should do its best to shun international engagement, but if it does engage, it should do so in a way that preserves national autonomy. They also share origins in the notion of U.S. exceptionalism, providing the nation an impetus to cordon itself off from the international system, but also to remake that system as America sees fit. It is precisely because isolationism and unilateralism are so deeply embedded in the country's political culture that they pose a dual threat to liberal internationalism, inducing the United States to retreat from the global stage even as it seeks to recreate the world in its image.[17]

The erosion of liberal internationalism in the United States is not a passing idiosyncrasy of the Bush administration. On the contrary, it is the product of secular changes in the geopolitical and political environment. The combination of unilateralism and isolationism toward which the United States is headed promises to be a dangerous mix. One day, America may well be alienating partners through its stiff-necked, go-it-alone ways, inducing the EU to emerge not just as a counterweight, but an angry one at that. The next, it may be leaving allies in the lurch as it backs away from an international system that it finds difficult to control. At the very moment that the United States will need the help of others to address mounting challenges, it may well find the world a lonely place.

Incorporating the trajectory of U.S. internationalism into analysis of the forces driving systemic change thus has profound implications for forecasting how and when America's unipolar moment is likely to end. In purely material terms, no single country is likely to catch the United States for decades, as Wohlforth has persuasively argued. But Wohlforth, like many other scholars, makes a critical analytic error in assuming that polarity emerges solely from the distribution of power. The willingness of states to deploy their resources, the manner in which they deploy them, and the ends to which they do so also play a role in shaping polarity. The emergence of a more reluctant and prickly American internationalism, even if U.S. preponderance remains uncontested, is a powerful engine of change in the global landscape.

The Evidence

I have thus far built what is primarily a deductive case for the proposition that liberal internationalism is in retreat in the United States. I now provide sup-

[17] See Arthur M. Schlesinger, Jr., *The Cycles of American History* (Boston: Houghton Mifflin, 1986).

porting empirical evidence, examining briefly public opinion, congressional behavior, and the early foreign policy of George W. Bush. I then take up the likely impact of terrorism on the trajectory of U.S. internationalism.

Numerous indicators suggest that U.S. internationalism is changing in step with the world's shifting geopolitics. Consider the picture that unfolded over the course of the last decade. America's diplomatic corps, once a magnet for the country's most talented, lost much of its professional allure. The few top candidates that the State Department did succeed in attracting often left in frustration after only a few years. According to a front-page story in the *New York Times*, "The State Department, the institution responsible for American diplomacy around the world, is finding it hard to adjust to an era in which financial markets pack more punch than a Washington-Moscow summit meeting. It is losing recruits to investment banks, dot-com companies and the Treasury and Commerce Departments, which have magnified their foreign policy roles."[18]

Public opinion surveys paint a similar picture. Regular surveys by the Chicago Council on Foreign Relations and other bodies indicate that Americans remained generally internationalist throughout the 1990s.[19] However, the public's interest in foreign affairs did decline sharply. During the cold war, some pressing geopolitical issue of the day usually ranked near the top of the public's concerns. By the end of the 1990s, only 2 to 3 percent of Americans viewed foreign policy as a primary concern. When Americans were asked to name the "two or three biggest foreign-policy problems facing the United States today," the most popular response was "don't know." A solid majority of Americans indicated that events in other parts of the world have "very little" impact on the United States. As James Lindsay of the Brookings Institution summed up the situation in an article in *Foreign Affairs*, "Americans endorse internationalism in theory but seldom do anything about it in practice."[20] At the opening of the twenty-first century, Americans thus did not oppose their country's engagement in the world. They had just become profoundly apathetic about it.

It is precisely because of this attention deficit that newspapers, magazines, and the television networks dramatically cut back foreign coverage. In a com-

[18] Jane Perlez, "As Diplomacy Loses Luster, Young Stars Flee State Dept.," *New York Times*, 5 September 2000. In 2001, the State Department launched a publicity campaign to reverse its recruiting woes. The campaign was an apparent success, with the number of applicants for the 2001 Foreign Service entrance exam substantially larger than for the 2000 exam. See David Stout, "Sign-Ups for Foreign Service Test Nearly Double After 10-Year Ebb," *New York Times*, 31 August 2001.

[19] The Chicago Council on Foreign Relations carries out a public opinion survey every four years. The 1998 survey indicated that 96 percent of U.S. leaders and 61 percent of the public "favor an active part for the US in world affairs." The figures for 1994 were 98 percent and 65 percent respectively, indicating only a slight drop. In general, public opinion surveys show only a minor decrease in internationalism since the end of the cold war. See John E. Reilly, ed., *American Public Opinion and U.S. Foreign Policy* (Chicago: Chicago Council on Foreign Relations, 1999), available at: http://www.ccfr.org/publications/opinion/AmPuOp99.pdf.

[20] James Lindsay, "The New Apathy," *Foreign Affairs* 79 (September/October 2000): 2–8. The public opinion data in this paragraph are also from the Lindsay article.

petitive industry driven by market-share and advertisement fees per second, the media gave America what it wanted. Coverage of foreign affairs on television and in newspapers and magazines dropped precipitously. The time allocated to international news by the main television networks fell by almost 50 percent between the late 1980s and the mid-1990s.[21] Between 1985 and 1995, the space devoted to international stories declined from 24 to 14 percent in *Time* and from 22 to 12 percent in *Newsweek*.[22]

The spillover into the political arena was all too apparent. With foreign policy getting so little traction among the public, it had all but fallen off the political radar screen. Virtually every foreign matter that came before Congress, including questions of war and peace, turned into a partisan sparring match. Peter Trubowitz has documented that partisan conflict over foreign policy increased dramatically in the recent past.[23] Bill Clinton's scandals and his repeated stand-offs with an alienated Republican leadership no doubt played a role in pushing relations between the two parties to the boiling point. But the fact that foreign policy was held hostage made clear that America's politics and priorities had entered a new era.

Partisan politics with worrisome regularity trumped the demands of international leadership. Important ambassadorial posts remained empty throughout the Clinton years because Republicans on the Senate Foreign Relations Committee, purely out of spite, refused to confirm the president's nominees. In August 2000, Peter Burleigh resigned from the State Department after waiting nine months for the Senate to confirm his appointment as ambassador to the Philippines.[24] Burleigh was widely recognized as one of America's most accomplished diplomats. America's dues to the United Nations went unpaid for most of the decade to keep happy the antiabortion wing of the Republican party, which thought the UN's approach to family planning too aggressive. The Senate in 1999 rejected the treaty banning the testing of nuclear weapons despite the administration's willingness to shelve it. Better to embarrass Clinton than to behave responsibly on matters of war and peace. Senator Chuck Hagel, a Republican from Nebraska, even admitted as much on the record. Reflecting on the apparent Republican assault on internationalism, Hagel commented that "what this is about on the Republican side is a deep dislike and distrust for President Clinton."[25] It is hard to imagine a more potent indicator of the direction of American internationalism than the defeat of a major treaty because of political animosities on the Senate floor.

[21] Andrew Tyndall, "Decline of International Network News Coverage since the End of the Cold War (in Minutes)," The Tyndall Report, cited in Media Studies Center, "The Decline of International News Coverage," available at http://www.mediastudies.org/international/international.html.

[22] Hall's Magazine Editorial Reports cited in James F. Hoge, Jr., "Foreign News: Who Gives a Damn?" *Columbia Journalism Review* 36 (November/December 1997): 48–52.

[23] Peter Trubowitz, University of Texas at Austin (draft paper presented at the Autonomous National University of Mexico, Mexico City, 20 August 2000).

[24] "Stymied by Senate, Would-Be Envoy Quits," *New York Times*, 1 September 2000.

[25] Alison Mitchell, "Bush and the G.O.P. Congress: Do the Candidate's Internationalist Leanings Mean Trouble?" *New York Times*, 19 May 2000.

Kosovo

The battle for Kosovo provides perhaps the best window into these new attitudes, largely because it entailed putting U.S. forces into combat. On the surface, NATO's battle for Kosovo appeared to confirm that American leadership was alive and well. The United States led NATO into battle, Washington effectively ran the air campaign, and Clinton held course until Slobodan Milosevic capitulated and withdrew his forces from Kosovo. Upon a closer reading, however, the war was anything but a resounding confirmation of U.S. internationalism.

America's effort in the Balkans was at best half-hearted and enjoyed only razor-thin political support. From the outset, President Clinton pledged to avoid the use of ground forces, severely constraining the military operation and weakening NATO's hand in coercive diplomacy. The Clinton team expected Yugoslav President Slobodan Milosevic to capitulate after a few days of air strikes; when he did not, the administration was shell-shocked and in a state of virtual paralysis.[26] Even after weeks of an air war that only exacerbated the humanitarian crisis, NATO was supposed to resolve and increase the probability of a southward spread of the war to Macedonia and Albania, President Clinton maintained his veto on ground troops. Moreover, he insisted that allied aircraft bomb from no lower than 15,000 feet to avoid being shot down.

Congressional opposition to the conflict only made matters worse. A month into a war that had not produced a single U.S. casualty, the House nevertheless expressed grave misgivings and voted 249–180 to refuse funding for sending U.S. ground troops to Yugoslavia without congressional approval. The House was not even willing to pass a resolution endorsing the bombing campaign (the vote was 213–213). Congress's behavior hardly represented a strong reaffirmation of America's commitment to stability in Europe.

American behavior after the end of the conflict over Kosovo gave further indication of Washington's clear intent to limit the scope of U.S. commitments in the Balkans. European forces picked up the bulk of peacekeeping responsibilities in Kosovo, and the EU took the lead on economic reconstruction. Even before the end of the fighting, President Clinton promised Americans in his Memorial Day address that "when the peacekeeping force goes in there [Kosovo], the overwhelming majority of people will be European; and that when the reconstruction begins, the overwhelming amount of investment will be Eu-

---

[26] Brookings Institution scholars Ivo Daalder and Michael O'Hanlon offer a damning critique of the alliance's strategy: "The allies viewed force simply as a tool of diplomacy, intended to push negotiations one way or another. They were unprepared for the possibility that they might need to directly achieve a battlefield result. . . . NATO's war against Serbia was a vivid reminder that when using military power, one must be prepared for things to go wrong and to escalate." Ivo H. Daalder and Michael E. O'Hanlon, *Winning Ugly: NATO's War to Save Kosovo* (Washington, DC: Brookings Institution Press, 2000), 105.

ropean."[27] When the peacekeepers were deployed, American troops (which represented less than 15 percent of the total force) were sent to the east of Kosovo, where the likelihood of violence was presumed to be lower. In February 2000, a small contingent of U.S. troops was dispatched to the northern city of Mitrovica to help quell ethnic violence. When the troops were stoned by angry Serbs, the Pentagon responded by ordering U.S. forces back to their sector, making clear that Washington was prepared to undercut the peacekeepers' commander on the ground and put U.S. forces under special restrictions.[28]

Despite the unusual protections afforded U.S. troops, American lawmakers continued to complain about the need for Europe to do more. Republican Senator John Warner, chairman of the Senate Armed Services Committee, in March 2000 pledged to seek to withhold half of the two billion dollar appropriation for American troops in Kosovo unless European nations increased their financial contributions to the UN efforts there.[29] Democratic Senator Robert Byrd proposed that the United States should turn over to the EU the peacekeeping and reconstruction effort in Kosovo and withdraw U.S. troops from the region in a timely fashion.[30]

Despite the facade of unity within NATO, America's deep ambivalence about the war and its aversion to casualties did not go unnoticed in Europe. It is no coincidence that in the aftermath of Kosovo, the European Union redoubled its efforts to forge a collective defense policy and a military force capable of operating independently of the United States. Europeans were acting on the recognition that they might well be on their own when the next military crisis emerged on the continent. As British Prime Minister Tony Blair asserted in justifying the initiative, "We Europeans should not expect the United States to have to play a part in every disorder in our own back yard."[31] As Europeans clearly noticed, the war over Kosovo made plain America's dissipating willingness to be Europe's chief peacemaker and its protector of last resort.

The New Unilateralism

These neoisolationist proclivities were accompanied by intensifying unilateralist instincts. According to its rhetoric, the Clinton administration was deeply committed to liberal internationalism, insisting that it would lead through multilateral institutions and shape international order through consensus, not fiat. The United States was "the indispensable nation" because of its ability to build coalitions of the willing and organize joint action.

[27] Remarks by the president at Memorial Day Service, 31 May 1999, The White House, Office of the Press Secretary.

[28] Carlotta Gall, "Serbs Stone U.S. Troops in Divided Kosovo Town," *New York Times*, 21 February 2000.

[29] Jane Perlez, "Kosovo's Unquenched Violence Dividing U.S. and NATO Allies," *New York Times*, 12 March 2000.

[30] Robert Byrd, "Europe's Turn to Keep the Peace," *New York Times*, 20 March 2000.

[31] Speech at the Royal United Services Institute, 8 March 1999.

But the record belies the rhetoric. On a regular basis, the United States opted out of multilateral efforts. In Kyoto in 1997, the international community reached agreement on new measures to protect the environment. Washington was a party to the negotiations, but then dragged its feet on implementation. A broadly successful effort to ban landmines won the 1997 Nobel Peace Prize for Jody Williams and the organization she headed, the International Campaign to Ban Landmines. The United States did not sign on; Washington preferred to play by its own rules. Clinton also withheld support for the International Criminal Court for years, changing his mind only at the end of his second term.

Signs of a diminishing appetite for liberal internationalism only intensified after George W. Bush succeeded Clinton. As a candidate, Bush promised to pursue a more "humble" foreign policy, scale back America's international commitments, be more selective in picking the country's fights, and focus more attention on its own hemisphere. After taking the helm, Bush generally adhered to these promises. During his first months in office, he drew down U.S. troop levels in Bosnia and kept U.S. troops in Kosovo on a tight leash despite the spread of fighting to Macedonia. He reduced America's role as a mediator in many different regional conflicts. Secretary of State Colin Powell followed suit by dropping from the State Department's roster more than one-third of the fifty-five special envoys that the Clinton administration had appointed to deal with trouble spots around the world. The *Washington Post* summed up the thrust of these moves in its headline, "Bush Retreats from U.S. Role as Peace Broker."[32]

In similar fashion, Bush made good on his promise to focus U.S. foreign policy on the Americas. President Bush's first two meetings with foreign leaders were with Canadian Prime Minster Jean Chrètien and Mexican President Vicente Fox. His first foreign trip was to Mexico. His first major international meeting was a Summit of the Americas in Quebec, at which he announced that he would host his first state dinner later in the year for Vicente Fox.

The Bush administration also stepped away from a host of multilateral commitments, preferring the autonomy that comes with unilateral initiative. Consider the fate of the Kyoto Protocol on climate change and the Anti-Ballistic Missile Treaty (ABM). During his first few months in office, George W. Bush, without first consulting with affected parties, announced that the United States would be withdrawing from both pacts. As to the fate of the Kyoto Protocol, Bush did not even try to hide his go-it-alone rationale: "We will not do anything that harms our economy, because first things first are the people who live in America."[33] As to the fate of the ABM Treaty, the administration did undertake consultations with numerous countries after making known its intention

---

[32] Alan Sipress, "Bush Retreats from U.S. Role as Peace Broker," *Washington Post*, 17 March 2001.
[33] Cited in Edmund Andrews, "Bush Angers Europe by Eroding Pact on Warming," *New York Times*, 1 April 2001.

to scrap the arms control pact. But Bush then proceeded to inform the world in August 2001 that, "We will withdraw from the ABM treaty on our timetable and at a time convenient to America."[34] In December, Bush made good on his promise.

The terror attacks of September 2001 were widely interpreted as an antidote to these unilateralist and isolationist trends. And they were, at least in the short run. Far from acting unilaterally, the Bush administration went out of its way to build a broad coalition against terrorism, enlisting the support of not just NATO allies, but also Russia, China, and moderate Arab regimes. Far from reining in America's commitments, Bush declared a war on terrorism and in 2002 destroyed the Taliban regime and the al Qaeda network in Afghanistan. The following year, he dispatched several hundred thousand troops to Iraq to topple the regime of Saddam Hussein. And Congress and the American people were fully engaged, with the Senate, the House, and the public strongly behind Bush's decision to use military force in both Afghanistan and Iraq.[35]

In the long run, however, the struggle against terror is unlikely to serve as a solid basis for ensuring either multilateral engagement or a robust brand of American internationalism. Despite the statements of support from abroad, U.S. forces were accompanied only by the British when the bombing campaign against Afghanistan began. A host of other countries offered logistical and intelligence support, but Americans did almost all the fighting. Only after the main battles were over did forces from Europe, Canada, Australia, and New Zealand arrive in significant numbers to serve as peacekeepers and help eliminate remaining pockets of resistance in the mountains.

America's unilateralist proclivities were even more pronounced in the war against Iraq. Bush made it amply clear amid the UN debate about whether to wage war against Iraq that the United States would act as it saw fit, asserting in his 2003 State of the Union Address that "this nation does not depend on the decisions of others."[36] He followed through on his pledge, launching an attack against Iraq despite Washington's failure to win the approval of the Security Council and despite the fact that France, Germany, Russia, China, and much of the world's population were strongly against the war. Terrorism is unlikely to make of America an avowed multilateralist.

[34] David Sanger, "Bush Flatly States U.S. Will Pull Out of Missile Treaty," *New York Times*, 24 August 2001.

[35] On 14 September 2001, both the Senate and the House voted on a resolution authorizing the president "to use all necessary and appropriate force" to respond to the attacks. The resolution passed 98–0 in the Senate and 420–1 in the House. In a poll conducted between 20 and 23 September 2001, 92 percent of the public supported military action against whoever was responsible for the attacks. See "Poll Finds Support for War and Fear on Economy," *New York Times*, 25 September 2001. In the lead-up to the war on Iraq, the House voted 296–133 to grant President Bush the authority to use military force against Iraq. The vote in the Senate was 77–23. These votes took place on 10 and 11 October 2002, respectively. As the campaign against Iraq began, 74 percent of the U.S. public approved of the decision to go to war to remove Saddam Hussein from power. Adam Nagourney and Janet Elder, "A Nation at War: The Poll; Support for Bush Surges at Home, but Split Remains," *New York Times*, 22 March 2003.

[36] Address on 28 January 2003.

It is also by no means clear that terrorism will eradicate, rather than fuel, isolationist strains within American society. The United States responded with alacrity and resolve to the attacks on New York and Washington. But the call for increased engagement in the global battle against terror was accompanied by an alternative logic, one that gained currency over time. A basic dictum of the country's Founding Fathers was that America should stay out of the affairs of other countries so that they stay out of America's affairs. The United States is a formidable adversary and is unlikely to let any attack on its own go unpunished. But should the price of hegemony mount and Americans come to believe that their commitments abroad are compromising their security at home, they will legitimately question whether the benefits of global engagement are worth the costs.

The potential allure of the Founding Fathers' admonition against foreign entanglement explains why, as one scholar put it, the attacks made "Israelis worry that Americans may now think that supporting Israel is too costly."[37] This logic similarly explains why François Heisbourg, one of France's leading analysts, commented in *Le Monde* the day after the attacks that, "It is to be feared that the same temptation [that led America to withdraw from the world after World War I] could again shape the conduct of the United States once the barbarians of September 11 have been punished. In this respect, the Pearl Harbor of 2001 could come to close the era opened by the Pearl Harbor of 1941."[38] So does this logic explain, at least in part, why Americans have begun debating whether to reduce the U.S. military presence in Saudi Arabia.[39] It is worth keeping in mind that amid the anti-American protests that broke out in South Korea late in 2002, even conservative U.S. voices urged Washington to consider withdrawing American troops from the Korean peninsula.[40]

It is also quite plausible that within the Bush administration forces that encourage retrenchment may well strengthen over time. Toppling Saddam Hussein enjoyed widespread support among Bush's top advisers. But only the neoconservative faction embraces an ambitious vision of political change in the Middle East and intends to use America's foothold in Iraq to pursue that vision. More traditional conservatives, especially those hailing from the heartland, are likely to show little enthusiasm for America's long-term occupation of Iraq or follow-on efforts to bring democracy to the Arab world.

The long-term consequences of the events of September 2001 could thus be an America that devotes much more attention and energy to the security of its homeland and much less attention to resolving problems far from its borders. The more time U.S. forces spend defending American territory, the less

[37] Shibley Telhami, "The Mideast Is Also Changed," *New York Times*, 19 September 2001.

[38] "De l'après guerre froide á l'hyperterrorisme," *Le Monde*, 12 September 2001.

[39] See Elaine Sciolino and Eric Schmitt, "U.S. Rethinks Its Role in Saudi Arabia," *New York Times*, 10 March 2002; and Shibley Telhami, "Shrinking Our Presence in Saudi Arabia," *New York Times*, 29 January 2002.

[40] See, for example, Richard Allen, "Seoul's Choice: The U.S. or the North," *New York Times*, 16 January 2003.

time they will spend defending the territory of others. The Bush administration admittedly showed no lack of enthusiasm for waging a comprehensive and resolute war against terrorism. Future attacks on U.S. territory would likely provoke a similarly sharp response. But prior to the events of September 2001, the initial instincts of Bush and his advisers were to scale back, not to deepen, America's involvement in distant disputes. In combination with the new focus on homeland defense and the political appeal of seeking to cordon off the country from foreign dangers, these instincts are a better indication of long-term trends than are actions taken amid shock and anger.

It is equally doubtful that the threat of terror will over the long run ensure a more responsible Congress and a more engaged and attentive public. Bipartisan rancor did disappear instantly on September 11, 2001, and the U.S. public stood firmly behind military retaliation. But these were temporary phenomena arising from the grief of the moment; after a few months, partisan wrangling returned to Capitol Hill, and the public mind again began to wander. As one reporter commented on 2 December 2002, "The post-Sept. 11 Congress has now almost fully abandoned its briefly adopted pose of high-minded bipartisanship."[41] Bipartisanship returned amid the preparations for war against Iraq, but it again dissipated as soon as the fighting was over.

The relatively rapid return to business as usual stems from the fact that the United States has embarked on a long march, not a prolonged war. After Pearl Harbor, American leaders had in Imperial Japan and Nazi Germany formidable and identifiable enemies against which to mobilize the nation and evoke continued sacrifice. The threat posed by the Soviet Union then kept America focused and determined during the long decades of the cold war. In Iraq, the United States similarly faced a tangible adversary with army divisions and clearly identified leadership targets. But much of the war against terrorism is against a far more elusive enemy. America confronts an enemy schooled in guerrilla tactics—a type of warfare that, as the Vietnam War demonstrated, plays to the strengths of neither America's armed forces nor its citizens. The United States handily defeated its foes in Afghanistan, but many supporters of al Qaeda escaped, melding into village life or fleeing to the tribal lands of Pakistan. In this battle, patience and tact are more useful weapons than military force.

With much of the struggle against terrorism occurring quietly beyond the public eye through intelligence, surveillance, and covert operations, this new challenge will not be accompanied by the evocative images that help rally the country around the flag. Rather than induce Americans to join the army or the production line to contribute to the war effort, terrorism's main impact on the average citizen is to induce him to stay at home. In the wake of the attacks on New York and Washington and the anthrax scare that followed, President Bush asked of Americans not that they make a special sacrifice but that they return to normal life by shopping in malls and traveling by air. Even as American

---

[41] Adam Clymer, "A House Divided. Senate, Too," *New York Times*, 2 December 2001.

soldiers were fighting and dying in Afghanistan, ABC was trying to woo David Letterman to its late-night slot to replace *Nightline*—one of the few network programs providing in-depth analysis of foreign news. As before September 2001, keeping the U.S. public engaged in international affairs promises to be an uphill battle.

MANAGING THE RETURN TO MULTIPOLARITY

Combine the rise of Europe and Asia with the decline of liberal internationalism in the United States and it becomes clear that America's unipolar moment is not long for this world. At the same time that alternative centers of power are taking shape, the United States is drawing away from multilateral institutions in favor of a unilateralism that risks estranging those power centers, raising the chances that their ascent will lead to a new era of geopolitical rivalry. As unipolarity gives way to multipolarity, the strategic competition now held in abeyance by U.S. primacy will return—and with a vengeance if America's unilateralist impulse prevails. No longer steadied by U.S. hegemony, processes of globalization and democratization are likely to falter, as are the international institutions currently dependent upon Washington's leadership to function effectively. Geopolitical fault lines will reemerge among centers of power in North America, Europe, and East Asia. The central challenge for U.S. grand strategy will be managing and taming the dangers arising from these new fault lines.

The United States cannot and should not resist the end of unipolarity and the return of a world of multiple centers of power. To do so would only risk alienating and risking conflict with a rising Europe and an ascendant Asia. And it would likely stoke an isolationist backlash in the United States by pursuing a level of foreign ambition for which there would be insufficient political support. Asking that the United States prepare for and manage its exit from global primacy, however, is a tall order. Great powers have considerable difficulty accepting their mortality; few in history have willfully made room for rising challengers and adjusted their grand strategies accordingly.

In managing the return of multipolarity, America should be guided by the principles of strategic restraint and institutional binding. Strategic restraint means making room for rising centers of power so that they array their rising strength with rather than against the United States. Institutional binding entails the use of international institutions to bind major powers to each other and to bound their behavior through adherence to common norms. Institutions also promise to fulfill another important function—that of guiding America down a multilateral path that offers a middle ground between unilateralism and isolationism.

Transatlantic Troubles—Managing the End of Alliance

Confronted with the rise of Europe and America's changing internationalism, the Atlantic alliance appears poised for demise. Its founder and primary patron, the United States, is losing interest in the alliance, resulting in a military pact that is hollowing out and of diminishing geopolitical relevance. Prior to the round of NATO enlargement that extended membership to Poland, Hungary, and the Czech Republic, Washington was abuzz with debate. In the weeks leading up to the 2002 Prague summit, which approved another round of enlargement, there was only a deafening silence; no one in the United States seemed to care. With the war against terrorism not just topping, but defining, America's strategic agenda, Europe is moving to the periphery of American grand strategy. The alliance is also of declining relevance to Europe. With the continent at peace and the European Union soon to take in the region's new democracies, Europe no longer needs its American pacifier—one of the main reasons France and Germany were prepared to stand their ground against the United States over Iraq.

Europe's security order is thus in the process of becoming much more European and much less Atlantic. As the United States prepares to decamp from the continent, the two sides of the Atlantic are heading toward a new division of labor. Europe will increasingly assume responsibility for its own security, while America focuses its attention and resources on other parts of the world—principally the Middle East and East Asia. Impressive levels of trade and investment promise to continue flowing across the Atlantic. But commercial ties will be unable to offset the forces of separation in the geopolitical arena. The traditional trans-Atlantic link, predicated upon the notion of the indivisibility of American and European security, will be no more.

To prepare the way for this new division of labor, Europe must redouble efforts to build a union capable of acting collectively on the international stage. The EU is currently in a no-man's-land. It is too strong to be Washington's lackey, but too weak and divided to be either an effective partner or a formidable counterweight. The result has been to invite Washington's disdain.

Although the debate over whether to wage war against Iraq unquestionably weakened European unity, that crisis may prove to be a turning point. Preserving the Atlantic link was one of the key motivations inducing Britain, Spain, Italy, and most Central European countries to side with the Bush administration. But now that the Atlantic alliance appears to be irreversibly headed toward demise, an Atlanticist Europe is no longer an option.

France and Germany have realized as much, one of the main reasons they are intensifying efforts to deepen defense cooperation. Poland and its neighbors have yet to give up hope of a strong NATO, but they can ignore reality for only so long; Warsaw and other like-minded capitals will soon realize they have no choice but to settle for a strong EU. The sooner current and prospective EU members face up to the fact that America is in the midst of leaving Europe for good, the sooner they will begin throwing their weight behind a more effective and collective union.

Several measures should be top priorities. The EU must complete the institutional adaptations already underway and work to establish efficient and effective mechanisms for the formulation and implementation of a common security policy. It must oversee the coordination and integration of national defense programs, seeking to map out on a collective basis the new force structures and procurement programs required to give Europe the more capable forces that it needs.[42] Europe must also build public support for the implementation of its new defense programs. Professionalizing and upgrading forces, merging the planning and procurement processes of individual states, increasing defense expenditure—these are tasks that will require public understanding and a new level of collective will. European leaders need to begin laying the necessary political foundation.

As a more capable Europe separates from the American imperium, Atlantic relations will likely get considerably worse before they get better. But an EU able to hold its own ultimately provides the only hope for building a new foundation for the Atlantic community. The United States will at least have the option of striking a more balanced and mature partnership with Europe. The EU, whether or not America has the good sense to rekindle multilateralism, will at least be prepared for the unforeseen dangers that will arise as America ends its days as Europe's protector.

On the American side, Washington would be wise to resist its unilateralist impulses and dismissive attitude toward Europe. Several steps are in order. The United States should stop its quiet but steady effort to block Europe's growing geopolitical ambition.[43] American officials have essentially been telling the Europeans that they welcome more European defense capability and a more equitable sharing of burdens, but that they are not interested in sharing power with the EU; Washington enjoys calling the shots. Instead, they should make clear to Europe that as its new capability becomes available, the United States will accord the EU greater voice. Warnings about decoupling should give way to a single, clear message: capabilities for influence. As Europe's defense capacities evolve, the United States should look for ways to forge a more mature and constructive relationship with the EU. This means more diplomatic contact with the EU as a collective entity rather than working primarily through national capitals. And it means consulting fully with the EU before pursuing important policy initiatives rather than briefing Europe after the fact.

Washington also needs to engage in a public education campaign if America and Europe are to pull off an amicable separation rather than a nasty divorce. In light of the isolationist and unilateralist instincts that have played such a central role in American history, today's leaders need to fashion a new political equilibrium and a new, even if reduced, level of American engagement in the world that enjoys the support of the public. Doing so entails rebuilding a liberal internationalism that guides America toward not just engagement but

---

[42] See Michael O'Hanlon, "Transforming NATO: The Role of European Forces," *Survival* 39 (Autumn 1997): 5–15.

[43] For a summary of U.S. concerns and why they are misguided, see Charles Kupchan, "In Defense of European Defense," *Survival* 42 (Summer 2000).

multilateral engagement through international institutions. Predicated upon the notion of sharing the rights and responsibilities of managing the international system with others, liberal internationalism offers a stable middle ground between isolationist and unilateralist extremes, providing the political foundations for an America that at once resists the urge to retreat and works with, rather than against, emerging centers of power. Before a backing away from the world becomes likely and go-it-alone impulses alienate potential partners, America needs to find this new internationalism.

East Asia: Sino-Japanese Rapprochement or Multipolar Balancing?

The implications of America's changing internationalism are less immediate for East Asia than for Europe. Unlike in Europe, the end of the cold war has not resolved the region's main geopolitical cleavages. As a result, the United States is likely to continue its role as East Asia's extraregional balancer. From this perspective, the United States will effectively gravitate to an Asia-first posture in the years ahead.

Nonetheless, it is still important for East Asian countries to work toward a regional security structure that is less dependent upon American power. If the United States does practice a more discriminating internationalism in the coming years, East Asia is likely to feel at least some of the consequences. The ongoing crisis on the Korean peninsula could affect the scope and tenor of America's strategic commitment in the region, with both Washington and Seoul in the midst of reevaluating the U.S. presence in Korea. Defending South Korea, at least in terms of public diplomacy, remains one of the main missions justifying America's forward presence in East Asia. If that mission disappears, it may be hard to make the case—in the United States as well as in America's regional allies such as Japan—that America's forward strategic posture should continue in its current form. At a minimum, the United States and East Asia's regional powers should begin a dialogue on how to move toward a more self-sustaining and stable regional order.

Preparing East Asia for less reliance on American power is far more complicated and dangerous than the parallel task in Europe. The key difference is that states in Europe took advantage of America's protective umbrella to deal with the past and pursue an ambitious agenda of regional cooperation and integration. Europeans have accordingly succeeded in fashioning a regional order that is likely to withstand the retraction of American power. In contrast, states in East Asia have hidden behind America's presence, pursuing neither reconciliation nor regional integration. East Asia's major powers remain estranged.

The United States, therefore, faces a severe trade-off in East Asia between the dependence upon American power arising from its predominant role in the region and the intraregional balancing that would ensue in the wake of an American retrenchment. America's sizable military presence keeps the peace and checks regional rivalries. But it also alienates China and holds in place a polarized political landscape. As China's economy and military capability grow, its efforts to balance against the United States could grow more pronounced. Were the United States to reduce its role as regional arbiter and protector, relations with China would likely improve, but at the expense of regional stability. Japan and Korea would no doubt increase their own military capabilities, risking a region-wide arms race and spiraling tensions.

If the United States is to escape the horns of this dilemma, it must help repair the region's main line of cleavage and facilitate rapprochement between East Asia's two major powers—Japan and China. Just as reconciliation between France and Germany was the critical ingredient in building a stable zone of peace in Europe, so too is Sino-Japanese rapprochement the sine qua non of a self-sustaining regional order in East Asia.

Primary responsibility for improving Sino-Japanese ties lies with Japan. With an economy and political system much more developed than China's, Japan has far more latitude in pushing their relationship forward. As in Europe, economic ties should serve as the vehicle for promoting closer political ties. Japan can also make a major step forward by finally acknowledging and formally apologizing for its behavior during World War II. The United States can further this process by welcoming and helping to facilitate overtures between Tokyo and Beijing. Washington should also help dislodge the inertia that pervades politics in Tokyo by making clear to the Japanese that they cannot indefinitely rely on American guarantees to ensure their security. Japan needs to take advantage of America's protective umbrella while it lasts, pursuing the policies of reconciliation and integration essential to constructing a regional security order resting on cooperation rather than deterrence.

China has its own work to do if its relationship with Japan is to move beyond cold peace. Beijing should respond with unequivocal enthusiasm should Japan address its past more openly. It would be particularly important for Beijing to take advantage of a resolute accounting and apology to shape public opinion and moderate the resentment toward Japan that still runs deep in Chinese society. According to a public opinion survey carried out in 1997, over 40 percent of Chinese has a "bad" impression of Japan, while 44 percent has an "average" impression, and only 14 percent has a "good" impression. Over 80 percent of respondents indicated that Japan's invasion of China during World War II remains their main association with Japan.[44] Loosening the domestic constraints stemming from these public attitudes is a necessity if rapprochement is to have any chance of getting off the ground.

If ties between China and Japan do markedly improve, the United States would be able to play a less prominent role in the region, making possible an improvement in its own relations with China. Washington should avoid rhetoric

[44] *Zhongguo Qingnian Bao* (China Youth Daily), 15 February 1997, cited in Kokubun Ryosei, "Japan-China Relations After the Cold War: Switching from the '1972 Framework,'" *Japan Echo* 28 (April 2001): 9.

and policies that might induce China to intensify its efforts to balance against Japan and the United States, instead buying time for Sino-Japanese rapprochement to get off the ground. In the great debate over China's future that is now taking place on America's op-ed pages and in its academic journals, both the optimists and the pessimists are way off the mark.[45] It is simply too early to pronounce China either a strategic partner or an implacable adversary. Talk of an impending Chinese military threat is both counterproductive and misguided; neither the Chinese military nor its economy is world-class.[46] The United States can, therefore, afford to adopt a wait-and-see attitude toward China while avoiding provocative moves, such as supporting a Taiwanese policy of moving toward formal independence. China can do its part to strengthen its relationship with the United States by containing saber-rattling over Taiwan, halting the export of weapons to rogue states, and avoiding actions and rhetoric that could inflame territorial disputes in the region.

The prospect of a meaningful rapprochement between China and Japan is obviously far off. Neither China nor Japan appears ready to embark down the path of reconciliation. Nor is the United States about to take steps to reduce its influence in the region; Washington enjoys being Asia's security hub. At the same time, no one imagined in 1945 that Germany and France would put their historical animosities aside and become the collective core of an integrated Europe. If China and Japan are to have a chance of heading in the same direction, they need to take the small steps now that will lead to lasting change down the road.

A Global Concert of Regional Powers

As this new century progresses, unipolarity will give way to a world of multiple centers of power. As this transition proceeds, American grand strategy should focus on making both Europe and East Asia less reliant on U.S. power, while at the same time working with major states in both regions to promote collective management of the global system. The ultimate vision that should guide U.S. grand strategy is the construction of a concert-like directorate of the major powers in North America, Europe, and East Asia. These major powers would together manage developments and regulate relations both within and among

[45] For optimistic views of China's future, see Robert S. Ross, "Beijing as a Conservative Power," *Foreign Affairs* 76 (March/April 1997): 33–44; and Nicholas Berry, "China is Not an Imperialist Power," *Strategic Review* 24 (Winter 2001): 4–10. For pessimistic views, see Richard Bernstein and Ross Munro, "The Coming Conflict with China," *Foreign Affairs* 76 (March/April 1997): 18–32; and Constantine Menges, "China: Myths and Reality," *Washington Times*, 12 April 2001.

[46] China's GDP in 1999 was $732 billion, while America's was $9.2 *trillion* — over twelve times larger. China's annual defense budget is roughly 5 percent of that of the United States. International Institute for Strategic Studies, *The Military Balance 2001–2002* (London: International Institute for Strategic Studies, 2000): 25, 194. See also Bates Gill and Michael O'Hanlon, "China's Hollow Military," *The National Interest* 56 (Summer 1999).

their respective regions. They would also coordinate efforts in the battle against terrorism, a struggle that will require patience and steady cooperation among many different nations.

Regional centers of power also have the potential to facilitate the gradual incorporation of developing nations into global flows of trade, information, and values. Strong and vibrant regional centers, for reasons of both proximity and culture, often have the strongest incentives to promote prosperity and stability in their immediate peripheries. North America might, therefore, focus on Latin America; Europe on Russia, the Middle East, and Africa; and East Asia on South Asia and Southeast Asia.

Mustering the political will and the foresight to pursue this vision will be a formidable task. The United States will need to begin ceding influence and autonomy to regions that have grown all too comfortable with American primacy. Neither American leaders, long accustomed to calling the shots, nor leaders in Europe and East Asia, long accustomed to passing the buck, will find the transition an easy one.

But it is far wiser and safer to get ahead of the curve and shape structural change by design than to find unipolarity giving way to a chaotic multipolarity by default. It will take a decade, if not two, for a new international system to evolve. But the decisions taken by the United States early in the twenty-first century will play a critical role in determining whether multipolarity reemerges peacefully or brings with it the competitive jockeying that has so frequently been the precursor to great power war in the past.*

* This article draws on material presented in my book, *The End of the American Era: U.S. Foreign Policy and the Geopolitics of the Twenty-first Century* (New York: Alfred A. Knopf, 2002), and on my article, "Hollow Hegemony or Stable Multipolarity?" in G. John Ikenberry, ed., *America Unrivalled: The Future of the Balance of Power* (Ithaca, NY: Cornell University Press, 2002).

How Countries Democratize

SAMUEL P. HUNTINGTON

Between 1974 and 1990 more than thirty countries in southern Europe, Latin America, East Asia, and Eastern Europe shifted from authoritarian to democratic systems of government. This "global democratic revolution" is probably the most important political trend in the late twentieth century. It is the third wave of democratization in the modern era.

A wave of democratization is a group of transitions from nondemocratic to democratic regimes that occurs within a specified period and that significantly outnumbers transitions in the opposite direction in the same period. The first wave began in America in the early nineteenth century and culminated at the end of World War I with about thirty countries having democratic regimes. Mussolini's march on Rome in 1922 began a reverse wave, and in 1942 there were only twelve democracies left in the world. The Allied victory in World War II and decolonization started a second movement toward democracy which, however, petered out by the early 1960s when about thirty-six countries had democratic regimes. This was then followed by a second reverse movement towards authoritarianism, marked most dramatically by military take-overs in Latin America and the seizure of power by personal despots such as Ferdinand Marcos.

The causes of the third wave, like those of its predecessors, were complex and peculiar to that wave. This article, however, is concerned not with the why of the third wave but rather with the question of how third wave democratizations occurred: the ways in which political leaders and publics in the 1970s and 1980s ended authoritarian systems and created democratic ones. The routes of change were diverse, as were the people primarily responsible for bringing

SAMUEL P. HUNTINGTON is Eaton Professor of the Science of Government and director of the John M. Olin Institute for Strategic Studies at Harvard University, and recent president of the American Political Science Association. He has published numerous books and articles on the processes and problems of democracies. This article is drawn from his recent book, *The Third Wave: Democratization in the Late Twentieth Century*, published by the University of Oklahoma Press.

about change. Moreover, the starting and ending points of the processes were asymmetric. Obvious differences exist among democratic regimes: some are presidential, some are parliamentary, some embody the Gaullist mixture of the two; so also some are two-party, some are multiparty, and major differences exist in the nature and strength of the parties. These differences have significance for the stability of the democratic systems that are created, but relatively little for the processes leading to them.[1] Of greater importance is that in all democratic regimes the principal officers of government are chosen through competitive elections in which the bulk of the population can participate. Democratic systems thus have a common institutional core that establishes their identity. Authoritarian regimes—as the term is used in this study—are defined simply by the absence of this institutional core. Apart from not being democratic they may have little else in common. It will, consequently, be necessary to start the discussion of change in authoritarian regimes by identifying the differences among those regimes and the significance of those differences for democratization processes.

AUTHORITARIAN REGIMES

Historically, nondemocratic regimes have taken a wide variety of forms. The regimes democratized in the first wave were generally absolute monarchies, lingering feudal aristocracies, and the successor states to continental empires. Those democratized in the second wave had been fascist states, colonies, and personalistic military dictatorships and often had had some previous democratic experience. The regimes that moved to and toward democracy in the third wave generally fell into three groups: one-party systems, military regimes, and personal dictatorships.

The one-party systems were created by revolution or Soviet imposition and included the communist countries plus Taiwan and Mexico (with Turkey also fitting this model before its second wave democratization in the 1940s). In these systems, the party effectively monopolized power, access to power was through the party organization, and the party legitimated its rule through ideology. These systems often achieved a relatively high level of political institutionalization.

The military regimes were created by coups d'etat replacing democratic or civilian governments. In them, the military exercised power on an institutional basis, with the military leaders typically either governing collegially as a junta or circulating the top governmental position among top generals. Military regimes existed in large numbers in Latin America (where some approximated the bureaucratic-authoritarian model) and also in Greece, Turkey, Pakistan, Nigeria, and South Korea.

---

[1] See G. Bingham Powell, Jr., *Contemporary Democracies: Participation, Stability, and Violence* (Cambridge, MA: Harvard University Press, 1982), chaps. 5–9; Juan J. Linz, "Perils of Presidentialism," *Journal of Democracy* 1 (Winter 1990): 51–69.

Personal dictatorships were a third, more diverse group of nondemocratic systems. The distinguishing characteristic of a personal dictatorship is that the individual leader is the source of authority and that power depends on access to, closeness to, dependence on, and support from the leader. This category included Portugal under António Salazar and Marcello Caetano, Spain under Francisco Franco, the Philippines under Ferdinand Marcos, India under Indira Ghandi, and Romania under Nicolae Ceausescu. Personal dictatorships had varied origins. Those in the Philippines and India were the result of executive coups. Those in Portugal and Spain began with military coups (which in the latter case led to civil war) with the dictators subsequently establishing bases of power independent of the military. In Romania, a personal dictatorship evolved out of a one-party system. Chile under Augusto Pinochet originated as a military regime but in effect became a personal dictatorship due to his prolonged tenure and his differences with and dominance over the leaders of the military services. Some personal dictatorships, such as those of Marcos and Ceausescu, like those of Anastasio Somoza, François Duvalier, Sese Seko Mobutu, and the shah, exemplified Weber's model of sultanistic regimes characterized by patronage, nepotism, cronyism, and corruption.

One-party systems, military regimes, and personal dictatorships suppressed both competition and participation. The South African system differed from these in that it was basically a racial oligarchy with more than 70 percent of the population excluded from politics but with fairly intense political competition occurring within the governing white community. Historical experience suggests that democratization proceeds more easily if competition expands before participation.[2] If this is the case, the prospects for successful democratization were greater in South Africa than in countries with the other types of authoritarian systems. The process in South Africa would, in some measure, resemble the nineteenth-century democratizations in Europe in which the central feature was the expansion of the suffrage and the establishment of a more inclusive polity. In those cases exclusion had been based on economic, not racial, grounds. Hierarchical communal systems, however, historically have been highly resistant to peaceful change.[3] Competition within the oligarchy thus favored successful South African democratization; the racial definition of that oligarchy created problems for democratization.

Particular regimes did not always fit neatly into particular categories. In the early 1980s, for instance, Poland combined elements of a decaying one-party system and of a military-based martial law system led by a military officer who was also secretary general of the Communist party. The communist system in

[2] Robert A. Dahl, *Polyarchy: Participation and Opposition* (New Haven: Yale University Press, 1971), 33–40.

[3] See Donald L. Horowitz, "Three Dimensions of Ethnic Politics," *World Politics* 23 (January 1971): 232–36; Samuel P. Huntington and Jorge I. Domínguez, "Political Development" in Fred I. Greenstein and Nelson W. Polsby, eds., *Handbook of Political Science*, vol. 3 (Reading, MA: Addison-Wesley, 1975), 74–75.

TABLE 1

Authoritarian Regimes and Liberalization/Democratization Processes, 1974–90

Processes	Regimes			
	One-Party	Personal	Military	Racial Oligarchy
Transformation	(Taiwan)ᵃ	Spain	Turkey	
	Hungary	India	Brazil	
	(Mexico)	Chile	Peru	
	(USSR)		Ecuador	
	Bulgaria		Guatemala	
			Nigeria*	
			Pakistan	
			Sudan*	
16	5	3	8	
Transplacement	Poland	(Nepal)	Uruguay	(South Africa)
	Czechoslovakia		Bolivia	
	Nicaragua		Honduras	
	Mongolia		El Salvador	
			Korea	
11	4	1	5	1
Replacement	East Germany	Portugal	Greece	
		Philippines	Argentina	
		Romania		
6	1	3	2	
Intervention	Grenada		(Panama)	
2	1		1	
Totals				
35	11	7	16	1

Note: The principal criterion of democratization is selection of a government through an open, competitive, fully participatory, fairly administered election.

ᵃ Parentheses indicate a country that significantly liberalized but did not democratize by 1990.

* Indicates a country that reverted to authoritarianism.

Romania (like its counterpart in North Korea) started out as a one-party system but by the 1980s had evolved into a sultanistic personal dictatorship. The Chilean regime between 1973 and 1989 was in part a military regime but also, in contrast to other South American military regimes, during its entire existence had only one leader who developed other sources of power. Hence it had many of the characteristics of a personal dictatorship. The Noriega dictatorship in Panama, on the other hand, was highly personalized but dependent almost entirely on military power. The categorizations in Table 1, consequently, should be viewed as rough approximations. Where a regime combined elements of two types it is categorized in terms of what seemed to be its dominant type as the transition got underway.

In the second wave, democratization occurred in large measure through foreign imposition and decolonization. In the third wave, as we have seen, those two processes were less significant, limited before 1990 to Grenada, Panama, and several relatively small former British colonies also mostly in the Caribbean area. While external influences often were significant causes of third wave democratizations, the processes themselves were overwhelmingly indigenous. These processes can be located along a continuum in terms of the relative importance of governing and opposition groups as the sources of democratization. For analytical purposes it is useful to group the cases into three broad types of processes. Transformation (or, in Juan J. Linz's phrase, *reforma*) occurred when the elites in power took the lead in bringing about democracy. Replacement (Linz's *ruptura*) occurred when opposition groups took the lead in bringing about democracy, and the authoritarian regime collapsed or was overthrown. What might be termed transplacement or "*ruptforma*" occurred when democratization resulted largely from joint action by government and opposition groups.[4] In virtually all cases groups both in power and out of power played some roles, and these categories simply distinguish the relative importance of government and opposition.

As with regime types, historical cases of regime change did not necessarily fit neatly into theoretical categories. Almost all transitions, not just transplacements, involved some negotiation—explicit or implicit, overt or covert—between government and opposition groups. At times transitions began as one type and then became another. In the early 1980s, for instance, P. W. Botha appeared to be initiating a process of transformation in the South African political system, but he stopped short of democratizing it. Confronting a different political environment, his successor, F. W. de Klerk, shifted to a transplacement process of negotiation with the principal opposition group. Similarly, scholars agree that the Brazilian government initiated and controlled the transition process for many years. Some argue that it lost control over that process as a result of popular mobilization and strikes in 1979–1980; others, however, point to the government's success in resisting strong opposition demands for direct election of the president in the mid-1980s. Every historical case combined elements of two or more transition processes. Virtually every historical case, however, more clearly approximated one type of process than others.

---

[4] For reasons that are undoubtedly deeply rooted in human nature, scholars often have the same ideas but prefer to use different words for those ideas. My tripartite division of transition processes coincides with that of Donald Share and Scott Mainwaring, but we have our own names for those processes:

Huntington		Linz		Share/Mainwaring
(1) transformation	=	*reforma*	=	transaction
(2) replacement	=	*ruptura*	=	breakdown/collapse
(3) transplacement	=	—	=	extrication

See Juan J. Linz, "Crisis, Breakdown, and Reequilibration" in Juan J. Linz and Alfred Stepan, eds., *The Breakdown of Democratic Regimes* (Baltimore: Johns Hopkins University Press, 1978), 35; Donald Share and Scott Mainwaring, "Transitions Through Transaction: Democratization in Brazil and Spain" in Wayne A. Selcher, ed., *Political Liberalization in Brazil: Dynamics, Dilemmas, and Future Prospects* (Boulder, CO: Westview Press, 1986), 177–79.

How did the nature of the authoritarian regime relate to the nature of the transition process? As Table 1 suggests, there was no one-to-one relation. Yet the former did have consequences for the latter. With three exceptions, all the transitions from military regimes involved transformation or transplacement. In the three exceptions—Argentina, Greece, and Panama—military regimes suffered military defeats and collapsed as a result. Elsewhere military rulers took the lead, at times in response to opposition and popular pressure, in bringing about the change in regime. Military rulers were better placed to terminate their regimes than were leaders of other regimes. The military leaders virtually never defined themselves as the permanent rulers of their country. They held out the expectation that once they had corrected the evils that had led them to seize power they would exit from power and return to their normal military functions. The military had a permanent institutional role other than politics and governorship. At some point, consequently, the military leaders (other than those in Argentina, Greece, and Panama) decided that the time had come to initiate a return to civilian democratic rule or to negotiate their withdrawal from power with opposition groups. Almost always this occurred after there had been at least one change in the top leadership of the military regime.[5]

Military leaders almost invariably posited two conditions or "exit guarantees" for their withdrawal from power. First, there would be no prosecution, punishment, or other retaliation against military officers for any acts they may have committed when they were in power. Second, the institutional roles and autonomy of the military establishment would be respected, including its overall responsibility for national security, its leadership of the government ministries concerned with security, and often its control of arms industries and other economic enterprises traditionally under military aegis. The ability of the withdrawing military to secure agreement of civilian political leaders to these conditions depended on their relative power. In Brazil, Peru, and other instances of transformation, the military leaders dominated the process and civilian political leaders had little choice but to acquiesce to the demands of the military. Where relative power was more equal, as in Uruguay, negotiations led to some modifications in the military demands. Greek and Argentinean military leaders asked for the same assurances other leaders did. Their requests, however, were rejected out of hand by civilian leaders, and they had to agree to a virtual unconditional surrender of power.[6]

[5] See Martin C. Needler, "The Military Withdrawal from Power in South America," *Armed Forces and Society* 6 (Summer 1980): 621–23.

[6] For discussion of the terms under which military rulers arranged their exits from power, see Robert H. Dix, "The Breakdown of Authoritarian Regimes," *Western Political Quarterly* 35 (December 1982): 567–68, for "exit guarantees"; Myron Weiner, "Empirical Democratic Theory and the Transition from Authoritarianism to Democracy," *PS* 20 (Fall 1987): 864–98; Enrique A. Baloyra, "Conclusion: Toward a Framework for the Study of Democratic Consolidation" in Enrique A. Baloyra, ed., *Comparing New Democracies: Transition and Consolidation in Mediterranean Europe and the Southern Cone* (Boulder, CO: Westview Press, 1987), 299–300; Alfred Stepan, *Rethinking Military Politics: Brazil and the Southern Cone* (Princeton, NJ: Princeton University Press, 1988), 64–65; Philip Mauceri, "Nine Cases of Transitions and Consolidations" in Robert A. Pastor, ed., *Democracy in the Americas:*

It was thus relatively easy for military rulers to withdraw from power and to resume professional military roles. The other side of the coin, however, is that it could also be relatively easy for them to return to power when exigencies and their own interests warranted. One successful military coup in a country makes it impossible for political and military leaders to overlook the possibility of a second. The third wave democracies that succeeded military regimes started life under this shadow.

Transformation and transplacement also characterized the transitions from one-party systems to democracy through 1989, except for those in East Germany and Grenada. One-party regimes had an institutional framework and ideological legitimacy that differentiated them from both democratic and military regimes. They also had an assumption of permanence that distinguished them from military regimes. The distinctive characteristic of one-party systems was the close interweaving of party and state. This created two sets of problems, institutional and ideological, in the transition to democracy.

The institutional problems were most severe with Leninist party states. In Taiwan as in communist countries the "separation of the party from the state" was "the biggest challenge of a Leninist party" in the process of democratization.[7] In Hungary, Czechoslovakia, Poland, and East Germany constitutional provisions for "the leading role" of the communist party had to be abrogated. In Taiwan comparable "temporary provisions" added to the constitution in 1950 were similarly challenged. In all Leninist party systems major issues arose concerning ownership of physical and financial assets—did they belong to the party or the state? The proper disposition of those assets was also in question—should they be retained by the party, nationalized by the government, sold by the party to the highest bidder, or distributed in some equitable manner among social and political groups? In Nicaragua, for instance, after losing the election in February 1990, the Sandinista government apparently moved quickly "to transfer large amounts of Government property to Sandinista hands." "They are selling houses to themselves, selling vehicles to themselves," alleged one anti-Sandinista businessman.[8] Similar allegations were made about the disposal of government property to the Communist party as Solidarity was about to take

---

Stopping the Pendulum (New York: Holmes and Meier, 1989), 225, 229; Luis A. Abugattas, "Populism and After: The Peruvian Experience" in James M. Malloy and Mitchell A. Seligson, eds., *Authoritarians and Democrats: Regime Transition in Latin America* (Pittsburgh: University of Pittsburgh Press, 1987), 137–39; Aldo C. Vacs, "Authoritarian Breakdown and Redemocratization in Argentina" in Malloy and Seligson, eds., *Authoritarians and Democrats*, 30–31; P. Nikiforos Diamandouros, "Transition to, and Consolidation of, Democratic Politics in Greece, 1974–83: A Tentative Assessment" in Geoffrey Pridham, ed., *The New Mediterranean Democracies: Regime Transition in Spain, Greece, and Portugal* (London: Frank Cass, 1984), 54; Harry J. Psomiades, "Greece: From the Colonels' Rule to Democracy" in John H. Herz, ed., *From Dictatorship to Democracy: Coping with the Legacies of Authoritarianism and Totalitarianism* (Westport, CT: Greenwood Press, 1982), 253–54.

[7] Tun-jen Cheng, "Democratizing the Quasi-Leninist Regime in Taiwan," *World Politics* 41 (July 1989): 496.

[8] *New York Times*, 9 March 1990; 11 March 1990.

over the government in Poland. (In a parallel move in Chile, the Pinochet government as it went out of power transferred to the military establishment property and records that had belonged to other government agencies.)

In some countries party militias had to be disbanded or brought under government control, and in almost all one-party states the regular armed forces had to be depoliticized. In Poland, as in most communist countries, for instance, all army officers had to be members of the Communist party; in 1989, however, Polish army officers lobbied parliament to prohibit officers from being members of any political party.[9] In Nicaragua the Sandinista People's Army had been the army of the movement, became also the army of the state, and then had to be converted into being only the latter. The question of whether party cells within economic enterprises should continue was also a highly controversial issue. Finally, where the single party remained in power, there was the question of the relation between its leaders in government and the top party bodies such as the Politburo and the central committee. In the Leninist state the latter dictated policy to the former. Yet this relationship was hardly compatible with the supremacy of elected parliamentary bodies and responsible cabinets in a democratic state.

The other distinctive set of problems was ideological. In one-party systems, the ideology of the party defined the identity of the state. Hence opposition to the party amounted to treason to the state. To legitimize opposition to the party it was necessary to establish some other identity for the state. This problem manifested itself in three contexts. First, in Poland, Hungary, Czechoslovakia, Romania, and Bulgaria, communist ideology and rule had been imposed by the Soviet Union. The ideology was not essential to defining the identity of the country. In fact, in at least three of these countries nationalism opposed communism. When the communist parties in these countries gave up their claim to undisputed rule based on that ideology, the countries redefined themselves from "people's republics" to "republics" and reestablished nationalism rather than ideology as the basis of the state. These changes hence occurred relatively easily.

Second, several one-party systems where democratization became an issue had been created by national revolutions. In these cases—China, Mexico, Nicaragua, and Turkey—the nature and purpose of the state were defined by the ideology of the party. In China the regime staunchly adhered to its ideology and identified democratic opposition to communism with treason to the state. In Turkey, the government followed an uncertain and ambivalent policy toward Islamic groups challenging the secular basis of the Kemalist state. In Mexico the leadership of the Partido Revolucionario Institucional (PRI) held somewhat comparable views concerning the liberal challenge of the opposition Partido Acción Nacional (PAN) to the revolutionary, socialist, corporatist

---

[9] Bronislaw Geremek, "Postcommuninism and Democracy in Poland," *Washington Quarterly* 13 (Summer 1990): 129.

character of the PRI state. In Nicaragua Sandinista ideology was the basis of not just the program of a party but also of the legitimacy of the state created by the Nicaraguan revolution.

Third, in some instances the ideology of the single party defined both the nature of the state and its geographical scope. In Yugoslavia and the Soviet Union communist ideology provided the ideological legitimacy for multi-national states. If the ideology were rejected, the basis for the state would disappear and each nationality could legitimately claim its own state. In East Germany communism provided the ideological basis for a separate state; when the ideology was abandoned, the rationale for an East German state disappeared. The ideology of the Kuomintang (KMT) defined the government on Taiwan as the government of China, and the regime saw opposition elements supporting an independent Taiwan as subversive. The problem here was less serious than in the other three cases because the ideology legitimated an aspiration rather than a reality. The KMT government functioned in fact as the highly successful government of Taiwan even though in its own eyes its legitimacy depended on the myth that it was the rightful government of all China.

When the military give up their control of government, they do not also give up their control of the instruments of violence with which they could resume control of government. Democratization of a one-party system, however, means that the monopolistic party places at risk its control of government and becomes one more party competing in a multiparty system. In this sense its separation from power is less complete than it is for the military when they withdraw. The party remains a political actor. Defeated in the 1990 election, the Sandinistas could hope "to fight again another day" and come back to power through electoral means.[10] In Bulgaria and Romania former communist parties won elections; in other East European countries they had less sanguine expectations of participating in a coalition government sometime in the future.

After democratization a former monopolistic party is in no better position than any other political group to reinstate an authoritarian system. The party gives up its monopoly of power but not the opportunity to compete for power by democratic means. When they return to the barracks, the military give up both, but they also retain the capacity to reacquire power by nondemocratic means. The transition from a one-party system to democracy, consequently, is likely to be more difficult than the transition from a military regime to democracy, but it is also likely to be more permanent.[11] The difficulties of transforming one-party systems are perhaps reflected in the fact that as of 1990 the leaders of such regimes in Taiwan, Mexico, and the Soviet Union had initiated the liberalization of their regimes but were moving only slowly toward full democratization.

[10] *New York Times*, 11 March 1990.

[11] For a similar conclusion, see I. William Zartman, "Transition to Democracy from Single-Party Regimes: Lessons from North Africa" (Paper presented to Annual Meeting, American Political Science Association, Atlanta, 31 August–3 September 1989), 2–4.

The leaders of personal dictatorships were less likely than those of military and one-party regimes to give up power voluntarily. Personal dictators in countries that transited to democracy as well as those that did not usually tried to remain in office as long as they could. This often created tensions between a narrowly based political system and an increasingly complex and modern economy and society.[12] It also led on occasion to the violent overthrow of the dictator, as happened in Cuba, Nicaragua, Haiti, and Iran, and the dictator's replacement by another authoritarian regime. In the third wave of democratization, uprisings similarly overthrew personal dictatorships in Portugal, the Philippines, and Romania. In Spain, the dictator died and his successors led a classic case of democratic transformation from above. In India and in Chile, the leaders in power submitted themselves to elections in the apparent but mistaken belief that the voters would confirm them in office. When this did not happen, they, unlike Marcos and Manuel Noriega, accepted the electoral verdict. In the cases of sultanistic regimes, the transitions to democracy were complicated by the weakness of political parties and other institutions. Transitions to democracy from personal dictatorship thus occurred when the founding dictator died and his successors decided on democratization, when the dictator was overthrown, and when he or she miscalculated the support that the dictator could win in an election.

TRANSITION PROCESSES

The third wave transitions were complex political processes involving a variety of groups struggling for power and for and against democracy and other goals. In terms of their attitudes toward democratization, the crucial participants in the processes were the standpatters, liberal reformers, and democratic reformers in the governing coalition, and democratic moderates and revolutionary extremists in the opposition. In noncommunist authoritarian systems, the standpatters within the government were normally perceived as right-wing, fascist, and nationalist. The opponents of democratization in the opposition were normally left-wing, revolutionary, and Marxist-Leninist. Supporters of democracy in both government and opposition could be conceived as occupying middle positions on the left-right continuum. In communist systems left and right were less clear. Standpatters were normally thought of as Stalinist or Brezhnevite. Within the opposition, the extremist opponents of democracy were not revolutionary left-wingers but often nationalist groups thought of as right-wing.

Within the governing coalition some groups often came to favor democratization, while others opposed it, and others supported limited reform or liberalization (see Figure 1). Opposition attitudes toward democracy were also usu-

---

[12] See Richard K. Betts and Samuel P. Huntington, "Dead Dictators and Rioting Mobs: Does the Demise of Authoritarian Rulers Lead to Political Instability?" *International Security* 10 (Winter 1985–86): 112–46.

FIGURE 1

Political Groups Involved in Democratization

	Attitudes Toward Democracy			
	Against	For		Against
Government		Reformers Democratizers	Liberals	Standpatters
Opposition	Radical Extremists	Democratic Moderates		

ally divided. Supporters of the existing dictatorship always opposed democracy; opponents of the existing dictatorship often opposed democracy. Almost invariably, however, they used the rhetoric of democracy in their efforts to replace the existing authoritarian regime with one of their own. The groups involved in the politics of democratization thus had both conflicting and common objectives. Reformers and standpatters divided over liberalization and democratization but presumably had a common interest in constraining the power of opposition groups. Moderates and radicals had a common interest in bringing down the existing regime and getting into power but disagreed about what sort of new regime should be created. Reformers and moderates had a common interest in creating democracy but often divided over how the costs of creating it should be borne and how power within it should be apportioned. Standpatters and radicals were totally opposed on the issue of who should rule but had a common interest in weakening the democratic groups in the center and in polarizing politics in the society.

The attitudes and goals of particular individuals and groups at times changed in the democratization process. If democratization did not produce the dangers they feared, people who had been liberal reformers or even standpatters might come to accept democracy. Similarly, participation in the processes of democratization could lead members of extremist opposition groups to moderate their revolutionary propensities and accept the constraints and opportunities democracy offered.

The relative power of the groups shaped the nature of the democratization process and often changed during that process. If standpatters dominated the government and extremists the opposition, democratization was impossible, as, for example, where a right-wing personal dictator determined to hang on to power confronted an opposition dominated by Marxist-Leninists. Transition to democracy was, of course, facilitated if prodemocratic groups were dominant in both the government and opposition. The differences in power between reformers and moderates, however, shaped how the process occurred. In 1976, for instance, the Spanish opposition urged a complete "democratic break" or *ruptura* with the Franco legacy and creation of a provisional government and a constituent assembly to formulate a new constitutional order. Adolfo Suárez was powerful enough, however, to fend this off and produce democratization working through the Franco constitutional mechanism.[13] If democratic groups were strong in the opposition but not in the government, democratization depended on events undermining the government and bringing the opposition to power. If democratic groups were dominant in the governing coalition, but not in the opposition, the effort at democratization could be threatened by insurgent violence and by a backlash increase in power of standpatter groups possibly leading to a coup d'etat.

The three crucial interactions in democratization processes were those between government and opposition, between reformers and standpatters in the governing coalition, and between moderates and extremists in the opposition. In all transitions these three central interactions played some role. The relative importance and the conflictual or cooperative character of these interactions, however, varied with the overall nature of the transition process. In transformations, the interaction between reformers and standpatters within the governing coalition was of central importance; and the transformation only occurred if reformers were stronger than standpatters, if the government was stronger than the opposition, and if the moderates were stronger than the extremists. As the transformation went on, opposition moderates were often coopted into the governing coalition while standpatter groups opposing democratization defected from it. In replacements, the interactions between government and opposition and between moderates and extremists were important; the opposition eventually had to be stronger than the government, and the moderates had to be stronger than the extremists. A successive defection of groups often led to the downfall of the regime and inauguration of the democratic system. In transplacements, the central interaction was between reformers and moderates not widely unequal in power, with each being able to dominate the antidemocratic groups on its side of the line between the government and the opposition. In some transplacements, government and former opposition groups agreed on at least a temporary sharing of power.

TRANSFORMATIONS

In transformations those in power in the authoritarian regime take the lead and play the decisive role in ending that regime and changing it into a democratic system. The line between transformations and transplacements is fuzzy and some cases might be legitimately classified in either category. Overall, however, transformations accounted for approximately sixteen out of thirty-five third wave transitions that had occurred or that appeared to be underway by the end of the 1980s. These sixteen cases of liberalization or democratization included changes from five one-party systems, three personal dictatorships, and eight

---

[13] See Raymond Carr, "Introduction: The Spanish Transition to Democracy in Historical Perspective" in Robert P. Clark and Michael H. Haltzel, eds., *Spain in the 1980s: The Democratic Transition and a New International Role* (Cambridge, MA: Ballinger, 1987), 3–4.

military regimes. Transformation requires the government to be stronger than the opposition. Consequently, it occurred in well-established military regimes where governments clearly controlled the ultimate means of coercion vis-à-vis the opposition and/or vis-à-vis authoritarian systems that had been successful economically, such as Spain, Brazil, Taiwan, Mexico, and, compared to other communist states, Hungary. The leaders of these countries had the power to move their countries toward democracy if they wanted to. In every case the opposition was, at least at the beginning of the process, markedly weaker than the government. In Brazil, for example, as Alfred Stepan points out, when "liberalization began, there was no significant political opposition, no economic crisis, and no collapse of the coercive apparatus due to defeat in war."[14] In Brazil and elsewhere the people best situated to end the authoritarian regime were the leaders of the regime—and they did.

The prototypical cases of transformation were Spain, Brazil, and, among communist regimes, Hungary. The most important case, if it materializes, will be the Soviet Union. The Brazilian transition was "liberation from above" or "regime-initiated liberalization." In Spain "it was a question of reformist elements associated with the incumbent dictatorship, initiating processes of political change from within the established regime."[15] The two transitions differed significantly, however, in their duration. In Spain in less than three and a half years after the death of Franco, a democratizing prime minister had replaced a liberalizing one, the Franco legislature had voted the end of the regime, political reform had been endorsed in a referendum, political parties (including the Communist party) were legalized, a new assembly was elected, a democratic constitution was drafted and approved in a referendum, the major political actors reached agreement on economic policy, and parliamentary elections were held under the new constitution. Adolfo Suárez reportedly told his cabinet that "his strategy would be based on speed. He would keep ahead of the game by introducing specific measures faster than the *continuistas* of the Francoist establishment could respond to them." While the reforms were compressed within a short period of time, however, they were also undertaken sequentially. Hence, it has also been argued that "By staggering the reforms, Suárez avoided antagonizing too many sectors of the franquist regime simultaneously. The last set of democratic reforms provoked open hostility from the military and other franquist hardliners, but the President [Suárez] had greatly gained considerable momentum and support." In effect, then, Suárez followed a highly compressed version of the Kemalist "Fabian strategy, blitzkrieg tactics" pattern of reform.[16]

[14] Alfred Stepan, "Introduction," in Stepan, ed., *Democratizing Brazil: Problems of Transition and Consolidation* (New York: Oxford University Press, 1989), ix.

[15] Ibid.; Scott Mainwaring, "The Transition to Democracy in Brazil," *Journal of Interamerican Studies and World Affairs* 28 (Spring 1986): 149; Kenneth Medhurst, "Spain's Evolutionary Pathway from Dictatorship to Democracy" in Pridham, ed., *New Mediterranean Democracies*, 30.

[16] Paul Preston, *The Triumph of Democracy in Spain* (London: Methuen, 1986), 93; Donald Share and Scott Mainwaring, "Transitions Through Transaction: Democratization in Brazil and Spain" in

In Brazil, in contrast, President Ernesto Geisel determined that political change was to be "gradual, slow, and sure." The process began at the end of the Médici administration in 1973, continued through the Geisel and Figueiredo administrations, jumped forward with the installation of a civilian president in 1985, and culminated in the adoption of a new constitution in 1988 and the popular election of a president in 1989. The regime-decreed movements toward democratization were interspersed with actions taken to reassure hardliners in the military and elsewhere. In effect, Presidents Geisel and Figueiredo followed a two-steps forward, one-step backward policy. The result was a creeping democratization in which the control of the government over the process was never seriously challenged. In 1973 Brazil had a repressive military dictatorship; in 1989 it was a full-scale democracy. It is customary to date the arrival of democracy in Brazil in January 1985, when the electoral college chose a civilian president. In fact, however, there was no clear break; the genius of the Brazilian transformation is that it is virtually impossible to say at what point Brazil stopped being a dictatorship and became a democracy.

Spain and Brazil were the prototypical cases of change from above, and the Spanish case in particular became the model for subsequent democratizations in Latin America and Eastern Europe. In 1988 and 1989, for instance, Hungarian leaders consulted extensively with Spanish leaders on how to introduce democracy, and in April 1989 a Spanish delegation went to Budapest to offer advice. Six months later one commentator pointed to the similarities in the two transitions:

> The last years of the Kadar era did bear some resemblance to the benign authoritarianism of Franco's decaying dictatorship. Imre Pozsgay plays the part of Prince Juan Carlos in this comparison. He is a reassuring symbol of continuity in the midst of radical change. Liberal-minded economic experts with links to the old establishment and the new entrepreneurial class provide a technocratic elite for the transition, much as the new bourgeois elites associated with Opus Dei did in Spain. The opposition parties also figure in this analogy, emerging from underground in much the same way the Spanish exiles did once it was safe to come out. And as in Spain, the Hungarian oppositionists—moderate in style, radically democratic in substance—are playing a vital role in the reinvention of democracy.[17]

Third wave transformations usually evolved through five major phases, four of which occurred within the authoritarian system.

Emergence of reformers. The first step was the emergence of a group of leaders or potential leaders within the authoritarian regime who believed that movement in the direction of democracy was desirable or necessary. Why did

Wayne A. Selcher, ed., *Political Liberalization in Brazil: Dynamics, Dilemmas, and Future Prospects* (Boulder, CO: Westview Press, 1986), 179; Samuel P. Huntington, *Political Order in Changing Societies* (New Haven: Yale University Press, 1968), 344–57.

[17] Jacques Rupnik, "Hungary's Quiet Revolution," *New Republic*, 20 November 1989, 20; *New York Times*, 16 April 1989.

they conclude this? The reasons why people became democratic reformers varied greatly from country to country and seldom were clear. They can, however, be grouped into five categories. First, reformers often concluded that the costs of staying in power—such as politicizing their armed forces, dividing the coalition that had supported them, grappling with seemingly unsolvable problems (usually economic), and increasing repression—had reached the point where a graceful exit from power was desirable. The leaders of military regimes were particularly sensitive to the corrosive effects of political involvement on the integrity, professionalism, coherence, and command structure of the military. "We all directly or indirectly," General Morales Bermudez observed as he led Peru toward democracy, "had been witnesses to what was happening to this institution fundamental to our fatherland, and in the same vein, to the other institutions. And we don't want that." In a similar vein, General Fernando Matthei, head of the Chilean air force, warned, "If the transition toward democracy is not initiated promptly, we shall ruin the armed forces in a way no Marxist infiltration could."[18]

Second, in some cases reformers wished to reduce the risks they faced if they held on to power and then eventually lost it. If the opposition seemed to be gaining strength, arranging for a democratic transition was one way of achieving this. It is, after all, preferable to risk losing office than to risk losing life.

Third, in some cases, including India, Chile, and Turkey, authoritarian leaders believed that they or their associates would not lose office. Having made commitments to restore democratic institutions and being faced with declining legitimacy and support these rulers could see the desirability of attempting to renew their legitimacy by organizing elections in anticipation that the voters would continue them in power. This anticipation was usually wrong.

Fourth, reformers often believed that democratizing would produce benefits for their country: increase its international legitimacy, reduce U.S. or other sanctions against their regime, and open the door to economic and military assistance, International Monetary Fund (IMF) loans, invitations to Washington, and inclusion in international gatherings dominated by the leaders of the Western alliance.

Finally, in many cases, including Spain, Brazil, Hungary, and Turkey and some other military regimes, reformers believed that democracy was the "right" form of government and that their country had evolved to the point where, like other developed and respected countries, it too should have a democratic political system.

Liberal reformers tended to see liberalization as a way of defusing opposition to their regime without fully democratizing the regime. They would ease up on repression, restore some civil liberties, reduce censorship, permit broader

---

[18] Quoted by Abugattas in Malloy and Seligson, eds., *Authoritarians and Democrats*, 129, and by Sylvia T. Borzutzky, "The Pinochet Regime: Crisis and Consolidation" in ibid., 85.

discussion of public issues, and allow civil society—associations, churches, unions, business organizations—greater scope to conduct their affairs. Liberalizers did not, however, wish to introduce fully participatory competitive elections that could cause current leaders to lose power. They wanted to create a kinder, gentler, more secure and stable authoritarianism without altering fundamentally the nature of their system. Some reformers were undoubtedly unsure themselves how far they wished to go in opening up the politics of their country. They also at times undoubtedly felt the need to veil their intentions: democratizers tended to reassure standpatters by giving the impression that they were only liberalizing; liberalizers attempted to win broader popular support by creating the impression they were democratizing. Debates consequently raged over how far Geisel, Botha, Gorbachev, and others "really" wanted to go.

The emergence of liberalizers and democratizers within an authoritarian system creates a first-order force for political change. It also, however, can have a second-order effect. In military regimes in particular it divides the ruling group, further politicizes the military, and hence leads more officers to believe that "the military as government" must be ended in order to preserve "the military as institution." The debate over whether or not to withdraw from government in itself becomes an argument to withdraw from government.

Acquiring power. Democratic reformers not only had to exist within the authoritarian regime, they also had to be in power in that regime. How did this come about? In three cases leaders who created the authoritarian regime presided over its transition to democracy. In India and Turkey, authoritarian regimes were defined from the start as interruptions in the formal pattern of democracy. The regimes were short-lived, ending with elections organized by the authoritarian leaders in the false anticipation that they or the candidates they supported would win those elections. In Chile General Pinochet created the regime, remained in power for seventeen years, established a lengthy schedule for the transition to democracy, implemented that schedule in anticipation that the voters would extend him in office for eight more years, and exited grudgingly from power when they did not. Otherwise those who created authoritarian regimes or who led such regimes for prolonged periods of time did not take the lead in ending those regimes. In all these cases, transformation occurred because reformers replaced standpatters in power.

Reformers came to power in authoritarian regimes in three ways. First, in Spain and Taiwan, the founding and long-ruling authoritarian leaders, Franco and Chiang Kai-shek died. Their designated successors, Juan Carlos and Chiang Ching-kuo, succeeded to the mantle, responded to the momentous social and economic changes that had occurred in their countries, and began the process of democratization. In the Soviet Union, the deaths in the course of three years of Leonid Brezhnev, Yuri Andropov, and Konstantine Chernenko allowed Gorbachev to come to power. In a sense, Franco, Chiang, and Brezhnev died in time; Deng Xiao-ping did not.

In Brazil and in Mexico, the authoritarian system itself provided for regular change in leadership. This made the acquisition of power by reformers possible but not necessary. In Brazil two factions existed in the military. Repression reached its peak between 1969 and 1972 during the presidency of General Emílio Médici, a hard-liner. In a major struggle within the military establishment at the end of his term, the soft-line Sorbonne group was able to secure the nomination of General Ernesto Geisel for president, in part because his brother was minister of war. Guided by his chief associate, General Golbery do Couto e Silva, Geisel began the process of democratization and acted decisively to ensure that he would, in turn, be succeeded in 1978 by another member of the Sorbonne group, General João Batista Figueiredo. In Mexico, outgoing President José Lopez Portillo in 1981 followed standard practice in selecting his minister of planning and budgets, Miguel de la Madrid, as his successor. De la Madrid was an economic and political liberalizer and, rejecting more traditional and old-guard candidates, chose a young reforming technocrat, Carlos Salinas, to continue the opening up process.

Where authoritarian leaders did not die and were not regularly changed, democratic reformers had to oust the ruler and install prodemocratic leadership. In military governments, other than Brazil, this meant the replacement by coup d'etat of one military leader by another: Morales Bermudez replaced Juan Velasco in Peru; Alfredo Poveda replaced Guillermo Rodríguez Lara in Ecuador; Oscar Mejía replaced Jose Rios Montt in Guatemala; Murtala Muhammed replaced Yacubu Gowon in Nigeria.[19] In the one-party system in Hungary, reformers mobilized their strength and deposed the long-ruling Janos Kadar at a special party conference in May 1988, replacing him as secretary general with Karoly Grosz. Grosz, however, was only a semireformer, and a year later the Central Committee replaced him with a four-person presidium dominated by reformers. In October 1989 one of them, Rezso Nyers, became party president. In Bulgaria in the fall of 1989, reform-minded Communist party leaders ousted Todor Zhivkov from the dominant position he had occupied for thirty-five years. The leadership changes associated with some liberalizing and democratizing reforms are summarized in Table 2.

The failure of liberalization. A critical issue in the third wave concerned the role of liberal reformers and the stability of a liberalized authoritarian polity. Liberal reformers who succeeded standpatter leaders usually turned out to be transition figures with brief stays in power. In Taiwan, Hungary, and Mexico, liberalizers were quickly succeeded by more democratically oriented reformers. In Brazil, although some analysts are dubious, it seems reasonably clear that Geisel and Golbery do Couto e Silva were committed to meaningful de-

---

[19] See Needler, "The Military Withdrawal," 621–23 on "second phase" coups and the observation that "the military government that returns power to civilian hands is not the same one that seized power from the constitutional government in the first place."

TABLE 2

Leadership Change and Reform, 1973–90

Country	Standpat Leader	Change	Reform Leader I	Change	Reform Leader II	First Democratic Election
Nigeria	Gowon	July 1975 coup	Murtala Mohammed	February 1976 death	Obasanjo	August 1979
Ecuador	Rodriguez Lara	January 1976 coup	Proveda	—	—	April 1979
Peru	Velasco	August 1975 coup	Morales Bermudez	—	—	May 1980
Brazil	Medici	March 1974 succession	Geisel	March 1979 succession	Figueiredo	January 1985
Guatemala	Rios Montt	August 1983 coup	Mejia	—	—	December 1985
Spain	Franco	November 1975 death	Juan Carlos	—	Juan Carlos	March 1979
	Carrero Blanco	December 1973 death	Arias	July 1976 ouster	Suárez	
Taiwan	Chiang Kai-shek	April 1975 death	Chaing Ching-kuo	January 1988 death	Lee Teng-hui	
Hungary	Kadar	May 1988 ouster	Grosz	May–October 1989 ouster	Nyers-Pozsgay	March 1990
Mexico	Portillo	December 1982 succession	De la Madrid	December 1988 succession	Salinas	
South Africa	Vorster	September 1978 ouster	Botha	September 1989 ouster	de Klerk	
USSR	Chernenko	March 1985 death	Gorbachev			
Bulgaria	Zhivkov	November 1989 ouster	Mladenov	—	—	June 1990

mocratization from the start.[20] Even if they did just intend to liberalize the authoritarian system rather than replace it, João Figueiredo extended the process to democratization. "I have to make this country into a democracy," he said in 1978 before taking office, and he did.[21]

In Spain the hard-line prime minister, Admiral Luis Carrero Blanco, was assassinated in December 1973, and Franco appointed Carlos Arias Navarro to succeed him. Arias was the classic liberal reformer. He wished to modify the Franco regime in order to preserve it. In a famous speech on 12 February 1974, he proposed an opening (*apertura*) and recommended a number of modest reforms including, for instance, permitting political associations to function but not political parties. He "was too much of a conservative and Francoist at heart to carry out a true democratization of the regime." His reform proposals were torpedoed by the standpatters of the "bunker," including Franco; at the same

[20] Stepan, *Rethinking Military Politics*, 32–40; and Thomas E. Skidmore, "Brazil's Slow Road to Democratization: 1974–1985" in Stepan, ed., *Democratizing Brazil*, 33. This interpretation coincides with my own impression of Golbery's intentions that I formed in 1974 working with him on plans for Brazil's democratization. For a contrary argument, see Silvio R. Duncan Baretta and John Markoff, "Brazil's *Abertura*: A Transition from What to What?" in Malloy and Seligson, eds., *Authoritarians and Democrats*, 45–46.

[21] Quoted in Francisco Weffort, "Why Democracy?" in Stepan, ed., *Democratizing Brazil*, 332.

time the proposals stimulated the opposition to demand a more extensive opening. In the end, Arias "discredited *aperturismo* just as Luis Carrero Blanco had discredited immobilism."[22] In November 1975 Franco died and Juan Carlos succeeded him as chief of state. Juan Carlos was committed to transforming Spain into a true, European-style parliamentary democracy, Arias resisted this change, and in July 1976 Juan Carlos replaced him with Adolfo Suárez, who moved quickly to introduce democracy.

The transition from liberalized authoritarianism, however, could move backward as well as forward. A limited opening could raise expectations of further change that could lead to instability, upheaval, and even violence; these, in turn, could provoke an antidemocratic reaction and replacement of the liberalizing leadership with standpatter leaders. In Greece, George Papadopoulos attempted to shift from a standpatter to a liberalizing stance; this led to the Polytechnic student demonstration and its bloody suppression; a reaction followed and the liberalizing Papadopoulos was replaced by the hard-line Dimitrios Ioannidis. In Argentina General Roberto Viola succeeded the hard-line General Jorge Videla as president and began to liberalize. This produced a reaction in the military, Viola's ouster, and his replacement by hard-line General Leopoldo Galtieri. In China ultimate power presumably rested with Deng Xiao-ping. In 1987, however Zhao Ziyang became general secretary of the Communist party and began to open up the political system. This led to the massive student demonstrations in Tiananmen Square in the spring of 1989, which, in turn, provoked a hard-line reaction, the crushing of the student movement, the ouster of Zhao, and his replacement by Li Peng. In Burma, General Ne Win, who had ruled Burma for twenty-six years, ostensibly retired from office in July 1988 and was replaced by General Sein Lwin, another hard-liner. Mounting protests and violence forced Sein Lwin out within three weeks. He was succeeded by a civilian and presumed moderate, Maung Maung, who proposed elections and attempted to negotiate with opposition groups. Protests continued, however, and in September the army deposed Maung Maung, took control of the government, bloodily suppressed the demonstrations, and ended the movement toward liberalization.

The dilemmas of the liberalizer were reflected in the experiences of P. W. Botha and Mikhail Gorbachev. Both leaders introduced major liberalizing reforms in their societies. Botha came to power in 1978 with the slogan "Adapt or die" and legalized black trade unions, repealed the marriage laws, established mixed trading zones, granted citizenship to urban blacks, permitted blacks to acquire freehold title, substantially reduced petty apartheid, increased significantly investment in black education, abolished the pass laws, provided for elected black township councils, and created houses of parliament representing coloureds and Asians, although not blacks. Gorbachev opened up pub-

[22] Raymond Carr and Juan Pablo Fusi Aizpurua, *Spain: Dictatorship to Democracy*, 2d ed. (London: Allen & Unwin, 1981), 198–206.

lic discussion, greatly reduced censorship, dramatically challenged the power of the Communist party apparat, and introduced at least modest forms of government responsibility to an elected legislature. Both leaders gave their societies new constitutions incorporating many reforms and also creating new and very powerful posts of president, which they then assumed. It seems probable that neither Botha nor Gorbachev, however, wanted fundamental change in their political systems. Their reforms were designed to improve and to moderate, but also to bolster the existing system and make it more acceptable to their societies. They themselves said as much repeatedly. Botha did not intend to end white power; Gorbachev did not intend to end communist power. As liberal reformers they wanted to change but also to preserve the systems that they led and in whose bureaucracies they had spent their careers.

Botha's liberalizing but not democratizing reforms stimulated intensified demands from South African blacks for their full incorporation into the political system. In September 1984 black townships erupted with protests that led to violence, repression, and the deployment of military forces into the townships. The efforts at reform simultaneously ended, and Botha the reformer was widely viewed as having become Botha the repressor. The reform process only got underway again in 1989 when Botha was replaced by F. W. de Klerk, whose more extensive reforms led to criticisms from Botha and his resignation from the National party. In 1989 and 1990 Gorbachev's liberalizing but not democratizing reforms appeared to be stimulating comparable upheaval, protests, and violence in the Soviet Union. As in South Africa, communal groups fought each other and the central authorities. The dilemma for Gorbachev was clear. Moving forward toward full-scale democratization would mean not only the end of communist power in the Soviet Union but very probably the end of the Soviet Union. Leading a hard-line reaction to the upheavals would mean the end of his efforts at economic reform, his greatly improved relations with the West, and his global image as a creative and humane leader. Andrei Sakharov put the choices squarely to Gorbachev in 1989: "A middle course in situations like these is almost impossible. The country and you personally are at a crossroads—either increase the process of change maximally or try to retain the administrative command system with all its qualities."[23]

Where it was tried, liberalization stimulated the desire for democratization in some groups and the desire for repression in others. The experience of the third wave strongly suggests that liberalized authoritarianism is not a stable equilibrium; the halfway house does not stand.

Backward legitimacy: subduing the standpatters. The achievement of power enabled the reformers to start democratizing but it did not eliminate the ability of the standpatters to challenge the reformers. The standpatter elements of what had been the governing coalition—the Francoist "bunker" in Spain, the

---

[23] Quoted in David Remnick, "The Struggle for Light," *New York Review of Books*, 16 August 1990, 6.

military hard-liners in Brazil and other Latin American countries, the Stalinists in Hungary, the mainlander old guard in the KMT, the party bosses and bureaucracy in the PRI, the *Verkrampte* wing of the National party—did not give up easily. In the government, military, and party bureaucracies standpatters worked to stop or slow down the processes of change. In the non-one-party systems—Brazil, Ecuador, Peru, Guatemala, Nigeria, and Spain—standpatter groups in the military attempted coups d'etat and made other efforts to dislodge the reformers from power. In South Africa and in Hungary, standpatter factions broke away from the dominant parties, charging them with betraying the basic principles on which the parties were based.

Reform governments attempted to neutralize standpatter opposition by weakening, reassuring, and converting the standpatters. Countering standpatter resistance often required a concentration of power in the reform chief executive. Geisel asserted himself as "dictator of the *abertura*" in order to force the Brazilian military out of politics.[24] Juan Carlos exercised his power and prerogatives to the full in moving Spain toward democracy, not least in the surprise selection of Suárez as prime minister. Botha and Gorbachev, as we have seen, created powerful new presidential offices for themselves. Salinas dramatically asserted his powers during his first years as Mexico's president.

The first requirement for reform leaders was to purge the governmental, military, and, where appropriate, party bureaucracies, replacing standpatters in top offices with supporters of reform. This was typically done in selective fashion so as not to provoke a strong reaction and so as to promote fissions within the standpatter ranks. In addition to weakening standpatters, reform leaders also tried to reassure and convert them. In military regimes, the reformers argued that it was time to go back, after a necessary but limited authoritarian interlude, to the democratic principles that were the basis of their country's political system. In this sense, they appealed for a "return to legitimacy." In the nonmilitary authoritarian systems, reformers invoked "backward legitimacy" and stressed elements of continuity with the past.[25] In Spain, for instance, the monarchy was reestablished and Suárez adhered to the provisions of the Franco constitution in abolishing that constitution: no Francoist could claim that there were procedural irregularities. In Mexico and South Africa the reformers in the PRI and National party cast themselves in the traditions of those parties. On Taiwan the KMT reformers appealed to Sun Yat-Sen's three principles.

Backward legitimacy had two appeals and two effects: it legitimated the new order because it was a product of the old, and it retrospectively legitimated the old order because it had produced the new. It elicited consensus from all

---

[24] See Stepan, *Rethinking Military Politics*, 42–43.

[25] Giuseppe Di Palma highlighted the significance of backward legitimacy in "Founding Coalitions in Southern Europe: Legitimacy and Hegemony," *Government and Opposition* 15 (Spring 1980): 170. See also Nancy Bermeo, "Redemocratization and Transition Elections: A Comparison of Spain and Portugal," *Comparative Politics* 19 (January 1987): 218.

except opposition extremists who had no use for either the old authoritarian regime or the new democratic one. Reformers also appealed to standpatters on the grounds that they were preempting the radical opposition and hence minimizing instability and violence. Suárez, for instance, asked the Spanish army to support him for these reasons and the dominant elements in the army accepted the transition because there "was no illegitimacy, no disorder in the streets, no significant threat of breakdown and subversion." Inevitably, the reformers also found that, as Geisel put it, they could "not advance without some retreats" and that hence, on occasion, as in the 1977 "April package" in Brazil, they had to make concessions to the standpatters.[26]

Coopting the opposition. Once in power the democratic reformers usually moved quickly to begin the process of democratization. This normally involved consultations with leaders of the opposition, the political parties, and major social groups and institutions. In some instances relatively formal negotiations occurred and quite explicit agreements or pacts were reached. In other cases, the consultations and negotiations were more informal. In Ecuador and Nigeria the government appointed commissions to develop plans and policies for the new system. In Spain, Peru, Nigeria, and eventually in Brazil elected assemblies drafted new constitutions. In several instances referenda were held to approve the new constitutional arrangements.

As the reformers alienated standpatters within the governing coalition, they had to reinforce themselves by developing support within the opposition and by expanding the political arena and appealing to the new groups that were becoming politically active as a result of the opening. Skillful reformers used the increased pressure from these groups for democratization to weaken the standpatters, and used the threat of a standpatter coup as well as the attractions of a share in power to strengthen moderate groups in the opposition.

To these ends, reformers in government negotiated with the principal opposition groups and arrived at explicit or tacit agreements with them. In Spain, for instance, the Communist party recognized that it was too weak to follow a "radical *rupturista* policy" and instead went along with a "*ruptura pactada*" even though the pact was "purely tacit." In October 1977 Suárez won the agreement of the Communist and Socialist parties to the *Pactos de la Moncloa* comprising a mixture of fairly severe economic austerity measures and some social reforms. Secret negotiations with Santiago Carrillo, the principal Communist leader, "played on the PCE [Partido Comunista de España] leader's anxiety to be near the levers of power and secured his backing for an austerity package."[27]

---

[26] Stanley G. Payne, "The Role of the Armed Forces in the Spanish Transition" in Clark and Haltzel, eds., *Spain in the 1980s*, 86; Stepan, *Rethinking Military Politics*, 36.

[27] Theses presented by the Central Committee, Ninth Congress, Communist Party of Spain, 5–9 April 1978, quoted in Juan J. Linz, "Some Comparative Thoughts on the Transition to Democracy in Portugal and Spain" in Jorge Braga de Macedo and Simon Serfaty, eds., *Portugal Since the Revolution: Economic and Political Perspectives* (Boulder, CO: Westview Press, 1981), 44; Preston, *Triumph of Democracy in Spain*, 137.

In Hungary explicit negotiations occurred in the fall of 1989 between the Communist party and the Opposition Round Table representing the principal other parties and groups. In Brazil informal understandings developed between the government and the opposition parties, the Movimento Democrático Brasileiro (MDB) and the Partido Movimento Democrático Brasileiro (PMDB). On Taiwan in 1986 the government and the opposition arrived at an understanding on the parameters within which political change would take place and, in a week-long conference in July 1990, agreed on a full schedule of democratization.

Moderation and cooperation by the democratic opposition—their involvement in the process as junior partners—were essential to successful transformation. In almost all countries, the principal opposition parties—the MDB-PMDB in Brazil, the Socialists and Communists in Spain, the Democratic Progressive Party (DPP) on Taiwan, the Civic Forum in Hungary, the Alianza Popular Revolucionaria Americana (APRA) in Peru, the Christian Democrats in Chile—were led by moderates and followed moderate policies, at times in the face of considerable provocation by standpatter groups in the government.

Thomas E. Skidmore's summary of what occurred in Brazil neatly catches the central relationship involved in transformation processes:

> In the end, liberalization was the product of an intense dialectical relationship between the government and the opposition. The military who favored *abertura* had to proceed cautiously, for fear of arousing the hardliners. Their overtures to the opposition were designed to draw out the "responsible" elements, thereby showing there were moderates ready to cooperate with the government. At the same time, the opposition constantly pressed the government to end its arbitrary excesses, thereby reminding the military that their rule lacked legitimacy. Meanwhile, the opposition moderates had to remind the radicals that they would play into the hands of the hardliners if they pushed too hard. This intricate political relationship functioned successfully because there was a consensus among both military and civilians in favor of a return to an (almost) open political system.[28]

Guidelines for Democratizers 1:
Reforming Authoritarian Systems

The principal lessons of the Spanish, Brazilian, and other transformations for democratic reformers in authoritarian governments include the following:

(1) Secure your political base. As quickly as possible place supporters of democratization in key power positions in the government, the party, and the military.

(2) Maintain backward legitimacy, that is, make changes through the established procedures of the nondemocratic regime and reassure standpatter groups with symbolic concessions, following a course of two steps forward, one step backward.

---

[28] Skidmore, "Brazil's Slow Road" in Stepan, ed., *Democratizing Brazil*, 34.

(3) Gradually shift your own constituency so as to reduce your dependence on government groups opposing change and to broaden your constituency in the direction of opposition groups supporting democracy.

(4) Be prepared for the standpatters to take some extreme action to stop change (for example, a coup attempt)—possibly even stimulate them to do so—and then crack down on them ruthlessly, isolating and discrediting the more extreme opponents of change.

(5) Seize and keep control of the initiative in the democratization process. Only lead from strength and never introduce democratization measures in response to obvious pressure from more extreme radical opposition groups.

(6) Keep expectations low as to how far change can go; talk in terms of maintaining an ongoing process rather than achieving some fully elaborated democratic utopia.

(7) Encourage development of a responsible, moderate opposition party, which the key groups in society (including the military) will accept as a plausible non-threatening alternative government.

(8) Create a sense of inevitability about the process of democratization so that it becomes widely accepted as a necessary and natural course of development even if to some people it remains an undesirable one.

REPLACEMENTS

Replacements involve a very different process from transformations. Reformers within the regime are weak or nonexistent. The dominant elements in government are standpatters staunchly opposed to regime change. Democratization consequently results from the opposition gaining strength and the government losing strength until the government collapses or is overthrown. The former opposition groups come to power and the conflict then often enters a new phase as groups in the new government struggle among themselves over the nature of the regime they should institute. Replacement, in short, involves three distinct phases: the struggle to produce the fall, the fall, and the struggle after the fall.

Most third wave democratizations required some cooperation from those in power. Only six replacements had occurred by 1990. Replacements were rare in transitions from one-party systems (one out of eleven) and military regimes (two out of sixteen) and more common in transitions from personal dictatorships (three out of seven). As we have pointed out, with some exceptions (Gandhi, Kenan Evren, Pinochet), leaders who created authoritarian regimes did not end those regimes. Changes of leadership within authoritarian systems were much more likely in military regimes through "second phase" coups or, in one-party systems, through regular succession or the action of constituted party bodies. Personal dictators, however, seldom retired voluntarily, and the nature of their power—personal rather than military or organizational—made it difficult for opponents within the regime to oust them and, indeed, made it unlikely that such opponents would exist in any significant numbers or strength. The personal dictator was thus likely to hang on until he died or until the regime itself came to an end. The life of the regime became the life of the dictator. Politically and at times literally (for example, Franco, Ceausescu) the deaths of the dictator and the regime coincided.

Democratic reformers were notably weak in or missing from the authoritarian regimes that disappeared in replacements. In Argentina and Greece, the liberalizing leaders Viola and Papadopoulos were forced out of power and succeeded by military hard-liners. In Portugal Caetano initiated some liberalizing reforms and then backed away from them. In the Philippines, Romania, and East Germany, the entourages of Marcos, Ceausescu, and Erich Honecker contained few if any democrats or even liberals. In all six cases standpatters monopolized power, and the possibility of initiating reform from within was almost totally absent.

An authoritarian system exists because the government is politically stronger than the opposition. It is replaced when the government becomes weaker than the opposition. Hence replacement requires the opposition to wear down the government and shift the balance of power in its favor. When they were initiated, the authoritarian regimes involved in the third wave were almost always popular and widely supported. They usually had the backing of a broad coalition of groups. Over time, however, as with any government, their strength deteriorated. The Greek and Argentine military regimes suffered the humiliation of military defeat. The Portuguese and Philippine regimes were unable to win counterinsurgency wars, and the Philippine regime created a martyr and stole an election. The Romanian regime followed policies that deeply antagonized its people and isolated itself from them; hence it was vulnerable to the cumulative snowballing of the antiauthoritarian movement throughout Eastern Europe. The case of East Germany was more ambiguous. Although the regime was relatively successful in some respects, the inevitable comparison with West Germany was an inherent weakness, and the opening of the transit corridor through Hungary dramatically undermined the regime's authority. The party leadership resigned in early December 1989, and a caretaker government took over. The regime's authority, however, evaporated, and with it the reasons for the East German state.

The erosion of support for the regime sometimes occurred openly, but, given the repressive character of authoritarian regimes, it was more likely to occur covertly. Authoritarian leaders were often unaware of how unpopular they were. Covert disaffection then manifested itself when some triggering event exposed the weakness of the regime. In Greece and Argentina it was military defeat. In Portugal and East Germany it was the explicit turning against the regime of its ultimate source of power—the army in Portugal, the Soviet Union in East Germany. The actions of the Turks, the British, the Portuguese military, and Gorbachev galvanized and brought into the open the disaffection from the regime of other groups in those societies. In all these cases, only a few weak groups rallied to the support of the regime. Many people had become disaffected from the regime but, because it was an authoritarian regime, a triggering event was required to crystalize the disaffection.

Students are the universal opposition; they oppose whatever regime exists in their society. By themselves, however, students do not bring down regimes. Lacking substantial support from other groups in the population, they were gunned down by the military and police in Greece in November 1973, Burma in September 1988, and China in June 1989. The military are the ultimate support of regimes. If they withdraw their support, if they carry out a coup against the regime, or if they refuse to use force against those who threaten to overthrow the regime, the regime falls. In between the perpetual opposition of the students and the necessary support of the military are other groups whose support for or opposition to the regime depends on circumstances. In noncommunist authoritarian systems, such as the Philippines, these groups tended to disaffect in sequence. The disaffection of the students was followed by that of intellectuals in general and then by the leaders of previously existing political parties, many of whom may have supported or acquiesced in the authoritarian takeover. Typically the broader reaches of the middle class—white-collar workers, professionals, small business proprietors—became alienated. In a Catholic country, Church leaders also were early and effective opponents of the regime. If labor unions existed and were not totally controlled by the government, at some point they joined the opposition. So also, and most important, did larger business groups and the bourgeoisie. In due course, the United States or other foreign sources of support became disaffected. Finally and conclusively, the military decided not to support the government or actively to side with the opposition against the government.

In five out of six replacements, consequently, the exception being Argentina, military disaffection was essential to bringing down the regime. In the personal dictatorships in Portugal, the Philippines, and Romania, this military disaffection was promoted by the dictator's policies weakening military professionalism, politicizing and corrupting the officer corps, and creating competing paramilitary and security forces. Opposition to the government normally (Portugal was the only exception) had to be widespread before the military deserted the government. If disaffection was not widespread, it was either because the most probable sources of opposition—the middle class, bourgeoisie, religious groups—were small and weak or because the regime had the support of these groups, usually as a result of successful policies for economic development. In Burma and China the armed forces brutally suppressed protests that were largely student-led. In societies that were more highly developed economically, opposition to authoritarianism commanded a wider range of support. When this opposition took to the streets in the Philippines, East Germany, and Romania, military units did not fire on broadly representative groups of their fellow citizens.

A popular image of democratic transitions is that repressive governments are brought down by "people power," the mass mobilization of outraged citizens demanding and eventually forcing a change of regime. Some form of mass action did take place in almost every third wave regime change. Mass demonstrations, protests, and strikes played central roles, however, in only about six transitions completed or underway at the end of the 1980s. These included the replacements in the Philippines, East Germany, and Romania, and the transplacements in Korea, Poland, and Czechoslovakia. In Chile frequent mass actions attempted, without success, to alter Pinochet's plan for transformation. In East Germany, uniquely, both "exit" and "voice," in Albert Hirschman's terms, played major roles, with protest taking the form first of massive departure of citizens from the country and then of massive street demonstrations in Leipzig and Berlin.[29]

In the Philippines, Portugal, Romania, and Greece, when the regime collapsed, it collapsed quickly. One day the authoritarian government was in power, the next day it was not. In Argentina and East Germany, the authoritarian regimes were quickly delegitimated but clung to power while attempting to negotiate terms for the change in regime. In Argentina, the successor military government of General Reynaldo Bignone, which took over in July 1982 immediately after the Falklands defeat, was "relatively successful" in maintaining some regime control over the transition for six months. In December 1982, however, mounting public opposition and the development of opposition organizations led to mass protests, a general strike, Bignone's scheduling of elections, and the rejection by the united opposition parties of the terms proposed by the military for the transfer of power. The authority of the lame-duck military regime continued to deteriorate until it was replaced by the Alfonsín government elected in October 1983. "The military government collapsed," one author observed; "it had no influence over the choice of candidates or the election itself, it excluded no one, and reserved neither powers nor veto prerogatives for itself in the future. In addition, it was unable to guarantee either its autonomy in relation to the future constitutional government or the promise of a future military policy, and, even less—given the winning candidate—the basis for an agreement on the ongoing struggle against the guerrillas."[30] In East Germany in early 1990 a somewhat similar situation existed, with a weak and discredited communist government clinging to power, and its prime minister, Hans Modrow, playing the role of Bignone.

The emphasis in transformations on procedural continuity and backward legitimacy was absent from replacements. The institutions, procedures, ideas, and individuals connected with the previous regime were instead considered

---

[29] Albert O. Hirschman, *Exit, Voice, and Loyalty: Responses to Decline in Firms, Organizations, and States* (Cambridge, MA: Harvard University Press, 1970).

[30] Virgilio R. Beltran, "Political Transition in Argentina: 1982 to 1985," *Armed Forces and Society* 13 (Winter 1987): 217; Scott Mainwaring and Eduardo J. Viola, "Brazil and Argentina in the 1980s," *Journal of International Affairs* 38 (Winter 1985): 206–9.

tainted and the emphasis was on a sharp, clean break with the past. Those who succeeded the authoritarian rulers based their rule on "forward legitimacy," what they would bring about in the future, and their lack of involvement in or connection with the previous regime.

In transformations and transplacements the leaders of the authoritarian regimes usually left politics and went back to the barracks or private life quietly and with some respect and dignity. Authoritarian leaders who lost power through replacements, in contrast, suffered unhappy fates. Marcos and Caetano were forced into exile. Ceausescu was summarily executed. The military officers who ran Greece and Argentina were tried and imprisoned. In East Germany punishments were threatened against Honecker and other former leaders in notable contrast to the absence of such action in Poland, Hungary, and Czechoslovakia. The dictators removed by foreign intervention in Grenada and Panama were similarly subjected to prosecution and punishment.

The peaceful collapse of an authoritarian regime usually produced a glorious if brief moment of public euphoria, or carnations and champagne, absent from transformations. The collapse also created a potential vacuum of authority absent from transformations. In Greece and the Philippines, the vacuum was quickly filled by the accession to power of Constantine Karamanlis and Corazon C. Aquino, popular political leaders who guided their countries to democracy. In Iran the authority vacuum was filled by the ayatollah, who guided Iran elsewhere. In Argentina and East Germany the Bignone and Modrow governments weakly filled the interim between the collapse of the authoritarian regimes and the election of democratic governments.

Before the fall, opposition groups are united by their desire to bring about the fall. After the fall, divisions appear among them and they struggle over the distribution of power and the nature of the new regime that must be established. The fate of democracy was determined by the relative power of democratic moderates and antidemocratic radicals. In Argentina and Greece, the authoritarian regimes had not been in power for long, political parties quickly reappeared, and an overwhelming consensus existed among political leaders and groups on the need quickly to reestablish democratic institutions. In the Philippines overt opposition to democracy, apart from the NPA insurgency, also was minimal.

In Nicaragua, Iran, Portugal, and Romania the abrupt collapse of the dictatorships led to struggles among the former opposition groups and parties as to who would exercise power and what sort of regime would be created. In Nicaragua and Iran the democratic moderates lost out. In Portugal, a state of revolutionary ferment existed between April 1974 and November 1975. A consolidation of power by the antidemocratic Marxist-Leninist coalition of the Communist party and left-wing military officers was entirely possible. In the end, after intense struggles between military factions, mass mobilizations, demonstrations, and strikes, the military action by António Ramalho Eanes settled Portugal on a democratic course. "What started as a coup," as Robert Harvey observed, "became a revolution which was stopped by a reaction before it became an anarchy. Out of the tumult a democracy was born."[31]

The choices in Portugal were between bourgeois democracy and Marxist-Leninist dictatorship. The choices in Romania in 1990 were less clear, but democracy also was not inevitable. The lack of effectively organized opposition parties and groups, the absence of previous experience with democracy, the violence involved in the overthrow of Ceausescu, the deep desire for revenge against people associated with the dictatorship combined with the widespread involvement of much of the population with the dictatorship, the many leaders of the new government who had been part of the old regime—all did not augur well for the emergence of democracy. At the end of 1989 some Romanians enthusiastically compared what was happening in their country to what had happened two hundred years earlier in France. They might also have noted that the French Revolution ended in a military dictatorship.

Guidelines for Democratizers 2:
Overthrowing Authoritarian Regimes

The history of replacements suggests the following guidelines for opposition democratic moderates attempting to overthrow an authoritarian regime:[32]

(1) Focus attention on the illegitimacy or dubious legitimacy of the authoritarian regime; that is its most vulnerable point. Attack the regime on general issues that are of widespread concern, such as corruption and brutality. If the regime is performing successfully (particularly economically) these attacks will not be effective. Once its performance falters (as it must), highlighting its illegitimacy becomes the single most important lever for dislodging it from power.

(2) Like democratic rulers, authoritarian rulers over time alienate erstwhile supporters. Encourage these disaffected groups to support democracy as the necessary alternative to the current system. Make particular efforts to enlist business leaders, middle-class professionals, religious figures, and political party leaders, most of whom probably supported creation of the authoritarian system. The more "respectable" and "responsible" the opposition appears, the easier it is to win more supporters.

(3) Cultivate generals. In the last analysis, whether the regime collapses or not depends on whether they support the regime, join you in opposition to it, or stand by on the sidelines. Support from the military could be helpful when

---

[31] Robert Harvey, *Portugal: Birth of a Democracy* (London: Macmillan, 1978), 2.

[32] Myron Weiner has formulated a similar and more concise set of recommendations: "For those who seek democratization the lessons are these: mobilize large-scale non-violent opposition to the regime, seek support from the center and, if necessary, from the conservative right, restrain the left and keep them from dominating the agenda of the movement, woo sections of the military, seek sympathetic coverage from the western media, and press the United States for support." "Empirical Democratic Theory and the Transition from Authoritarianism to Democracy," *PS* 20 (Fall 1987): 866.

the crisis comes, but all you really need is military unwillingness to defend the regime.

(4) Practice and preach nonviolence. Among other things, this will make it easier for you to win over the security forces: soldiers do not tend to be sympathetic to people who have been hurling Molotov cocktails at them.

(5) Seize every opportunity to express opposition to the regime, including participation in elections it organizes.

(6) Develop contacts with the global media, foreign human rights organizations, and transnational organizations such as churches. In particular, mobilize supporters in the United States. American congressmembers are always looking for moral causes to get publicity for themselves and to use against the American administration. Dramatize your cause to them and provide them with material for TV photo opportunities and headline-making speeches.

(7) Promote unity among opposition groups. Attempt to create comprehensive umbrella organizations that will facilitate cooperation among such groups. This will be difficult and, as the examples of the Philippines, Chile, Korea, and South Africa show, authoritarian rulers are often expert in promoting opposition disunity. One test of your qualifications to become a democratic leader of you country is your ability to overcome these obstacles and secure some measure of opposition unity. Remember Gabriel Almond's truth: "Great leaders are great coalition builders."[33]

(8) When the authoritarian regime falls, be prepared quickly to fill the vacuum of authority that results. This can be done by: pushing to the fore a popular, charismatic, democratically inclined leader; promptly organizing elections to provide popular legitimacy to a new government; and building international legitimacy by getting support of foreign and transnational actors (international organizations, the United States, the European Community, the Catholic Church). Recognize that some of your former coalition partners will want to establish a new dictatorship of their own and quietly organize the supporters of democracy to counter this effort if it materializes.

TRANSPLACEMENTS

In transplacements democratization is produced by the combined actions of government and opposition. Within the government the balance between standpatters and reformers is such that the government is willing to negotiate a change of regime—unlike the situation of standpatter dominance that leads to replacement—but it is unwilling to initiate a change of regime. It has to be pushed and/or pulled into formal or informal negotiations with the opposition. Within the opposition democratic moderates are strong enough to prevail over

---

[33] Gabriel A. Almond, "Approaches to Developmental Causation" in Gabriel A. Almond, Scott C. Flanagan, and Robert J. Mundt, eds., *Crisis, Choice, and Change: Historical Studies of Political Development* (Boston: Little, Brown, 1973), 32.

antidemocratic radicals, but they are not strong enough to overthrow the government. Hence they too see virtues in negotiation.

Approximately eleven of thirty-five liberalizations and democratizations that occurred or began in the 1970s and 1980s approximated the transplacement model. The most notable ones were in Poland, Czechoslovakia, Uruguay, and Korea; the regime changes in Bolivia, Honduras, El Salvador, and Nicaragua also involved significant elements of transplacement. In El Salvador and Honduras the negotiations were in part with the United States government, acting as a surrogate for democratic moderates. In 1989 and 1990, South Africa began a transplacement process, and Mongolia and Nepal appeared to be moving in that direction. Some features of transplacement were also present in Chile. The Pinochet regime was strong enough, however, to resist opposition pressure to negotiate democratization and stubbornly adhered to the schedule for regime change that it laid down in 1980.

In successful transplacements, the dominant groups in both government and opposition recognized that they were incapable of unilaterally determining the nature of the future political system in their society. Government and opposition leaders often developed these views after testing each other's strength and resolve in a political dialectic. Initially, the opposition usually believed that it would be able to bring about the downfall of the government at some point in the not too distant future. This belief was on occasion wildly unrealistic, but so long as opposition leaders held to it, serious negotiations with the government were impossible. In contrast, the government usually initially believed that it could effectively contain and suppress the opposition without incurring unacceptable costs. Transplacements occurred when the beliefs of both changed. The opposition realized that it was not strong enough to overthrow the government. The government realized that the opposition was strong enough to increase significantly the costs of nonnegotiation in terms of increased repression leading to further alienation of groups from the government, intensified divisions within the ruling coalition, increased possibility of a hard-line takeover of the government, and significant losses in international legitimacy.

The transplacement dialectic often involved a distinct sequence of steps. First, the government engaged in some liberalization and began to lose power and authority. Second, the opposition exploited this loosening by and weakening of the government to expand its support and intensify its activities with the hope and expectation it would shortly be able to bring down the government. Third, the government reacted forcefully to contain and suppress the mobilization of political power by the opposition. Fourth, government and opposition leaders perceived a standoff emerging and began to explore the possibilities of a negotiated transition. This fourth step was not, however, inevitable. Conceivably, the government, perhaps after a change of leadership, could brutally use its military and police forces to restore its power, at least temporarily. Or the opposition could continue to develop its strength, further eroding the power of the government and eventually bringing about its downfall. Transplacements thus required some rough equality of strength between government and opposition as well as uncertainty on each side as to who would prevail in a major test of strength. In these circumstances, the risks of negotiation and compromise appeared less than the risks of confrontation and catastrophe.

The political process leading to transplacement was thus often marked by a seesawing back and forth of strikes, protests, and demonstrations, on the one hand, and repression, jailings, police violence, states of siege, and martial law, on the other. Cycles of protest and repression in Poland, Czechoslovakia, Uruguay, Korea, and Chile eventually led to negotiated agreements between government and opposition in all cases except that of Chile.

In Uruguay, for instance, mounting protests and demonstrations in the fall of 1983 stimulated the negotiations leading to the military withdrawal from power. In Bolivia in 1978 "a series of conflicts and protest movements" preceded the military's agreeing to a timetable for elections.[34] In Korea as in Uruguay, the military regime had earlier forcefully suppressed protests. In the spring of 1987, however, the demonstrations became more massive and broadbased and increasingly involved the middle class. The government first reacted in its usual fashion but then shifted, agreed to negotiate, and accepted the central demands of the opposition. In Poland the 1988 strikes had a similar impact. As one commentator explained, "The strikes made the round table not only possible, but necessary—for both sides. Paradoxically, the strikes were strong enough to compel the communists to go to the round table, yet too weak to allow Solidarity's leaders to refuse negotiations. That's why the round table talks took place."[35]

In transplacements, the eyeball-to-eyeball confrontation in the central square of the capital between massed protesters and serried ranks of police revealed each side's strengths and weaknesses. The opposition could mobilize massive support; the government could contain and withstand opposition pressure.

Politics in South Africa in the 1980s also evolved along the lines of the four-step model. In the late 1970s P. W. Botha began the process of liberalizing reform, arousing black expectations and then frustrating them when the 1983 constitution denied blacks a national political role. This led to uprisings in the black townships in 1984 and 1985, which stimulated black hopes that the collapse of the Afrikaner-dominated regime was imminent. The government's forceful and effective suppression of black and white dissent then compelled the opposition drastically to revise their hopes. At the same time, the uprisings attracted international attention, stimulated condemnation of both the apartheid system

---

[34] *Washington Post*, 7 October 1983; Laurence Whitehead, "Bolivia's Failed Democratization, 1977–1980" in Guillermo O'Donnell, Philippe C. Schmitter, and Laurence Whitehead, eds., *Transitions from Authoritarian Rule: Latin America* (Baltimore: Johns Hopkins University Press, 1986), 59.

[35] "Leoplitax" (identified as a "political commentator in the Polish underground press"), *Uncaptive Minds* 2 (May–June–July 1989): 5.

and the government's tactics, and led the United States and European governments to intensify economic sanctions against South Africa. As the hopes for revolution of the African National Congress (ANC) radicals declined, the worries of the National party government about international legitimacy and the economic future increased. In the mid-1970s, Joe Slovo, head of the South African Communist party and the ANC's military organization, argued that the ANC could overthrow the government and win power through sustained guerrilla warfare and revolution. In the late 1980s he remained committed to the use of violence, but saw negotiations as the more likely route for achieving ANC goals. After becoming president of South Africa in 1989, F. W. de Klerk also emphasized the importance of negotiations. The lesson of Rhodesia, he said, was that "When the opportunity was there for real, constructive negotiation, it was not grasped. . . . It went wrong because in the reality of their circumstances they waited too long before engaging in fundamental negotiation and dialogue. We must not make that mistake, and we are determined not to repeat that mistake."[36] The two political leaders were learning from their own experience and that of others.

In Chile, in contrast, the government was willing and able to avoid negotiation. Major strikes erupted in the spring of 1983, but a national general strike was suppressed by the government. Beginning in May 1983 the opposition organized massive monthly demonstrations on "Days of National Protest." These were broken up by the police, usually with several people being killed. Economic problems and opposition protests forced the Pinochet government to initiate a dialogue with the opposition. The economy then began to recover, however, and the middle classes became alarmed at the breakdown of law and order. A national strike in October 1984 was put down with considerable bloodshed. Shortly thereafter the government reimposed the state of siege that had been cancelled in 1979. The opposition efforts thus failed to overthrow the government or to induce it to engage in meaningful negotiations. The opposition had "overestimated its strength and underestimated the government's."[37] It had also underestimated Pinochet's tenacity and political skill and the willingness of Chilean security forces to shoot unarmed civilian demonstrators.

Transplacements required leaders on both sides willing to risk negotiations. Divisions of opinion over negotiations usually existed within governing elites. At times, the top leaders had to be pressured by their colleagues and by circumstances to negotiate with the opposition. In 1989, for instance, Adam Michnik argued that Poland, like Hungary, was following "the Spanish way to democracy." At one level, he was right in that both the Spanish and Polish transitions were basically peaceful. At a more particular level, however, the Spanish analogy did not hold for Poland because Wojciech Jaruzelski was not a Juan Carlos

---

[36] Steven Mufson, "Uncle Joe," *New Republic*, 28 September 1987, 22–23; *Washington Post National Weekly*, 19–25 February 1990, 7.

[37] Edgardo Boeninger, "The Chilean Road to Democracy," *Foreign Affairs* 64 (Spring 1986): 821.

or Suárez (whereas Imre Pozsgay in Hungary in considerable measure was). Jaruzelski was a reluctant democrat who had to be pushed by the deterioration of his country and his regime into negotiations with Solidarity.[38] In Uruguay the president, General Gregorio Alvarez, wanted to prolong his power and postpone democratization and had to be forced by the other members of the military junta to move ahead with the regime change. In Chile, General Pinochet was somewhat similarly under pressure from other junta members, especially the air force commander, General Fernando Matthei, to be more forthcoming in dealing with the opposition, but Pinochet successfully resisted this pressure.

In other countries changes occurred in the top leadership before serious negotiations with the opposition began. In Korea the government of General Chun Doo Hwan followed a staunch standpatter policy of stonewalling opposition demands and suppressing opposition activity. In 1987, however, the governing party designated Roh Tae Woo as its candidate to succeed Chun. Roh dramatically reversed Chun's policies, announced a political opening, and entered into negotiations with the opposition leader.[39] In Czechoslovakia the long-in-power standpatter Communist party general secretary, Gustav Husak, was succeeded by the mildly reformist Milos Jakes in December 1987. Once the opposition became mobilized in the fall of 1989, however, Jakes was replaced by the reformer Karel Urbanek. Urbanek and the reformist prime minister, Ladislav Adamec, then negotiated arrangements for the transition to democracy with Vaclav Havel and the other leaders of the opposition Civic Forum. In South Africa, de Klerk moved beyond his predecessor's aborted transformation process from above to transplacement-type negotiations with black opposition leaders. Uncertainty, ambiguity, and division of opinion over democratization thus tended to characterize the ruling circles in transplacement situations. These regimes were not overwhelmingly committed either to holding on to power ruthlessly or to moving decisively toward democracy.

Disagreement and uncertainty existed not only on the government side in transplacements. In fact, the one group more likely to be divided against itself than the leaders of a decaying authoritarian government are the opposition leaders who aspire to replace them. In replacement situations the government suppresses the opposition and the opposition has an overriding common interest in bringing down the government. As the Philippine and Nicaraguan examples indicate, even under these conditions securing unity among opposition leaders and parties may be extremely difficult, and the unity achieved is often tenuous and fragile. In transplacements, where it is a question not of overthrowing the government but of negotiating with it, opposition unity is even more difficult to achieve. It was not achieved in Korea, and hence the govern-

---

[38] Anna Husarska, "A Talk with Adam Michnik," *New Leader*, 3–17 April 1989, 10; Marcin Sulkowski, "The Dispute About the General," *Uncaptive Minds* 3 (March–April 1990): 7–9.

[39] See James Cotton, "From Authoritarianism to Democracy in South Korea," *Political Studies* 37 (June 1989): 252–53.

mental candidate, Roh Tae Woo, was elected president with a minority of the vote, as the two opposition candidates split the antigovernment majority by opposing each other. In Uruguay, because its leader was still imprisoned, one opposition party—the National party—rejected the agreement reached between the two other parties and the military. In South Africa a major obstacle to democratic reform was the many divisions within the opposition between parliamentary and nonparliamentary groups, Afrikaner and English, black and white, and among black ideological and tribal groups. At no time before the 1990s did the South African government confront anything but a bewildering multiplicity of opposition groups whose differences among themselves were often as great as their differences with the government.

In Chile the opposition was seriously divided into a large number of parties, factions, and coalitions. In 1983, the moderate centrist opposition parties were able to join together in the Democratic Alliance. In August 1985 a broader group of a dozen parties joined in the National Accord calling for a transition to democracy. Yet conflicts over leadership and tactics continued. In 1986 the Chilean opposition mobilized massive protests, hoping to duplicate in Santiago what had just happened in Manila. The opposition, however, was divided and its militancy frightened conservatives. The problem, as one observer put it at the time, was that "the general is not being challenged by a moderate opposition movement that has got itself together under the leadership of a respected figure. There is no Chilean Cory."[40] In Poland, on the other hand, things were different. Lech Walesa was a Polish Cory, and Solidarity dominated the opposition for most of a decade. In Czechoslovakia the transplacement occurred so quickly that differences among opposition political groups did not have time to materialize.

In transplacements democratic moderates have to be sufficiently strong within the opposition to be credible negotiating partners with the government. Almost always some groups within the opposition reject negotiations with the government. They fear that negotiations will produce undesirable compromises and they hope that continued opposition pressure will bring about the collapse or the overthrow of the government. In Poland in 1988–89, right-wing opposition groups urged a boycott of the Round Table talks. In Chile left-wing opposition groups carried out terrorist attacks that undermined the efforts of the moderate opposition to negotiate with the government. Similarly, in Korea radicals rejected the agreement on elections reached by the government and the leading opposition groups. In Uruguay, the opposition was dominated by leaders of moderate political parties and extremists were less of a problem.

For negotiations to occur each party had to concede some degree of legitimacy to the other. The opposition had to recognize the government as a worthy partner in change and implicitly if not explicitly acquiesce in its current right to

---

[40] *Economist*, 10 May 1986, 39; Alfred Stepan, "The Last Days of Pinochet?" *New York Review of Books*, 2 June 1988, 34.

rule. The government, in turn, had to accept the opposition groups as legitimate representatives of significant segments of society. The government could do this more easily if the opposition groups had not engaged in violence. Negotiations were also easier if the opposition groups, such as political parties under a military regime, had previously been legitimate participants in the political process. It was easier for the opposition to negotiate if the government had used only limited violence against it and if there were some democratic reformers in the government whom it had reason to believe shared its goals.

In transplacements, unlike transformations and replacements, government leaders often negotiated the basic terms of the regime change with opposition leaders they had previously had under arrest: Lech Walesa, Vaclav Havel, Jorge Batile Ibanez, Kim Dae Jung and Kim Young Sam, Walter Sisulu and Nelson Mandela. There were good reasons for this. Opposition leaders who have been in prison have not been fighting the government, violently or nonviolently; they have been living with it. They have also experienced the reality of government power. Governmental leaders who released their captives were usually interested in reform, and those released were usually moderate enough to be willing to negotiate with their former captors. Imprisonment also enhanced the moral authority of the former prisoners. This helped them to unite the opposition groups, at least temporarily, and to hold out the prospect to the government that they could secure the acquiescence of their followers to whatever agreement was reached.

At one point in the Brazilian transition, General Golbery reportedly told an opposition leader, "You get your radicals under control and we will control ours."[41] Getting radicals under control often requires the cooperation of the other side. In transplacement negotiations, each party has an interest in strengthening the other party so that he can deal more effectively with the extremists on his side. In June 1990, for instance, Nelson Mandela commented on the problems F. W. de Klerk was having with white hard-liners and said that the ANC had appealed "to whites to assist de Klerk. We are also trying to address the problems of white opposition to him. Discussions have already been started with influential sectors in the right wing." At the same time, Mandela said that his own desire to meet with Chief Mengosuthu Buthelezi had been vetoed by militants within the ANC and that he had to accept that decision because he was "a loyal and disciplined member of the A.N.C."[42] De Klerk obviously had an interest in strengthening Mandela and helping him deal with his militant left-wing opposition.

[41] Quoted by Weffort, "Why Democracy" in Stepan, ed., *Democratizing Brazil*, 345, and by Thomas G. Sanders, "Decompression" in Howard Handelman and Thomas G. Sanders, eds., *Military Government and the Movement Toward Democracy in South America* (Bloomington: Indiana University Press, 1981), 157. As Weffort points out, this advice was somewhat beside the point in Brazil. Before starting its transformation process the Brazilian military regime had physically eliminated most of the serious radicals. The aide's advice is much more relevant in transplacement situations.

[42] *Time*, 25 June 1990, 21.

Negotiations for regime change were at times preceded by "prenegotiations" about the conditions for entering into negotiations. In South Africa, the government precondition was that the ANC renounce violence. ANC preconditions were that the government unban opposition groups and release political prisoners. In some cases prenegotiations concerned which opposition individuals and groups would be involved in the negotiations.

Negotiations were sometimes lengthy and sometimes brief. They often were interrupted as one party or the other broke them off. As the negotiations continued, however, the political future of each of the parties became more engaged with their success. If the negotiations failed, standpatters within the governing coalition and radicals in the opposition stood ready to capitalize on that failure and to bring down the leaders who had engaged in negotiations. A common interest emerged and the sense of common fate. "[I]n a way," Nelson Mandela observed in August 1990, "there is an alliance now" between the ANC and the National party. "We are on one boat, one ship," agreed National Party leader P. W. Botha, "and the sharks to the left and the sharks to the right are not going to distinguish between us when we fall overboard."[43] Consequently, as negotiations continued, the parties became more willing to compromise in order to reach an agreement.

The agreements they reached often generated attacks from others in government and opposition who thought the negotiators had conceded too much. The specific agreements reflected, of course, issues peculiar to their countries. Of central importance in almost all negotiations, however, was the exchange of guarantees. In transformations former officials of the authoritarian regime were almost never punished; in replacements they almost always were. In transplacements this was often an issue to be negotiated; the military leaders in Uruguay and Korea, for instance, demanded guarantees against prosecution and punishment for any human rights violations. In other situations, negotiated guarantees involved arrangements for the sharing of power or for changes in power through elections. In Poland each side was guaranteed an explicit share of the seats in the legislature. In Czechoslovakia positions in the cabinet were divided between the two parties. In both these countries coalition governments reassured communists and the opposition that their interests would be protected during the transition. In Korea the governing party agreed to a direct, open election for the presidency on the assumption, and possibly the understanding, that at least two major opposition candidates would run, thereby making highly probable victory for the government party's candidate.

The risks of confrontation and of losing thus impel government and opposition to negotiate with each other; and guarantees that neither will lose everything become the basis for agreement. Both get the opportunity to share in power or to compete for power. Opposition leaders know they will not be sent back to prison; government leaders know they will not have to flee into exile.

---

[43] Mandela quoted in Pauline H. Baker, "A Turbulent Transition," *Journal of Democracy* 1 (Fall 1990): 17; Botha quoted in *Washington Post National Weekly Edition*, 14–20 May 1990, 17.

Mutual reduction in risk prompts reformers and moderates to cooperate in establishing democracy.

Guidelines for Democratizers 3:
Negotiating Regime Changes

For democratic reformers in government. (1) Following the guidelines for transforming authoritarian systems, first isolate and weaken your standpatter opposition and consolidate your hold on the government and political machinery.

(2) Also following those guidelines, seize the initiative and surprise both opposition and standpatters with the concessions you are willing to make, but never make concessions under obvious opposition pressure.

(3) Secure endorsement of the concept of negotiations from leading generals or other top officials in the security establishment.

(4) Do what you can to enhance the stature, authority, and moderation of your principal opposition negotiating partner.

(5) Establish confidential and reliable back-channels for negotiating key central questions with opposition leaders.

(6) If the negotiation succeeds, you very probably will be in the opposition. Your prime concern, consequently, should be securing guarantees and safeguards for the rights of the opposition and of groups that have been associated with your government (e.g., the military). Everything else is negotiable.

For democratic moderates in the opposition. (1) Be prepared to mobilize your supporters for demonstrations when these will weaken the standpatters in the government. Too many marches and protests, however, are likely to strengthen them, weaken your negotiating partner, and arouse middle-class concern about law and order.

(2) Be moderate; appear statesmanlike.

(3) Be prepared to negotiate and, if necessary, make concessions on all issues except the holding of free and fair elections.

(4) Recognize the high probability that you will win those elections and do not take actions that will seriously complicate your governing your country.

For both government and opposition democratizers. (1) The political conditions favorable to a negotiated transition will not last indefinitely. Seize the opportunity they present and move quickly to resolve the central issues.

(2) Recognize that your political future and that of your partner depend on your success in reaching agreement on the transition to democracy.

(3) Resist the demands of leaders and groups on your side that either delay the negotiating process or threaten the core interest of you negotiating partner.

(4) Recognize that that agreement you reach will be the only alternative; radicals and standpatters may denounce it, but they will not be able to produce an alternative that commands broad support.

(5) When in doubt, compromise.

Islam, Democracy, and Constitutional Liberalism

FAREED ZAKARIA

It is always the same splendid setting, and the same sad story. A senior U.S. diplomat enters one of the grand presidential palaces in Heliopolis, the neighborhood of Cairo from which President Hosni Mubarak rules over Egypt. He walks through halls of marble, through rooms filled with gilded furniture—all a bad imitation of imperial French style that has been jokingly called "Louis Farouk" (after the last king of Egypt). Passing layers of security guards, he arrives at a formal drawing room, where he is received with great courtesy by the Egyptian president. The two talk amiably about U.S.-Egyptian relations, regional affairs, and the state of the peace process between Israel and the Palestinians. Then the American gently raises the issue of human rights and suggests that Egypt's government might ease up on political dissent, allow more press freedoms, and stop jailing intellectuals. Mubarak tenses up and snaps, "If I were to do what you ask, Islamic fundamentalists will take over Egypt. Is that what you want?" The conversation moves back to the latest twist in the peace process.

Over the years, Americans and Arabs have had many such exchanges. When President Clinton urged Palestinian leader Yasser Arafat to agree to the Camp David peace plan that had been negotiated in July 2001, Arafat reportedly responded with words to this effect: "If I do what you want, Hamas will be in power tomorrow." The Saudi monarchy's most articulate spokesman, Prince Bandar bin Sultan, often reminds American officials that if they press his government too hard, the likely alternative to the regime is not Jeffersonian democracy but a Taliban-style theocracy.

FAREED ZAKARIA has published articles on democracy and Islam in scholarly journals. Dr. Zakaria is now Editor of *Newsweek International* and a columnist for *Newsweek*. His most recent book, *The Future of Freedom: Illiberal Democracy at Home and Abroad*, is being translated into fifteen languages.

187

The worst part of it is, they may be right. The Arab rulers of the Middle East are autocratic, corrupt, and heavy-handed. But they are still more liberal, tolerant, and pluralistic than those who would likely replace them. Elections in many Arab countries would produce politicians who espouse views that are closer to those of Osama bin Laden than those of Jordan's liberal monarch, King Abdullah. Last year, the emir of Kuwait, with American encouragement, proposed giving women the vote. But the democratically elected Kuwaiti parliament—filled with Islamic fundamentalists—roundly rejected the initiative. Saudi crown prince Abdullah tried something much less dramatic when he proposed that women in Saudi Arabia be allowed to drive. (They are currently forbidden to do so, which means that Saudi Arabia has had to import half a million chauffeurs from places like India and the Philippines.) But the religious conservatives mobilized popular opposition and forced him to back down.

A similar dynamic is evident elsewhere in the Arab world. In Oman, Qatar, Bahrain, Jordan, and Morocco, on virtually every political issue, the monarchs are more liberal than the societies over which they reign. Even in the Palestinian territories, where secular nationalists like Arafat and his Palestine Liberation Organization have long been the most popular political force, militant and religious groups such as Hamas and Islamic Jihad are gaining strength, especially among the young. And although they speak the language of elections, many of the Islamic parties have been withering in their contempt for democracy, which they see as a Western form of government. They would happily come to power through an election, but then would set up their own theocratic rule. It would be one man, one vote, one time.

Compare, for example, the wildly opposite reactions of state and society to the November 2001 videotape of a gloating bin Laden found by U.S. armed forces in an al-Qaeda hideout in Kabul. On tape, bin Laden shows an intimate knowledge of the September 11 attacks and delights in the loss of life they caused. Most of the region's governments quickly noted that the tape seemed genuine and proved bin Laden's guilt. Prince Bandar issued a statement: "The tape displays the cruel and inhumane face of a murderous criminal who has no respect for the sanctity of human life or the principles of his faith." Abdul Latif Arabiat, head of Jordan's Islamic party, the Islamic Action Front, asked, "Do Americans really think the world is that stupid that they would believe that this tape is evidence?"

In most societies, dissidents force their country to take a hard look at its own failings. In the Middle East, those who advocate democracy are the first to seek refuge in fantasy, denial, and delusion. The region is awash in conspiracy theories, such as those claiming that the Israeli intelligence service, Mossad, was actually behind the World Trade Center attacks. In a CNN poll conducted across nine Muslim countries in February 2002, 61 percent of those polled said that they did not believe that Arabs were responsible for the September 11 attacks. Al-Jazeera, the first independent satellite television station in the region, which has an enormous pan-Arab audience, is populist and modern. Many of its anchors are women. It broadcasts news that the official media routinely censor. And yet it fills its airwaves with crude appeals to Arab nationalism, anti-Americanism, anti-Semitism, and religious fundamentalism.

The Arab world today is trapped between autocratic states and illiberal societies, neither of them fertile ground for liberal democracy. The dangerous dynamic between these two forces has produced a political climate filled with religious extremism and violence. As the state becomes more repressive, opposition within society grows more pernicious, goading the state into further repression. It is the reverse of the historical process in the Western world, where liberalism produced democracy and democracy fueled liberalism. The Arab path has instead produced dictatorship, which has bred terrorism. But terrorism is only the most noted manifestation of this dysfunction, social stagnation, and intellectual bankruptcy.

The Middle East today stands in stark contrast to the rest of the world, where freedom and democracy have been gaining ground over the past two decades. In its 2002 survey, Freedom House finds that 75 percent of the world's countries are currently "free" or "partly free." Only 28 percent of the Middle Eastern countries could be so described, a percentage that has fallen during the last twenty years. By comparison, more than 60 percent of African countries today are classified as free or partly free.

Since September 11, the political dysfunctions of the Arab world have suddenly presented themselves on the West's doorstep. In the back of everyone's mind—and in the front of many—is the question why. Why is this region the political basket case of the world? Why is it the great holdout, the straggler in the march of modern societies?

ISLAM'S WIDE WORLD

Bin Laden has an answer. For him the problem with Arab regimes is that they are insufficiently Islamic. Only by returning to Islam, he tells his followers, will Muslims achieve justice. Democracy, for bin Laden, is a Western invention. Its emphasis on freedom and tolerance produces social decay and licentiousness. Bin Laden and those like him seek the overthrow of the regimes of the Arab world—perhaps of the whole Muslim world—and their replacement by polities founded on strict Islamic principles, ruled by Islamic law (*sharia*) and based on the early Caliphate (the seventh-century Islamic kingdom of Arabia). Their more recent role model was the Taliban regime in Afghanistan.

There are those in the West who agree with bin Laden that Islam is the key to understanding the Middle East's turmoil. Preachers such as Pat Robertson and Jerry Falwell and writers such as Paul Johnson and William Lind have made the case that Islam is a religion of repression and backwardness. More serious scholars have argued—far more insightfully—that the problem is more complex: for fundamentalist Muslims, Islam is considered a template for all life, including politics. But classical Islam, developed in the seventh and eighth centuries, contains few of the ideas that we associate with democracy today. Elie Kedourie, an eminent student of Arab politics, wrote "The idea of representation, of elections, of popular suffrage, of political institutions being regulated by laws laid down by a parliamentary assembly, of these laws being guarded and upheld by an independent judiciary, the ideas of the secularity of state . . . all these are profoundly alien to the Muslim political tradition."[1]

Certainly the Koranic model of leadership is authoritarian. The Muslim holy book is bursting with examples of the just king, the pious ruler, the wise arbiter. But the Bible has its authoritarian tendencies as well. The kings of the Old Testament were hardly democrats. The biblical Solomon, held up as the wisest man of all, was, after all, an absolute monarch. The Bible also contains passages that seem to justify slavery and the subjugation of women. The truth is that little is to be gained by searching in the Koran for clues to Islam's true nature. The Koran is a vast book, filled with poetry and contradictions—much like the Bible and the Torah. All three books praise kings, as do most religious texts. As for mixing spiritual and temporal authority, Catholic popes combined religious and political power for centuries in a way that no Muslim ruler has ever been able to achieve. Judaism has had much less involvement with political power because, until Israel's founding, Jews were a minority everywhere in the modern world. Yet the word "theocracy" was coined by Josephus to describe the political views of ancient Jews.[2] The founding religious texts of all faiths were, for the most part, written in another age, one filled with monarchs, feudalism, war, and insecurity. They bear the stamp of their times.

Still, Western scholars of the nineteenth and early twentieth centuries often argued that Islam encourages authoritarianism. This assertion was probably influenced by their view of the Ottoman Empire, a community of several hundred million Muslims laboring docilely under the sultan in distant Constantinople, singing hosannas to him before Friday prayers. But most of the world at the time was quite similar in its deference to political authority. In Russia, the czar was considered almost a god. In Japan, the emperor was a god. On the whole, Asian empires were more despotic than Western ones, but Islamic rule was no more autocratic than were Chinese, Japanese, or Russian versions.

Indeed, if any intrinsic aspect of Islam is worth noting, it is not its devotion to authority, but the opposite: Islam has an antiauthoritarian streak that is evident in every Muslim land today. It originates, probably, in several *hadith*—sayings of the Prophet Mohammed—in which obedience to the ruler is incumbent on the Muslim only so far as the ruler's commands are in keeping with God's law.[3] If the ruler asks you to violate the faith, all bets are off. ("If he is

---

[1] Elie Kedourie, *Democracy and Arab Political Culture* (Washington, DC: Washington Institute for Near East Studies, 1992), 5.

[2] Bernard Lewis, *What Went Wrong: Western Impact and Middle Eastern Response* (Oxford: Oxford University Press, 2002), 97.

[3] The *hadith* are often more important than the Koran because they tell Muslims how to implement the sometimes general Koranic injunctions. For example, the Koran commands Muslims to pray, but it does not tell them how to pray; this is found in the *hadith*. (There are, of course, many *hadith*, many of dubious authenticity, and sometimes they contradict each other.)

ordered to do a sinful act, a Muslim should neither listen to [his leader] nor should he obey his orders."[4]) Religions are vague, of course. This means that they are easy to follow—you can interpret their prescriptions as you like. But it also means that it is easy to slip up—there is always some injunction you are violating. But Islam has no religious establishment—no popes or bishops—that can declare by fiat which is the correct interpretation. As a result, the decision to oppose the state on the grounds that it is insufficiently Islamic can be exercised by anyone who wishes to do so. This much Islam shares with Protestantism. Just as a Protestant with just a little training—Jerry Falwell, Pat Robertson—can declare himself a religious leader, so also can any Muslim opine on issues of faith. In a religion without an official clergy, bin Laden has as much—or as little—authority to issue *fatwas* (religious orders) as does a Pakistani taxi driver in New York City. The problem, in other words, is the absence of religious authority in Islam, not its dominance.

Consider the source of the current chaos in Arab lands. In Egypt, Saudi Arabia, Algeria, and elsewhere, Islamist[5] groups wage bloody campaigns against states that they accuse of betraying Islam. Bin Laden and his deputy, the Egyptian Ayman Zawahiri, both laymen, began their careers by fighting their own governments because of policies they deemed un-Islamic (for Zawahiri, it was Egyptian president Anwar Sadat's 1978 peace treaty with Israel; for bin Laden, it was King Fahd's decision to allow American troops on Saudi soil in 1991). In his 1996 declaration of jihad, bin Laden declared that the Saudi government had left the fold of Islam, and so it was permissible to take up arms against it: "The regime betrayed the *ummah* (community of believers) and joined the *kufr* (unbelievers), assisting and helping them against the Muslims." Bin Laden called for rebellion against rulers, and many responded to his call. The rulers of the Middle East probably wish that Muslims were more submissive toward authority.

There is also the question of timing: if Islam is the problem, then why is this conflict taking place now? Why did Islamic fundamentalism take off only after the 1979 Iranian revolution? Islam and the West have coexisted for fourteen centuries. There have been periods of war but many more periods of peace. Many scholars have pointed out that, until the 1940s, minorities, and particularly Jews, were persecuted less under Muslim rule than under any other majority religion. That is why the Middle East was for centuries home to many minorities. It is commonly noted that a million Jews left or were expelled from Arab countries after the creation of Israel in 1948. No one asks why so many were living in Arab countries in the first place.

The trouble with thundering declarations about "Islam's nature" is that Islam, like any religion, is not what books make it but what people make it. Forget

---

[4] *Sahih Muslim*, book 20, *hadith* 4533.

[5] "Islamist" refers to people, like bin Laden, who want to use Islam as a political ideology, setting up an Islamic state that follows Islamic law strictly. I use this term interchangeably with the more commonly used "Islamic fundamentalist," although many scholars prefer the former.

the rantings of the fundamentalists, who are a minority. Most Muslims' daily lives do not confirm the idea of a faith that is intrinsically anti-Western or anti-modern. The most populous Muslim country in the world, Indonesia, has had secular government since its independence in 1949, with a religious opposition that is tiny (although now growing). As for Islam's compatibility with capitalism, Indonesia was until recently the World Bank's model Third World country, having liberalized its economy and grown at 7 percent a year for almost three decades. It has now embraced democracy (still a fragile experiment) and has elected a woman as its president. After Indonesia, the three largest Muslim populations in the world are in Pakistan, Bangladesh, and India (India's Muslims number more than 120 million.) Not only have these countries had much experience with democracy, all three have elected women as prime ministers, and they did so well before most Western countries. So although some aspects of Islam are incompatible with women's rights, the reality on the ground is sometimes quite different. And South Asia is not an anomaly with regard to Islamic women. In Afghanistan, before its twenty-year descent into chaos and tyranny, 40 percent of all doctors were women and Kabul was one of the most liberated cities for women in all of Asia. Although bin Laden may have embraced the Taliban's version of Islam, most Afghans did not — as was confirmed by the sight of men in post-Taliban Kabul and Mazar-e-Sharif lining up to watch movies, listen to music, dance, shave, and fly kites.

The real problem lies not in the Muslim world but in the Middle East. When you get to this region, you see in lurid color all the dysfunctions that people conjure up when they think of Islam today. In Iran,[6] Egypt, Syria, Iraq, the West Bank, the Gaza Strip, and the Persian Gulf states, dictatorships pose in various stripes and liberal democracy appears far from reach. The allure of Islamic fundamentalism seems strong, whether spoken of urgently behind closed doors or declared in fiery sermons in mosques. This is the land of flag burners, fiery mullahs, and suicide bombers. America went to war in Afghanistan, but not a single Afghan was linked to any terrorist attack against Americans. Afghanistan was the campground from which an Arab army was battling America.

The Arab world is an important part of the world of Islam — its heartland. But it is only one part and, in numerical terms, a small one. Of the 1.2 billion Muslims in the world, only 260 million live in Arabia. People in the West often use the term "Islamic," "Middle Eastern," and "Arab" interchangeably. But they do not mean the same thing.

THE ARAB MIND

Today, characterizations of "the Oriental" have about them the whiff of illegitimacy, reminders of the days when ideas such as phrenology passed for science.

---

[6] I often lump Iran together with Arab countries. It is technically not one of them; Iranians speak Farsi not Arabic. But Iran's Islamic Revolution of 1979 gave an enormous fillip to the broader fundamentalist movement and, for now, has dulled the age-old divide between the two largest sects of Islam, Sunni (mostly Arabs) and Shia (mostly Iranians).

(And if "Orientals" are to include the Chinese and the Indians—as they did then—then what to make of the stunning success of these groups at science, math, and other such manifestations of rationality?) But things have moved from one extreme to the other. Those who have resorted to such cultural stereotypes, the "Orientalists," have been succeeded by a new generation of politically correct scholars who will not dare to ask why it is that Arab countries seem to be stuck in a social and political milieu very different from that of the rest of the world. Nor is there any self-criticism in this world. Most Arab writers are more concerned with defending their national honor against the pronouncements of dead Orientalists than with trying to understand the predicament of the Arab world.

The reality is impossible to deny. Of the twenty-two members of the Arab League, not one is an electoral democracy, whereas 63 percent of all the counties in the world are. And although some—Jordan, Morocco—have, in some senses, liberal authoritarian regimes, most do not. The region's recent history is bleak. Its last five decades are littered with examples of Arab crowds hailing one dictator after another as a savior. Gamal Abdel Nasser in Egypt, Mu'ammer Qaddafi in Libya, and Saddam Hussein in Iraq all have been the recipients of the heartfelt adulation of the Arab masses.

The few Arab scholars who venture into the cultural field point out that Arab social structure is deeply authoritarian. The Egyptian-born scholar Bahgat Korany writes that "Arab political discourse [is] littered with descriptions of the enlightened dictator, the heroic leader, the exceptional Za'im, the revered head of family."[7] The Lebanese scholar Halim Barakat suggests that the same patriarchal relations and values that prevail in the Arab family seem also to prevail at work, at school, and in religious, political, and social organizations. In all of these, a father figure rules over others, monopolizing authority, expecting strict obedience, and showing little tolerance of dissent. Projecting a paternal image, those in positions of responsibility (as rulers, leaders, teachers, employers, or supervisors) securely occupy the top of the pyramid of authority. Once in this position, the patriarch cannot be dethroned except by someone who is equally patriarchal.[8]

THE FAILURE OF POLITICS

It is difficult to conjure up the excitement in the world in the late 1950s as Nasser consolidated power in Egypt. For decades Arabs had been ruled by colonial governors and decadent kings. Now they were achieving their dreams of independence, and Nasser was their new savior, a modern man for the postwar era. He had been born under British rule, in Alexandria, a cosmopolitan city that

[7] Bahgat Korany, "Arab Democratization: A Poor Cousin?" *PS: Political Science and Politics* 27, no. 3 (September 1994), 511.

[8] Halim Barakat, *The Arab World: Society, Culture, and State* (Berkeley: University of California Press, 1993), 23.

was more Mediterranean than Arab. His formative years had been spent in the army, the most Westernized segment of Egyptian society. With his tailored suits and fashionable dark glasses, he cut a daring figure on the world stage. "The Lion of Egypt" spoke for all the Arab world.

Nasser believed that Arab politics needed to be fired by ideas such as self-determination, socialism, and Arab unity. These were modern notions; they were also Western ones. Like many Third World leaders of the time, Nasser was a devoted reader of the British *New Statesman.* His "national charter" of 1962 reads as if it had been written by left-wing intellectuals in Paris or London. Even his most passionately pursued goal, pan-Arabism, was European inspired. It was a version of the nationalism that had united first Italy and then Germany in 1870—the idea that those who spoke one language should be one nation.

Before wealth fattened the Gulf states into golden geese, Egypt was the leader of the Middle East. Thus, Nasser's vision became the region's. Every regime, from the Baathists and generals in Syria and Iraq to the conservative monarchies of the Gulf, spoke in similar terms and tones. They were not simply aping Nasser. The Arab world desperately wanted to become modern, and it saw modernity in an embrace of Western ideas, even if it went hand in hand with a defiance of Western power.

The colonial era of the late nineteenth and early twentieth centuries raised hopes of British friendship that were to be disappointed, but still Arab elites remained fascinated with the West. Future kings and generals attended Victoria College in Alexandria, learning the speech and manners of British gentlemen. Many then went to Oxford, Cambridge, or Sandhurst—a tradition that is still maintained by Jordan's royal family, although now they go to American schools. After World War I, a new liberal age flickered briefly in the Arab world, as ideas about opening politics and society gained currency in places like Egypt, Lebanon, Iraq, and Syria. But the liberal critics of kings and aristocrats were swept away along with those old regimes. A more modern, coarser ideology of military republicanism, state socialism, and Arab nationalism came into vogue. These ideas, however, were still basically Western; the Baathists and Nasserites all wore suits and wanted to modernize their countries.

The new politics and policies of the Arab world went nowhere. For all their energy Arab regimes chose bad ideas and implemented them in worse ways. Socialism produced bureaucracy and stagnation. Rather than adjusting to the failures of central planning, the economies never really moved on. Instead of moving toward democracy, the republics calcified into dictatorships. Third World "non-alignment" became pro-Soviet propaganda. Arab unity cracked and crumbled as countries discovered their own national interests and opportunities. An Arab "Cold War" developed between the countries led by pro-Western kings (the Gulf states, Jordan) and those ruled by revolutionary generals (Syria, Iraq). Worst of all, Israel dealt the Arabs a series of humiliating defeats on the battlefield. Their swift, stunning defeat in 1967 was in some ways the turning point, revealing that behind the rhetoric and bombast lay societies that were failing. When Saddam invaded Kuwait in 1990, he destroyed the last remnants of the pan-Arab idea.

By the late 1980s, while the rest of the world was watching old regimes from Moscow to Prague to Seoul to Johannesburg crack, the Arabs were stuck with their corrupt dictators and aging kings. Regimes that might have seemed promising in the 1960s were now exposed as tired kleptocracies, deeply unpopular and thoroughly illegitimate. In an almost unthinkable reversal of a global pattern, almost every Arab country today is less free than it was forty years ago. There are few places in the world about which one can say that.

The Failure of Economics

At almost every meeting or seminar on terrorism organized by think tanks and universities since September 11, 2001, whenever someone wanted to sound thoughtful and serious, he would say in measured tones, "We must fight not just terrorism but also the roots of terrorism." This platitude has been invariably followed by a suggestion for a new Marshall Plan to eradicate poverty in the Muslim world. Who can be opposed to eradicating poverty? But the problem with this diagnosis is that it overlooks an inconvenient fact: the al-Qaeda terrorist network is not made up of the poor and dispossessed.

This is obviously true at the top; bin Laden was born into a family worth more than $5 billion. But it is also true of many of his key associates, such as his deputy, Zawahiri, a former surgeon in Cairo who came from the highest ranks of Egyptian society. His father was a distinguished professor at Cairo University, his grandfather the chief imam of Al Azhar (the most important center of mainstream Islam in the Arab world), and his uncle the first secretary general of the Arab League. Mohammed Atta, the pilot of the first plane to hit the World Trade Center, came from a modern—and moderate—Egyptian family. His father was a lawyer. He had two sisters, a professor and a doctor. Atta himself studied in Hamburg, as had several of the other terrorists. Even the lower-level al-Qaeda recruits appear to have been educated, middle-class men. In this sense, John Walker Lindh, the California kid who dropped out of American life and tuned into the Taliban, was not that different from many of his fellow fundamentalists. In fact, with his high school diploma against their engineering degrees, one could say that he was distinctly undereducated by comparison.

In fact, the breeding grounds of terror have been places that have seen the greatest influx of wealth over the last thirty years. Of the nineteen hijackers, fifteen were from Saudi Arabia, the world's largest petroleum exporter. It is unlikely that poverty was at the heart of their anger. Even Egypt—the other great feeder country for al Qaeda—is not really a poor country by international standards. Its per capita income, $3,690, places it in the middle rank of nations, and it has been growing at a decent 5 percent for the last decade. That may not be enough when you take population growth into account—its population growth has been about 3 percent—but many countries around the world are doing far worse. Yet, they have not spawned hordes of men who are willing to drive planes into Manhattan skyscrapers. If poverty were the source of terror, the recruits should have come from sub-Saharan Africa or South Asia, not the Middle East.

There is, however, a powerful economic dimension to the crisis in the Arab world. The problem is wealth, not poverty. Regimes that get rich through natural resources tend never to develop, modernize, or gain legitimacy. The Arab world is the poster child for this theory of trust-fund states. And this is true not only for the big oil producers. Consider Egypt, which is a small but significant exporter of oil and gas. It also earns $2 billion a year in transit fees paid by ships crossing the Suez Canal, and gets another $2.2 billion a year in aid from the United States. In addition, it gets large sums in remittances—money sent home—from Egyptians who work in the Gulf states. All told, it gets a hefty percent of its GDP from unearned income. Or consider Jordan, a progressive state that is liberalizing; it gets $1 billion a year in aid from the United States. Although that may seem to be a small figure, keep in mind that Jordan's GDP is only $17 billion. Almost 6 percent of its annual income is foreign aid from one country.

Easy money means little economic or political modernization. The unearned income relieves the government of the need to tax its people—and in return provide something to them in the form of accountability, transparency, even representation.[9] History shows that a government's need to tax its people forces it to become more responsive and representative of its people. Middle Eastern regimes ask little of their people and, in return, give little to them. Another bad effect of natural-resource-derived wealth is that it makes the government rich enough to become repressive. There is always money enough for the police and the army. Saudi Arabia, for example, spends 13 percent of its GDP

---

[9] John Waterbury has demonstrated that, far from being undertaxed, the Middle East is the "most heavily taxed of the developing regions." Using World Bank data from 1975 to 1985, Waterbury showed that "tax revenues as a proportion of GNP averaged 25 percent for Middle Eastern states while Latin America averaged 12 percent. This reflects not merely the effect of the preponderant weight of captive petroleum corporations in several Middle Eastern countries, which can be easily and heavily taxed. On average, 19 percent of overall tax revenues in the Middle East came from corporate profits tax, while the corresponding figure for Africa was 20 percent, for Asia 19 percent, and for Latin America 10 percent." But Waterbury errs by neglecting to disaggregate Arab states by type and amount of unearned income. If he had done so, he would have found that the oil-producing states—such as Saudi Arabia and Kuwait—levy few or no taxes, whereas the larger non–oil-producing states such as Egypt and Syria do levy substantial direct and indirect taxes. Although the unearned income that non–oil-producing states receive is significant, it is not enough to live on. Most of the unearned income in such states goes straight to the military. So the absence of demands for democracy in the Middle East can be chalked up to two separate factors: mass bribery in the really rich states, and mass repression in the poorer ones. But both are courtesy of income that flows into the governments' coffers and requires very little real economic activity.

on the military, as does Oman. Kuwait spends around 8 percent. Various estimates of Iraqi military spending before the Gulf War have put its military spending at somewhere between 25 and 40 percent of annual GDP, an unusually high rate no doubt sustained, in part, by the Iran-Iraq War, but also by the massive internal intelligence network maintained by Saddam Hussein and his Baath Party.

For years, many in the oil-rich states argued that their enormous wealth would bring modernization. They pointed to the impressive appetites of Saudis and Kuwaitis for things Western, from McDonald's hamburgers to Rolex watches to Cadillac limousines. But importing Western goods is easy; importing the inner stuffing of modern society—a free market, political parties, accountability, the rule of law—is difficult and even dangerous for the ruling elites. The Gulf states, for example, have gotten a bastardized version of modernization, with the goods and even the workers imported from abroad. Little of their modernness is homegrown; if the oil evaporated tomorrow, these states would have little to show for decades of wealth except, perhaps, an overdeveloped capacity for leisure.

FEAR OF WESTERNIZATION

There is a sense of pride and fall at the heart of the Arab problem. It makes economic advance impossible and political progress fraught with difficulty. America thinks of modernity as all good—and it has been almost all good for America. But for the Arab world, modernity has been one failure after another. Each path followed—socialism, secularism, nationalism—has turned into a dead end. People often wonder why the Arab countries will not try secularism. In fact, for most of the last century, most of them did. Now Arabs associate the failure of their governments with the failure of secularism and of the Western path. The Arab world is disillusioned with the West when it should be disillusioned with its own leaders.

The new, accelerated globalization that flourished in the 1990s has hit the Arab world in a strange way. Its societies are open enough to be disrupted by modernity, but not so open that they can ride the wave. Arabs see the television shows, eat the fast foods, and drink the sodas, but they do not see genuine liberalization in their societies, with ordinary opportunities and dynamism—just the same elites controlling things. Globalization in the Arab world is the critic's caricature of globalization, a slew of Western products and billboards with little else. For the elites in Arab societies, it means more things to buy. But for some of them, it is also an unsettling phenomenon that threatens their comfortable base of power.

This mixture of fascination and repulsion with the West—with modernity—has utterly disoriented the Arab world. Young men, often better educated than their parents, leave their traditional villages to find work. They arrive in the noisy, crowded cities of Cairo, Beirut, or Damascus, or go to work in the oil states. (Almost 10 percent of Egypt's working population has worked in the Gulf states at some point.) In their new world, they see great disparities in wealth and the disorienting effects of modernity; most unsettlingly, they see women, unveiled and in public places, taking buses, eating in cafes, and working alongside them. They come face to face with the contradictions of modern life, seeking the wealth of the new world but the tradition and certainty of the old.

THE RISE OF RELIGION

Nasser was a reasonably devout Muslim, but he had no interest in mixing religion with politics, which struck him as moving backward. This became painfully apparent to the small Islamic parties that supported Nasser's rise to power. The most important one, the Muslim Brotherhood, began opposing him vigorously, often violently, by the early 1950s. Nasser cracked down on it ferociously, imprisoning more than a thousand of its leaders and executing six of them in 1954. One of those jailed was Sayyid Qutb, a frail man with a fiery pen, who wrote a book in prison called *Signposts on the Road*, which in some ways marked the beginning of modern political Islam or what is often called Islamic fundamentalism.[10]

In his book, Qutb condemned Nasser as an impious Muslim and his regime as un-Islamic. Indeed, he went on, almost every modern Arab regime was similarly flawed. Qutb envisioned a better, more virtuous polity based on strict Islamic principles, a core goal of orthodox Muslims since the 1880s.[11] As the regimes of the Middle East grew more distant, oppressive, and hollow in the decades following Nasser, fundamentalism's appeal grew. It flourished because the Muslim Brotherhood and organizations like it at least tried to give people a sense of meaning and purpose in a changing world, something no leader in the Middle East tried to do. In his seminal work, *The Arab Predicament*, which best explains the fracture of Arab political culture, Fouad Ajami explains, "The fundamentalist call has resonance because it invited men to participate . . . [in] contrast to a political culture that reduces citizens to spectators and asks them to leave things to their rulers. At a time when the future is uncertain, it connects them to a tradition that reduces bewilderment." Fundamentalism gave Arabs who were dissatisfied with their lot a powerful language of opposition.

[10] In many ways, the original fundamentalist was Qutb's contemporary, the Pakistani scholar Abul Ala Maududi. Qutb was an admirer of Maududi and translated his writings into Arabic. But it is Qutb who is read throughout the Islamic world today.

[11] The Pakistani Islamic scholar Abul Ala Maududi argued that the colonial powers could be viewed in the same manner as the pagan tribes at the dawn of Islam. Just as the pagans were fought and resisted by the Prophet, so too should a jihad be waged by Muslims against their colonial oppressors. Qutb adopted Maududi's reasoning and extended it to propose jihad against irreligious Muslim governments. Sayyid Qutb, *Milestones* (Indianapolis: American Trust Publications, 1990). The best introduction to Qutb is Gilles Kepel, *Muslim Extremism in Egypt: The Prophet and Pharaoh* (Berkely: University of California Press, 1985).

On that score, Islam had little competition. The Arab world is a political desert with no real political parties, no free press, and few pathways for dissent. As a result, the mosque became the place to discuss politics. As the only place that cannot be banned in Muslim societies, it is where all the hate and opposition toward the regimes collected and grew. The language of opposition became, in these lands, the language of religion. This combination of religion and politics has proven to be combustible. Religion, at least the religion of the Abrahamic traditions (Judaism, Christianity, and Islam), stresses moral absolutes. But politics is all about compromise. The result has been a ruthless, winner-take-all attitude toward political life.

Islamic fundamentalism got a tremendous boost in 1979 when Ayatollah Ruhollah Khomeini toppled the staunchly pro-American shah of Iran. The Iranian Revolution demonstrated that a powerful ruler could be taken on by groups within the society. It also revealed how, in a developing society, even seemingly benign forces of progress—for example, education—can add to the turmoil. Until the 1970s most Muslims in the Middle East were illiterate and lived in villages and towns. They practiced a kind of village Islam that had adapted itself to local cultures and to normal human desires. Pluralistic and tolerant, these villages often worshipped saints, went to shrines, sang religious hymns, and cherished art—all technically disallowed in Islam. By the 1970s, however, these societies were being urbanized. People had begun moving out of the villages to search for jobs in towns and cities. Their religious experience was no longer rooted in a specific place with local customs and traditions. At the same time, they were learning to read, and they discovered that a new Islam was being preached by a new generation of writers, preachers, and teachers. This was an abstract faith not rooted in historical experience but literal and puritanical—the Islam of the high church as opposed to the Islam of the street fair.

In Iran, Ayatollah Khomeini used a powerful technology—the audiocassette. Even when he was exiled in Paris in the 1970s, his sermons were distributed throughout Iran and became the vehicle of opposition to the shah's repressive regime. But they also taught people a new, angry, austere Islam in which the West is evil, America is the "Great Satan," and the unbeliever is to be fought. Khomeini was not alone in using the language of Islam as a political tool. Intellectuals, disillusioned by the half-baked or overly rapid modernization that was throwing their world into turmoil, were writing books against "Westoxification" and calling the modern Iranian man—half Western, half Eastern—"rootless." Fashionable intellectuals, often writing from the comfort of London or Paris, would criticize American secularism and consumerism and endorse an Islamic alternative. As theories like these spread across the Arab world, they appealed not to the poorest of the poor, for whom Westernization was magical, since it meant food and medicine; rather, they appealed to the educated hordes entering the cities of the Middle East or seeking education and jobs in the West. They were disoriented and ready to be taught that their disorientation would be solved by recourse to a new, true Islam.

In the Sunni world, the rise of Islamic fundamentalism was shaped and quickened by the fact that Islam is a highly egalitarian religion. This for most of its history has proved an empowering call for people who felt powerless. But it also means that no Muslim really has the authority to question whether someone is a "proper Muslim." In the Middle Ages, there was an informal understanding that a trained scholarly-clerical community, the *ulama*, had the authority to pronounce on such matters.[12] But fundamentalist thinkers, from Pakistani Maulana Maududi and Qutb to their followers, have muscled in on that territory. They loudly and continuously pronounce judgment as to whether people are "good Muslims." In effect, they excommunicate those whose Islam does not match their own. This process has terrified the Muslim world. Leaders dare not take on the rising tide of Islamists. Intellectual and social elites, widely discredited by their slavish support of the official government line, are also scared to speak out against a genuinely free-thinking clergy. As a result, moderate Muslims are loath to criticize or debunk the fanaticism of the fundamentalists. Some worry, like the moderates in Northern Ireland, about their safety if they speak their mind. Even as venerated a figure as Naguib Mahfouz was stabbed in Egypt for his mildly critical comments about the Islamists.

Nowhere is this more true than in the moderate monarchies of the Persian Gulf, particularly Saudi Arabia. The Saudi regime has played a dangerous game: it has tried to deflect attention away from its spotty economic and political record by allowing free reign to its most extreme clerics, hoping to gain legitimacy by association. Saudi Arabia's educational system is run by medieval-minded religious bureaucrats. Over the past three decades, the Saudis—mostly through private trusts—have funded religious schools (*madrasas*) and centers that spread Wahhabism (a rigid, desert variant of Islam that is the template for most Islamic fundamentalists) around the world. In the past thirty years, Saudi-funded *madrasas* have churned out tens of thousands of half-educated, fanatical Muslims who view the modern world and non-Muslims with great suspicion. America in this world-view is almost always uniquely evil.

This exported fundamentalism has infected not just other Arab societies but countries outside the Arab world. It often carries with it a distinctly parochial Arab political program. Thus, Indonesian Muslims, who twenty years ago did not know where Palestine was, are today militant in their support of its cause. The Arab influence extends even into the realm of architecture. In its buildings, the Islamic world has always mixed Arab influences with local ones— Hindu, Javan, Russian. But local cultures are now being ignored in places such as Indonesia and Malaysia because they are seen as insufficiently Islamic (meaning Arab).

---

[12] On the power of the medieval *ulama*, see Richard W. Bulliet, *Islam: The View from the Edge* (New York: Columbia University Press, 1994).

Pakistan has had a particularly bad experience with exported fundamentalism. During the eleven-year reign of General Zia ul-Haq during the 1980's, the dictator decided that he needed allies, since he had squashed political dissent and opposition parties. He found them in the local fundamentalists, who became his political allies. With the aid of Saudi financiers and functionaries, he set up scores of *madrasas* throughout the country. The Afghan war attracted religious zealots, eager to fight godless communism. These "jihadis" came mostly from Arabia. Without Saudi money and men, the Taliban would not have existed, nor would Pakistan have become the hotbed of fundamentalism that it is today. Zia's embrace of Islam brought him a kind of legitimacy, but it has eroded the social fabric of Pakistan. The country is now full of armed radicals, who first supported the Taliban, then joined in the struggle in Kashmir, and are now trying to undermine the secular regime of General Pervez Musharraf. They have infected the legal and political system with medieval ideas of blasphemy, the subordinate role of women, and the evils of modern banking.

Pakistan is not alone. A similar process has been at work in countries as diverse as Yemen, Indonesia, and the Philippines. During the 1980s and 1990s, a kind of competition emerged between Iran and Saudi Arabia, the two most religious states in the Middle East, to see who would be the greater religious power in the Islamic World. As a result, what were once small, extreme strains of Islam, limited to parts of the Middle East, have taken root around the world—in the globalization of radical Islam.

THE ROAD TO DEMOCRACY

For the most part, the task of reform in the Middle East must fall to the peoples of the region. No one can make democracy, liberalism, or secularism take root in these societies without their own search, efforts, and achievements. But the Western world in general, and the United States in particular, can help enormously. The United States is the dominant power in the Middle East; every country views its relations with Washington as the most critical tie they have. Oil, strategic ties, and the unique U.S. relationship with Israel ensure American involvement. Washington will continue to aid the Egyptian regime, protect the Saudi monarchy, and broker negotiations between Israel and the Palestinians. The question really is, Should it not ask for something in return? By not pushing these regimes, the United States would be making a conscious decision to let things stay as they are—to opt for stability. This is a worthwhile goal, except that the current situation in the Middle East is highly unstable. Even if viewed from a strategic perspective, it is in America's immediate security interests to try to make the regimes of the Middle East less prone to breeding fanatical and terrorist opposition movements.

As a start, the West must recognize that it does not seek democracy in the Middle East—at least not yet. We seek first constitutional liberalism, which is very different. Clarifying our immediate goals will actually make them more easily attainable. The regimes in the Middle East will be delighted to learn that we will not try to force them to hold elections tomorrow. They will be less pleased to know that we will continually press them on a whole array of other issues. The Saudi monarchy must do more to end its governmental and nongovernmental support for extreme Islam, which is now the kingdom's second largest export to the rest of the world. If this offends advocates of pure free speech, so be it. It must rein in its religious and educational leaders and force them to stop flirting with fanaticism. In Egypt, we must ask President Mubarak to insist that the state-owned press drop its anti-American and anti-Semitic rants and begin opening itself up to other voices in the country. Some of these voices will be worse than those we hear now, but some will be better. Most important, people in these countries will begin to speak about what truly concerns them—not only the status of Jerusalem or American policies in the Gulf, but also the regimes they live under and the politics they confront.

Israel has become the great excuse for much of the Arab world, the way for regimes to deflect attention from their own failures. Other countries have foreign policy disagreements with one another—think of China and Japan—but they do not have the sometimes poisonous quality of the Israeli-Arab divide. Israel's occupation of the West Bank and Gaza Strip has turned into the great cause of the Arab world. But even if fomented by cynical Arab rulers, this cause is now a reality that cannot be ignored. There is a new Arab street in the Middle East, built on Al-Jazeera and Internet chat sites. And the talk is all about the plight of the Palestinians. If unaddressed, this issue will only grow in importance, infecting America's relations with the entire Muslim world and ensuring permanent insecurity for Israel. The United States should maintain its unyielding support for the security of Israel. But it should also do what is in the best interest of itself, Israel, and the Palestinians, which is to press hard to broker a settlement that provides Israel and the Palestinians a viable state. Peace between the Israelis and Palestinians will not solve the problem of Arab dysfunction, but it would ease some of the tensions between the Arab world and the West.

The more lasting solution is economic and political reform. Economic reforms must come first, for they are fundamental. Even though the problems facing the Middle East are not purely economic, their solution may lie in economics. Moving toward capitalism, as we have seen, is the surest path to creating a limited, accountable state and a genuine middle class. And just as in Spain, Portugal, Chile, Taiwan, South Korea, and Mexico, economic reform means the beginnings of a genuine rule of law (capitalism needs contracts), openness to the world, access to information, and, perhaps most important, the development of a business class. If you talk with Arab businessmen and women, they want the old system to change. They have a stake in openness, in rules, and in stability. They want their societies to modernize and move forward rather than staying trapped in factionalism and war. Instead of the romance of ideology, they seek the reality of material progress. In the Middle East today, there are too many people consumed by political dreams and too few interested in practical plans.

There is a dominant business class in the Middle East, but it owes its position to oil or to connections to the ruling families.[13] Its wealth is that of feudalism, not capitalism, and its political effects remain feudal as well. A genuinely entrepreneurial business class would be the single most important force for change in the Middle East, pulling along all others in its wake. If culture matters, this is one place it would help. Arab culture for thousands of years has been full of traders, merchants, and businessmen. The bazaar is probably the oldest institution in the Middle East. And Islam has been historically highly receptive to business—Mohammed himself was a businessman. Ultimately, the battle for reform is one that Middle Easterners will have to fight, which is why there needs to be some group within these societies that advocates and benefits from economic and political reform.

This is not as fantastic an idea as it might sound. Already stirrings of genuine economic activity can be seen in parts of the Middle East. Jordan has become a member of the World Trade Organization (WTO), signed a free-trade pact with the United States, privatized key industries, and even encouraged cross-border business ventures with Israel. Saudi Arabia is seeking WTO membership. Egypt has made some small progress on the road to reform. Among the oil-rich countries, Bahrain and the United Arab Emirates are trying to wean themselves of their dependence on oil. Dubai, part of the United Arab Emirates, has already gotten oil down to merely 8 percent of its GDP and has publicly announced its intention of becoming a trading and banking center— the "Singapore of the Middle East." (It would do well to emulate Singapore's tolerance of its ethnic and religious minorities.) Even Saudi Arabia recognizes that its oil economy can provide only one job for every three of its young men coming into the work force. In Algeria, President Abdelaziz Bouteflika desperately wants foreign investment to repair his tattered economy.

If we could choose one place to press hardest to reform, it should be Egypt. Although Jordan has a more progressive ruler, and Saudi Arabia is more critical because of its oil, Egypt is the intellectual soul of the Arab world. If Egypt were to progress economically and politically, it would demonstrate more powerfully than any essay or speech that Islam is compatible with modernity, and that Arabs can thrive in today's world. In East Asia, Japan's economic success proved a powerful example that others in the region looked to and followed. The Middle East needs one such homegrown success story.

There is another possible candidate for the role: Iraq. Before it became a playpen for Saddam's megalomania, Iraq was one of the most advanced, literate, and secular countries in the region. It has oil, but more importantly, it has water. Iraq is the land of one of the oldest river-valley civilizations of the world.

---

[13] There are some exceptions to this rule in Gulf states such as Dubai, Bahrain, and even Saudi Arabia.

Its capital, Baghdad, is home to one of the wonders of the ancient world, the Hanging Gardens of Babylon, and has been an important city for thousands of years. Iraq in the 1950s was a country with a highly developed civil society, with engineers, doctors, and architects, many of whom were women. Now that Saddam has been dislodged, the United States must engage in a serious long-term project of nation-building, because Iraq could well become the first major Arab country to combine Arab culture with economic dynamism, religious tolerance, liberal politics, and a modern outlook on the world. And success is infectious.

THE IMPORTANCE OF CONSTITUTIONALISM

Spreading democracy is tough. But that does not mean that the West—in particular the United States—should stop trying to assist the forces of liberal democracy. Nor does it imply accepting blindly authoritarian regimes as the least bad alternative. It does, however, suggest the need for a certain sophistication. The haste to press countries into elections over the last decade has been, in many cases, counterproductive. In countries such as Bosnia, which went to the polls within a year of the Dayton peace accords, elections only made more powerful precisely the kinds of ugly ethnic forces that have made it more difficult to build genuine liberal democracy there. The ethnic thugs stayed in power and kept the courts packed and the police well fed. The old system has stayed in place, delaying real change for years, perhaps decades. In East Timor and Afghanistan, a longer period of state-building has proved useful. In general, a five-year period of transition, political reform, and institutional development should precede national multiparty elections. In a country with strong regional, ethnic, or religious divisions—like Iraq—this is crucial. It ensures that elections are held after civic institutions, courts, political parties, and the economy have all begun to function. As with everything in life, timing matters.

Although it is easy to impose elections on a country, it is more difficult to push constitutional liberalism on a society. The process of genuine liberalization and democratization, in which an election is only one step, is gradual and long-term. Recognizing this, governments and nongovernmental organizations are increasingly promoting an array of measures designed to bolster constitutional liberalism in developing countries. The National Endowment for Democracy promotes free markets, independent labor movements, and political parties. The U.S. Agency for International Development funds independent judiciaries. In the end, however, elections trump everything. If a country holds elections, Washington and the world will tolerate a great deal from the resulting government, as they did with Russia's Boris Yeltsin, Kyrgystan's Askar Akayev, and Argentina's Carlos Menem. In an age of images and symbols, elections are easy to capture on film. But how to do you televise the rule of law? Yet there is life after elections, especially for the people who live there.

Conversely, the absence of free and fair elections should be viewed as one flaw, not the definition of tyranny. Elections are an important virtue of governance, but they are not the only virtue. It is more important that governments be judged by yardsticks related to constitutional liberalism. Economic, civil, and religious liberties are at the core of human autonomy and dignity. If a government with limited democracy steadily expands these freedoms, it should not be branded a dictatorship. Despite the limited political choice they offer, countries such as Singapore, Malaysia, Jordan, and Morocco provide a better environment for the life, liberty, and happiness of citizens than do the dictatorships in Iraq and Libya or the illiberal democracies of Venezuela, Russia, or Ghana. And the pressures of global capitalism can push the process of liberalization forward, as they have in China. Markets and morals can work together.

The most difficult task economically is reforming the trust-fund states. It has proved nearly impossible to wean them of their easy money. In 2002, the World Bank began experimenting with a potentially pathbreaking model in the central African country of Chad. Chad has major oil fields, but foreign companies were wary of major investments to extract and transport the oil because of the country's history of political instability. The World Bank agreed to step in, bless the project, and loan the government money to partner with a multinational consortium—led by ExxonMobil—to get the oil flowing. But it also put in place certain conditions. Chad's parliament had to pass a law guaranteeing that 80 percent of the oil revenues would be spent on health, education, and rural infrastructure, 5 percent would be spent on locals near the oil fields, and 10 percent would be put into an escrow account for future generations. That leaves the government 5 percent to spend as it wishes. To ensure that the system works in practice as well as in theory, the bank required that all oil revenues be deposited in an offshore account that is managed by an independent oversight committee (made up of some of Chad's leading citizens). It is too soon to tell if this model works, but if it does, it could be copied elsewhere. Even in countries that do not need the World Bank's help, it could have a demonstration effect. The Chad model provides a method by which natural-resource revenues can become a blessing for countries rather than the curse they currently are.

Finally, we need to revive constitutionalism. One effect of the overemphasis of pure democracy is that little effort is given to creating imaginative constitutions for transitional countries. Constitutionalism, as it was understood by its greatest eighteenth-century exponents, such as Montesquieu and Madison, is a complicated system of checks and balances designed to prevent the accumulation of power and the abuse of office. This is accomplished not by simply writing up a list of rights but by constructing a system in which government will not violate those rights. Various groups must be included and empowered because, as Madison explained, "ambition must be made to counteract ambition."

Constitutions were also meant to tame the passions of the public, creating not simply democratic but also deliberative government. The South African constitution is an example of an unusually crafted, somewhat undemocratic structure. It secures power for minorities, both those regionally based, such as the Zulus, and those that are dispersed, such as the whites. In doing so it has increased that country's chances of success as a democracy, despite its poverty and harrowing social catastrophes.

Unfortunately, the rich variety of unelected bodies, indirect voting, federal arrangements, and checks and balances that characterized so many of the formal and informal constitutions of Europe are now regarded with suspicion. What could be called the Weimar syndrome—named after Germany's beautifully constructed constitution, which nevertheless failed to avert fascism—has made people regard constitutions as simply paperwork that cannot make much difference (as if any political system in Germany would have easily weathered military defeat, social revolution, the Great Depression, and hyperinflation). Procedures that inhibit direct democracy are seen as inauthentic, muzzling the voice of the people. Today, around the world, we see variations on the same majoritarian theme. But the trouble with these winner-take-all systems is that, in most democratizing countries, the winner really does take all.

Of course, cultures vary, and different societies will require different frameworks of government. This is a plea not for the wholesale adoption of any one model of government but rather for a more variegated conception of liberal democracy, one that emphasizes both words in that phrase. Genuine democracy is a fragile system that balances not just these two but other forces—what Tocqueville called "intermediate associations"—to create, in the end, a majestic clockwork. Understanding this system requires an intellectual task of recovering the constitutional liberal tradition, central to Western experience and to the development of good government throughout the world.

This recovery will be incomplete if we limit it in our minds to what is happening in faraway countries that are troubled and poor and utterly different from the prosperous, democratic West. Democracy is a work in progress, abroad as well as at home. The tension between democracy and liberalism is one that flourished in the West's own past. In a very different form, it still exists and is growing in the Western world. It is most widely prevalent in one country in particular: the United States of America.